NHL
THE WORLD OF PROFESSIONAL ICE HOCKEY

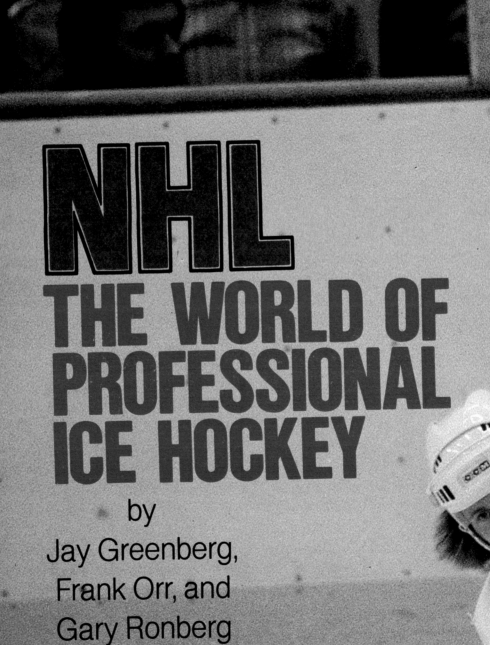

NHL
THE WORLD OF PROFESSIONAL ICE HOCKEY

by
Jay Greenberg,
Frank Orr, and
Gary Ronberg

The Rutledge Press
New York, New York

Acknowledgments

The authors and editors wish to express their thanks to the players, coaches, and administrators of the National Hockey League for their cooperation in the execution of this book. In particular, the unfailing good humor and thoroughness of Jack Driscoll, Rodger Gottlieb, and Dan Leary were always appreciated. And finally, to the fans and families of the NHL, for whom this book is intended.

Designed by Allan Mogel
Edited by Deborah Weiss

Published by The Rutledge Press
A Division of W.H. Smith Publishers Inc.
112 Madison Avenue, New York, New York 10016

First printing 1981
Printed in Italy by A. Mondadori, Verona

Library of Congress Cataloging in Publication Data
Greenberg, Jay.
    NHL, the world of professional hockey.

    1. National Hockey League.   I. Orr, Frank.
    II. Ronberg, Gary.   III. Title.
GV847.8.N3G73   796.96'26   81-5934
ISBN 0-8317-6370-1   AACR2

Preceding pages: *A check from Buffalo Sabre Rob
McClanahan (15), sends New York Islander scoring ace Mike
Bossy onto the ice.* Left: *Trying to gain control of the puck,
Buffalo's Andre Savard and New York Ranger Ron Duguay
collide.*

1
Living
the
Dream
Introduction
by Gary
Ronberg

It happened the night of April 1, 1978, during a game between the Philadelphia Flyers and the Los Angeles Kings at The Forum in Inglewood, California. A seemingly routine maneuver is what it appeared to be, one I had seen on numerous occasions in the past, yet when the surgeon's report arrived it sent shivers through press row and two entire teams of grizzled hockey professionals. "It's one of the desperate plays that sometimes you have to make, but you've got to be careful," Bill Barber, a Philadelphia left wing, would say later. "When you dive with your stick out there, you try to keep your arms in front of your face when [your opponent] turns. His skates can come up, and they can kill."

Early in the second period, the Kings were on a power play when Marcel Dionne, their mercurial center, seized the puck and flitted toward the Flyers' net: as he did, Rick MacLeish sprawled headfirst, his stick extended, in an effort to bump the puck from Dionne's. "He turned away, and as he did, his skate caught the side of my neck," MacLeish would say afterward. "All I felt was his boot hit my ear. Then I felt there with my hand, and found a little blood."

"As you got to the bench it really started bleeding," Wayne Stephenson, the Flyers' backup goaltender, would tell MacLeish. "That's when the blood really started to come."

"The cuts were so deep it was unbelievable," said Barry Dean, a teammate who helped guide MacLeish from the bench to the Philadelphia clubhouse. "They had sliced right through the fat and everything.... You could see everything. And you know the skates, how they're hollow ground? You could see those two little track marks; they'd sliced through so clean."

"Rick MacLeish is a very lucky man," Dr. Everett Borghsani declared later, after using eighty stitches to close gashes of one and a half and three inches in MacLeish's throat and the left side of his neck. "The cuts were dangerously close to everything. They were about three-quarters of an inch deep, and just missed all the major blood vessels of his neck, as well as the thyroid and the submaxillary gland. Two other doctors were cutting the stitches as I was doing the sewing. It took about forty-five minutes."

"Typical of a hockey player, though," Barry Dean recalled. "After the Doc was finished sewing him

up, Hawk [MacLeish] wanted to go out and play again. He was serious, too... but the Doc made me take his skates off."

By the time the game was over and writers traveling with the team were admitted to the Flyers' clubhouse, MacLeish was standing before a mirror, in a smart blue vest and slacks, blowing his hair dry. Taped bandages roamed from his left ear down to the collar of his white shirt, underneath his chin to the throat. He conceded that his wounds were "starting to get sore," that they "were too close for comfort," and that it was all "kinda scary when you think about it." But traditional to his breed is the hockey player's sense of humor and, as he shrugged into his suit coat, MacLeish turned to me and said: "It's funny. I took a puff on a cigarette and the smoke came out the side of my neck."

By that night in California, I had been following professional hockey—as both a writer and a fan—for almost 20 years. In two years of covering the Flyers for the Philadelphia *Inquirer*, I had already seen Tom Bladon almost lose his thumb when the skate of Boston's Terry O'Reilly accidentally stepped on his bare hand during an exhibition game in Portland, Maine, and Ross Lonsberry and Jimmy Watson almost lose an eye on different occasions in St. Louis. Later, during the 1978–79 season, I would watch MacLeish almost lose an eye when Mike Milbury's stick flew into his face in Boston Garden, hear about ex-Flyer Joe Watson's leg being shattered in 13 places during a game in St. Louis, watch Philadelphia's Bob Dailey swallow his tongue after colliding with the Red Wings' Perry Miller in Detroit, and see Bernie Parent's illustrious career end abruptly in a game against the New York Rangers at the Spectrum when a stick pierced the eyelet of his facemask.

"It could be categorized as a freak occurrence," the Flyers' team physician, Dr. Edward Viner, would say at the press conference announcing Parent's retirement. "Like a stone thrown from a lawn mower that happens to strike you, just right, in the eye. If the stick had been a fraction of an inch larger, or the eyelet a fraction smaller, this never would have happened. But as it was, that stick fit the opening perfectly."

Hockey at its ultimate is a game of extravagant beauty. I know that; from high in the press box, it

Preceding pages: *Mario Tremblay, one of the talented players who began his career with the Canadiens in the mid-1970s, demonstrates some skillful stickhandling.*
Opposite: *At the age of 20, Edmonton's Wayne Gretzky is just beginning to rewrite the pages of the NHL record books.*

Left: *St. Louis Blues' goaltender Doug Grant pauses a moment to wipe perspiration from beneath his mask.* Top: *Ex-Los Angeles Kings' goalie Ron Grahame makes a stick save on a point-blank shot.* Above: *The Kings' Triple Crown line takes the ice—(left to right) right wing Dave Taylor, center Marcel Dionne, and left wing Charlie Simmer.*

11

frequently acquires qualities that are almost lyrical to behold. For all the thunder against the boards and into the glass, the game's basic impressions can be those of continuous skating and whirling, starting and stopping, delicate but haphazard patterns building toward the inevitable crack of a shot on goal. The Ice Capades it is not, but from high in the stands, the punishment of professional hockey may appear so remote as to go unnoticed. Indeed, the crunch and the clang of bodies, armed with sticks, chasing and flailing at a frozen missile, may play mere counterpoint to the symphony unfolding below.

One night, Cheryl Dornhoefer—wife of the Flyers' Gary—happened to sit close to the ice instead of in her usual seat high in the stands of Philadelphia's Spectrum. And there, with her nose all but pressed against the glass, a brave new world of sheer violence developed before her eyes. Initially, it was the constant blur of color, the Minnesota green and Flyer white sweeping in upon her, colliding before her, then departing as quickly as it came. But the lasting impression was the dense clamor of it all, and it was as they were driving home afterward that Cheryl Dornhoefer turned to her husband and said: "Gary, you may find this a little hard to believe, but I couldn't imagine what I saw and heard down there tonight. One time Moose [Andre Dupont] carried one of their players into the boards in front of me and I could just *hear* the grunts and groans and the bones crunching. I never realized how rough it is down there."

Through the years, Dornhoefer had heard similar thoughts expressed, particularly by his parents, who every time the Flyers played in Toronto drove from their home in Kitchener, Ontario, for the game and dinner the night before. It was over those dinners, especially when their son was on the limp, that Dornhoefer's parents would look across the table and say, "Gary, when are you going to get out of this game?"

It was on other occasions—like the night MacLeish was almost killed in suburban Los Angeles, when Bladon's thumb was hanging by the tendons, when rookie Behn Wilson saved Bob Dailey's life by prying open his mouth with pressure on the jaw bones, when Jimmy Watson was writhing in silent agony on a

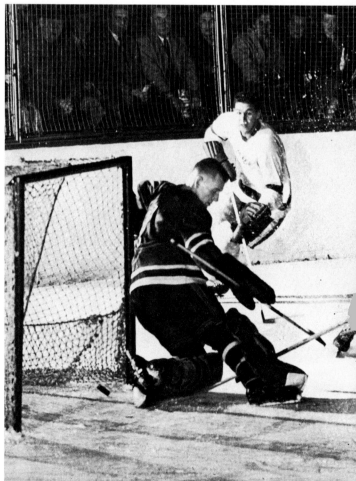

charter flight home after suffering his eye injury in St. Louis—that I would ask myself, "Why does *anybody* play this game?"

I'm convinced it all begins with the cold. The cold of Floral, Saskatchewan, in western Canada where, Gordie Howe recalls, "If you stuck your head out of the door at night you could hear a guy walking two blocks away." The cold of Parry Sound, Ontario, where, Bobby Orr recalls, when the harsh boreas came in from the north, the trees were left permanently starched to the south. The cold of Hamilton, Ontario, where, the mother of Philadelphia coach Pat Quinn recalls when she used to watch her son out in the backyard, just shooting a puck against a wooden fence, "He'd have a scarf wrapped so tight around his face I could never figure out how he could even *see*."

It's the Canadian cold, after all, that makes the ice. So much ice that in 1740, Frenchmen exploring the St. Lawrence River Valley came upon a band of Indians pursuing a hard ball over the ice with sticks and reacting to errant blows with cries of "ho-gee!" which meant, "It hurts!" Ice so thick that, 115 years later, off the shores of southern Ontario, the first organized hockey game in history was played on the ice of Kingston Harbour.

It's the cold that produces natural ice rinks. The first few snowfalls build up the banks, then the snow melts and runs off the banks and quickly freezes again. "And when the warm wind—the Chinook—would come to Saskatchewan," Howe remembers, "the water would run into the low areas, and then it would freeze, and we'd skate for seven miles."

Because of all the cold and ice, they often learn to skate before they know how to walk. Perhaps it's the mother, taking her toddler down to the neighborhood pond where they can skate together; or else it's the father, gently pushing his tiny son onto the edge of the rink and chuckling softly as he watches him use the hockey stick as a prop—a third leg, so to speak.

"I was about five when I got my first pair of skates," says Howe. "We were on relief at the time; a woman came to the door one night with a whole potato sack full of things, and my mother paid her a dollar and a quarter for it. I remember digging into that bag and there were four or five old pairs of skates in there, and I grabbed a pair. They were so big I had to wear a couple pairs of extra socks."

It was the sun that gave us baseball, the bite of autumn and early winter that gave us football. It was the desire for some indoor activity during the winter that gave us basketball. But it was the cold, the bitter, relentless cold, that gave Canadians something to do

Opposite top: *Center Howie Morenz was one of the NHL's first superstars and a member of the 1933 Stanley Cup-winning Chicago Black Hawks.* Opposite bottom: *A young Gordie Howe scores career goal 215 for Detroit in 1953 against New York.* Left: *Tough Bruins' defenseman Eddie Shore asked to play in a benefit game for Ace Bailey, whose career he had ended with a bone-jarring check.*

13

with all that ice.

"Back home when we'd skate, we'd have our oatmeal in the morning," says Howe, who is now 52 years old. "That would last you practically all day, if you didn't want to take time out to eat. After breakfast we'd put on our skates at home and skate down the ruts in the road to the rink. If we came home for lunch, my mother would have newspapers down on the floor so we could keep our skates on. Sometimes there'd be a whole flock of guys, and she'd give us stew or a thick soup. We'd do that again for supper if we were gonna skate again at night.

"I guess the coldest it would get would be fifty below. A lot of times it would be twenty-five below. When I played goalie, I remember I used to skate a mile from my house to the rink, holding the pads up in front of me to cut the wind. At the Avenue F Rink they had a heated shack, and a guy would ring a cowbell and the forward lines and the defense for both teams would go off and sit in the shack by the potbellied stove while the alternates played. After awhile he'd ring the bell again. The other guys would come in and somebody'd say, 'Who's winnin'?' "

I remember one particular night in October 1979 when I was standing in the backyard of a modest home in Brantford, Ontario. The inevitable cold had yet to come to the town of 30,000, but the man of the house was showing me precisely what would happen when it did. First, all the baseball bats and gloves, lacrosse sticks, soccer balls, and basketballs would be removed from the lawn and the grass mowed down to a stubble. Then, every night for the next week or so, the lawn sprinkler would be turned on and left on until morning.

"What you want is a fine spray, almost a mist," I was told. "The sprinkler shoots the water way up in the air and by the time it comes down it's a wet ice already. Then, when you've got a good, level base, you just flood it with a hose. By the time I get it built up to about a foot thick, it's a perfect surface. Takes about nine days in all."

The man was Walter Gretzky, father of the Edmonton Oilers' 20-year-old phenom, Wayne Gretzky, who grew up skating on that 40-foot by 60-foot backyard rink. Now, when the cold comes to Brantford, Walter Gretzky continues to flood his backyard

for sons Keith, 14; Glen, 12; Brent, 9; and daughter Kim, 18.

"They come home from school, get on their skates, and they're out there till about five-thirty or six, when it's time to come in for dinner," their mother, Phyllis, told me. "Then they're back out there until eight or so, until I can convince them it's time for bed. Of course, on Friday nights they're skating until about eleven or so—Walter turns the spotlight on when it's getting dark—and on weekends, too. Actually, if they're not at games or hockey practice, that's where you'll usually find them, skating in the backyard rink."

"It may have been the best ice in Canada," Wayne Gretzky said over dinner a few nights later in Buffalo, where the Oilers were playing the Sabres. "It was so good that your skates didn't have to be all that sharp to skate on it. I don't know why, but I think natural ice is softer than artificial ice. Whatever, it's better to skate on. Skates you can skate on natural ice with, you'll fall down the moment you step onto artificial ice with, 'cause it's so hard.

"I remember, we'd get out of school at a quarter after three, come home, put our skates on in the kitchen doorway, and out we'd go. Other kids, maybe fifteen or sixteen of 'em, would come over. They'd come clomping up our driveway, with their skates already on, and then we'd play. Sometimes we'd play tournaments, four to a side, and we'd finish the tournament by five-thirty, when it was time for dinner.

"After dinner, we'd go back out and skate some more until it was time to go to bed, 'cause my Dad would have the light on. Except on Tuesday, Wednesday, and Saturday nights. There were always hockey games on TV on Tuesday, Wednesday, and Saturday nights, so I'd go in at eight to watch them. But because I'd have to go to bed, I could watch only the first two periods, so after the second period I'd go out in the backyard and skate for twenty more minutes until it was time to go to bed. I could never watch a hockey game on TV without skating some afterward.

"No, without that backyard rink, I wouldn't be where I am now."

That, of course, is the way it has been in Canada since the turn of the century: cold, ice, skating—and

Preceding pages: *Rick MacLeish of the Philadelphia Flyers narrowly evades the check of New York Islander defenseman Ken Morrow (6).* Top: *The cold winters in Canada produce an abundance of natural ice rinks for youngsters to learn to skate on. However, in many parts of the United States, the climate dictates that anyone interested in hockey must play in leagues like this one in Hicksville, New York. Here, Wally Livingston, the league's director, holds a class.* Left: *Joe Cotton takes a breather and contemplates his next strategic play.* Above: *Two energetic competitors demonstrate the kind of effort and skill that make any coach proud.*

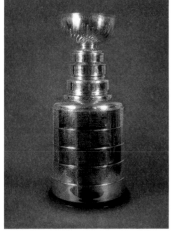

Opposite: *New York Islander captain Denis Potvin hoists the 1980 Stanley Cup above his head, leading teammate Butch Goring in celebration.* Above left: *Wayne Gretzky and his Edmonton teammates rejoice after a hard-won goal.* Above right: *Concentration, that quality that turns skill into winning, shows on the face of Curt Bennett.* Left: *The Stanley Cup, hockey's ultimate prize.* Right: *New York Ranger Don Maloney can't help jumping for joy.*

19

hockey. It wasn't until the mid-1930s, however—when Gordie Howe was still seven years old or so—that Canadians began looking forward with great anticipation to every Saturday night during the winter, when they would cozy up to the radio and listen to the voice of Foster Hewitt from Maple Leaf Gardens in Toronto. The game so many played for fun had, by then, become a source of glamorous employment in what was known as the National Hockey League. And from the speed and flair of Montreal's Howie Morenz to the cold-blooded ruthlessness of Boston's Eddie Shore, the NHL's first two superstars, the names that came crackling over that radio were veritable jewels in the night.

One night, against Toronto, Shore leveled Ace Bailey from behind with such force that the Maple Leaf player was rendered unconscious for 20 minutes, then hovered near death for days. Bailey recovered, never to play again; but after Shore specifically asked to be included in an All-Star game that was being staged for Bailey's benefit, then embraced him at center ice, there wasn't a dry eye in Maple Leaf Gardens. "It was," one veteran journalist wrote years later, "the most completely dramatic event I ever saw in hockey."

Only a few years after that, however, in 1937, Morenz was wheeling through one of his finest seasons when he caught his skate in a rut and tumbled to the ice, breaking four bones in his left leg and ankle. What had appeared to be an unfortunate injury became a tragedy five weeks later, when Morenz fell to the floor

Above: *Former Philadelphia Flyer right wing Gary Dornhoefer was known more for his tough, robust positional play than for any of his 200 career goals.* Opposite: *Dornhoefer, now retired, feels that hockey provided a good life for him and his family. It even opened up a new career for him as a broadcaster for "Hockey Night in Canada."*

of a Montreal hospital and died, at the age of 34, of a coronary embolism. As 25,000 people filed into the Montreal Forum to pay their respects to Morenz, an entire nation mourned his passing.

There is no way of measuring how much Foster Hewitt contributed to Canada's infatuation with hockey, of course; yet I think it's safe to say that by transforming Saturday night into "Hockey Night in Canada"—a weekly celebration of what had become the country's national pastime—his dramatic, cascading play-by-play sent countless youths to bed with dreams of playing in the NHL some day.

"When I was a kid, if you sent a Bee Hive Corn Syrup label to Toronto you'd get a picture of an NHL player," says Gordie Howe. "All of us kids would be down the alleys looking in the ash cans for labels. I was the champion. I had about one hundred pictures." (In fact, when Howe signed his first contract with the Red Wings, his "bonus" was a red Detroit jacket with the team's crest on the chest. And, when he was called up by the big club, he saved every newspaper article that mentioned his name. "Not because I had a big ego, 'cause I didn't," he says. "It was because I expected to last only a year or two, and later on, if anyone asked, I wanted to be able to prove that I had played in the National Hockey League.")

Indeed, to skate onto the ice of Maple Leaf Gardens or the Forum in Montreal, glance down and see Toronto's maple leaf or the "C" with the "H" in the middle, representing Le Club de Hockey Canadiens, was to have become a member of Canada's elite. As it did every other facet of life in North America, World War II had a profound influence on hockey and those who played it professionally: many careers and potential careers were interrupted or terminated as players joined the armed forces. Still, by the end of the 1940s, the NHL was literally feeding on its lore, traditions, and such stars as Montreal's Maurice ("Rocket") Richard, Toe Blake, and Elmer Lach; Boston's Woody Dumart, Bobby Bauer, and Milt Schmidt; and Detroit's "Production Line" of Sid Abel, Ted Lindsay, and Gordie Howe.

There was also a matter known as the Stanley Cup. It seems that back in 1888, the Right Honourable Sir Frederick Arthur Stanley, Baron Stanley of Preston, in the County of Lancaster, in the Peerage of Great Britain, Knight Grand Cross of the Most Honourable Order of the Bath, had crossed the Atlantic to become governor general of the Dominion. After assessing the state of the nation, Lord Stanley began to think that "it would be a good thing if there were a challenge cup," and "worth considering whether [the matches] could not be arranged so that each team would play once at home and once where their opponents hail from."

As a result, Lord Stanley ordered the purchase—for $48.50—of a silver bowl that in the last 90 years has become the oldest, most cherished trophy in contemporary professional sport. How significant is the Cup? "When I was holding the Cup, I could feel all the names," Bryan Trottier recalled after the New York Islanders prevailed over the Flyers in the spring of 1980. "The names are small, but you can feel them. It's more than they say. You say, 'Wow, it's the Stanley Cup!' It's more than wow. When I would see Guy Lafleur, I would say congratulations, but I really didn't know what I was congratulating him about. Now I know."

The annual wire-service photo of toothless hockey players pouring champagne into the Cup is also a hint as to what the game exacts from its participants. On the shelf of practically every dressing cubicle in the NHL is a small plastic cup in which the occupant deposits his dentures before a game or practice, then clicks them back into his mouth before departing for a beer with the guys. "It's the price you pay," Walter Gretzky told me, explaining the absence of Wayne's two front teeth at the age of 10. "Problem was, he didn't lose 'em until I'd spent a bundle straightening 'em."

The facial scars, from all manner of flying sticks, pucks, skates, and fists, are a matter of course. One time early in his career, Bobby Clarke was on a flight to St. Louis with the Flyers when a stewardess noticed a cut on his cheek, his blackened right eye, and asked, "Were you in an automobile accident?"

"No," Clarke replied. "I'm a professional hockey player."

"Oh," she said. "I thought you were only a teenager."

From the inevitable visit of the hockey tooth fairy to an experience so chilling as Rick MacLeish's, the

Preceding pages: *The puck is lost in this pileup of Los Angeles Kings and Hartford Whalers, both teams relatively new to the NHL. Above: Gary Dornhoefer (center), fore-checking Boston's Dallas Smith, realized a dream by playing in the NHL and on two Stanley Cup–winning teams.*

game clearly represents considerable punishment and risk; and from its very birth in Canada, hockey has borne the trademark of a hard-working, hard-living people who pushed back the frontiers with fierce pride in their ability to accept risk and endure physical agony. "Hockey reflects us," the late Canadian physical therapist Lloyd Percival once said. "In a game like hockey you have to have the emotional ability to keep going despite the knocks, without overreacting to the dangers."

It's interesting to note that few players who reach the NHL are products of affluent families. This would seem to suggest that while rich kids tend to give up passionate pursuit of a career in professional hockey as too rigorous and even dangerous, almost no price to be paid is too high for the youth of poor or modest means who sees the game as his only way out of a lifetime in a copper mine, a logging camp, or a paper mill. I remember discussing this aspect of hockey one night with Bob Plager, a defenseman who spent 14 years in pro hockey—8 with St. Louis—before becoming a scout for the Blues.

"My dad and my relatives all worked in the mines," said Plager, who was born and raised in Kirkland Lake, Ontario. "I did as a kid, and it was so dark down there that all I could think was, 'Please God, get me out of here. Let me see what the world is all about.' Hockey was the only way out. So I took it."

Still, as hockey flourished in four NHL cities and numerous minor-league sites south of the border, American fans could never quite understand why the Canadian hockey player appeared so anxious to fight at the drop of the gloves, to accept stitches without the benefit of anesthetics, to perform with injuries that would have relegated any U.S. athlete to the sidelines. But Buffalo general manager Scotty Bowman, whose own promising career as a player was terminated by a severe head injury in Junior A hockey, understands their puzzlement.

"Take a forty-year-old American guy," he says. "He's never played hockey. He sits up there in the stands and he sees someone give someone else a two-hander. He can't believe grown men do this to one another, but hockey players understand it. They expect it. It's part of the knocks you take to make the NHL and then stay there."

Opposite: *The Edmonton Oilers' "Whiz Kid" Wayne Gretzky attempts to outshadow Ranger defensive specialist Walt Tzachuk.* Above: *In his first two NHL seasons, Gretzky won the Hart Trophy as the league's MVP, broke Phil Esposito's regular-season scoring record, and Bobby Orr's regular-season record for assists.*

To get there, a Canadian youth almost invariably must make a choice between education and hockey, and, unfortunately, the two work at cross-purposes with each other: most youths showing any potential whatsoever ultimately have to decide, in their mid-teens, whether to remain in school or leave the hearth to play elsewhere for a team in Canada's highly competitive junior leagues. "Sure, there were drop-outs," says Aldo ("Bep") Guidolin, who coached for years in Junior A and B hockey. "Homesickness and poor grades were the big reasons. They played a seventy-game schedule, with overnight bus trips, and a lot of them never finished high school because of it. I mean, when a kid gets home at three or four in the morning, and he's got to get up for school at six or seven, it's not easy."

Especially when their teams were being sponsored by NHL clubs, the junior leagues were absolute crucibles of development; competition was fierce, rough, and intimidating, and Canada became inhabited by thousands of men who discovered—too late and with much regret—that by foresaking an education for hockey they had shortchanged themselves for life. One of the more fortunate souls is Jimmy Roberts, who played 16 years in the NHL and is now an assistant coach with the Buffalo Sabres—but who still flinches at memories of life in the junior leagues. "There were times when I was eighteen years old that I was really scared," Roberts told me. "Other clubs, like the Toronto Marlboros, they'd have some animals out there who acted like they were training to become wrestlers instead of hockey players. There were nights, lots of nights, when I was really scared to go out there against those guys. But somehow I got through it. The NHL isn't half as rough as it was in some of the amateur leagues."

Wilf Paiement, a rugged right wing who played for the Kansas City Scouts–Colorado Rockies before joining the Maple Leafs, remembers dropping out of school at 15 to play Junior A hockey for Niagara Falls, 500 miles away from his home in Earlton, Ontario. And the fact that he spoke French in a league dominated by English-speaking youngsters two and three years his senior made the experience all the more frightening. "They would push you around, try to make you run," Paiement told me. "Especially

somebody like me, who was only fifteen. The average guy was eighteen years old and some of them really wanted to make the NHL. Jim Schoenfeld [of the Buffalo Sabres] was there when I was, and Shonnie really wanted to make it, eh? He wouldn't turn away from anything. Some of the other guys, they didn't want to make it as bad as Shonnie. Me, I was young. I couldn't defend myself in English when they said something to me, so I just turned red, eh? I didn't go looking for fights, but I didn't back down. I *couldn't* back down if I wanted to stay."

Wally Harris, who is now an NHL referee, agrees. "In the amateurs, everything is simplified," he says. "It's player versus player. Fan versus fan. Town versus town. Everybody knows everybody else. There are no secrets. Rivalries are intense. It's not like the NHL, where the only time a fan sees a player is on the ice or on TV."

Then there were the hockey rinks themselves. "In the amateurs, they were nothing more than four walls with a tin roof on top to keep the wind out," Harris recalls. "There's no heat, so when it's twenty below outside, it feels like forty below inside because of the humidity. So the only way those fans could keep from freezing was by drinking that cheap Geneva gin. By the second period, they were bombed, smashed out of their minds. Compared to fans like that, the crowds in Boston or New York are a piece of cake."

If he survived the junior leagues, than several more years in the minor leagues—which were just about as turbulent—a player would do almost anything to stay in the NHL. "Before expansion I was with Toronto," says Philadelphia coach Pat Quinn. "Punch Imlach would walk into our dressing room before a game and wave a plane ticket to Pittsburgh under your nose. He'd already have it made out, in your name. That was intimidation, and intimidation of the worst kind. The threat of being sent down, not knowing if you'd ever be back again—that in itself made an awful lot of chickens courageous."

NHL sponsorship of junior teams also instilled great loyalty to the organization at a very young age; many, in fact, wore hand-me-down uniforms from the parent club. And this, combined with a schedule that pitted one NHL team against the other five 14 times during the regular season (7 home, 7 away), produced

Opposite: *Although it may appear as if ex-Pittsburgh Penguin Dave Schultz is readying to hit New York Islander Bob Lorimer over the head, Schultz is actually at the top of smashing his stick on the ice in frustration after a missed scoring opportunity.*

29

the fiercest rivalries that the league has ever known.

"I used to hate our home-and-home series with the Canadiens because after the Saturday night game in Montreal, I had to ride on the same train with them to Detroit," recalls Ted Lindsay, former coach and general manager of the Red Wings. "I can remember walking into the dining car on Sunday mornings and checking to see if somebody like the Rocket or Butch Bouchard was in there. I wouldn't go in until he had left. It was the same with the other teams. Everybody would try to finish their breakfast before the guys on the other club woke up. That way they wouldn't have to bump into them in the dining car."

For whatever inspired a youth to set his sights on a career in the NHL, however—be it his environment, the prestige of playing in the big league, having his name inscribed on the Stanley Cup—financial security was hardly one reason. In fact, even when the NHL was playing to capacity houses in two cities in Canada and four in the United States, its players were notoriously underpaid. Maurice Richard, for instance, is said to have never earned more than $50,000 a year from the Canadiens. Bobby Hull created a *cause célèbre* in the late 1960s when he sought to become the league's first $100,000 player with the Chicago Black Hawks, a figure even Howe did not reach until his final years with the Red Wings. Many players had to take jobs during the summer to make ends meet, and, when their NHL careers were over, were lost as to what to do with the rest of their lives.

Indeed, it was very early in his professional hockey career, when he was playing for Knoxville in the Central League, that Pat Quinn made a firm promise to himself that—one way or another—he would obtain a college degree. "Our first year in Knoxville, Pat had watched teammates who were thirty-five, thirty-eight, even forty years old, who couldn't do anything else but play hockey in the Central League," recalls Quinn's wife, Sandra. "He made up his mind right then and there that that wasn't going to happen to him. To a lot of those players, hockey had been the only way out of the copper mine or the steel mill. But to Pat, especially after our first year in Knoxville, hockey was his way of getting an education."

"It took him ten years [and courses at five

Preceding pages: *Playing goalie in hockey has been described as the single, most difficult task in sport. At times the goaltender is the last line of defense; at other times he finds himself alone with the ice before him.* Above: *In 1977, Ranger Ron Greschner required 32 stitches to close this cut in his ear caused by Chicago's John Marks' skate.*

Buffalo coach Roger ("Captain Video") Neilson (seated, left), who has earned a reputation as one of the game's most advanced thinkers, and assistant coach Jim Roberts, who communicates with a spotter in the press box during a game, are successful examples of Scotty Bowman's two-coach system.

universities from Toronto to Tulsa] to get his degree, and when he did, I never saw him so proud," says Quinn's mother, Jean. "It was very difficult then, because neither he nor Sandra was really able to enjoy their summers together. While he was going to classes, studying, taking the examinations, she was taking care of the [two baby] girls. Believe me, they've both had to give a lot in that marriage."

Now, less than 15 years later, much has changed so far as the NHL is concerned and why young men seek a career in the big league. In 1967, when the NHL expanded from 6 teams to 12, its 120 spots on player rosters doubled to 240; with the addition of 6 more franchises in the next 7 years, that number expanded to 360. Meanwhile, in 1972, the World Hockey Association was established in direct competition with the NHL; Bobby Hull and Derek Sanderson jumped from the NHL for multi-million-dollar contracts in the WHA. Many other players also went, lured by financial windfalls never dreamed of only a few years earlier.

Following a seven-year price war that drove the average player's salary to $96,000 annually in the NHL and teams in both leagues into seas of red ink, the two leagues merged. By that time there had at one point been 28 WHA and NHL teams offering spots for 560 players. Merger only accelerated the consideration of American and European hockey players as candidates for the NHL, and their numbers in the big league have been increasing ever since. At the same time, the NHL Players Association has grown into a powerful and highly influential body that would appear to be a positive force upon the long-range future of professional hockey.

So while many observers and fans contend that the NHL currently offers a new brand of hockey, and that those fierce rivalries Ted Lindsay remembers are now a remnant of the past, there is no denying that a career in the contemporary NHL offers far more to a player than it ever has offered before. Indeed, what once may have been a dream based upon the sheer romance of the game itself has become one that holds the potential of a career in medicine, law, or successful private enterprise.

Gary Dornhoefer is 38 years old now, a color commentator for "Hockey Night in Canada," and he lived the Dream. Not in the fashion of a Howe, a Richard, an Orr, or the way Gretzky will, for an unusually gifted athlete he was not. But if the fabric of professional hockey is old, erratic, and coarsely woven, highlighted by the colors of its most accomplished contributors, what has held the pattern through the decades has been the strong, firm thread of players like Dornhoefer.

He was a right wing and a member of the "old school," a genre that, unlike that of so many contemporary players, paid its dues in the minor leagues before rising to the NHL. In fact, until he was selected by Philadelphia in the twelfth round of the NHL's first expansion draft, Dornhoefer had—except for a few cups of coffee with the Boston Bruins—traveled from Minneapolis of the Central League to San Francisco of the Western to Hershey of the American. And in 11 years with the Flyers, Dornhoefer would become known more for his tough, robust, positional play than for any of the 200 goals that he scored along the way.

"I can name you any number of guys I've coached who are younger than Dornhoefer, who are better than him, but who are playing in some pickup league somewhere for thirty-five or forty-five dollars a game," Fred Shero once told me when he was still coaching the Flyers. "Their excuse is that coach was no good, or that the referee was no good, or that they just ran into tough luck. The Gary Dornhoefers don't make excuses; but then, they don't have to."

"All I know is that as a coach, you really have to be careful who you put out there when Dornhoefer's on the ice," Scotty Bowman noted when he was coaching the Montreal Canadiens. "The only way you can keep things even when he's out there is to make sure he's playing against someone he respects. Otherwise, he just runs over a guy, really takes advantage, and he'll keep it up all night. That sort of thing can lose us a hockey game."

Dornhoefer was born and raised by parents of solid German stock in Kitchener, Ontario, where his father was a mechanic at the Smiles and Chuckles Candy factory. By the time Gary was 9 years old, string-beaned and frail with talent that was only marginal at best, his dream of playing in the NHL should have come eyeball-to-eyeball with reality; but at the age of 18 he was playing Junior A hockey for the team Boston sponsored in Niagara Falls, Ontario, 150 miles from home. When he was called aside one day by the Bruins' general manager, Happ Emms, Dornhoefer's fantasy assumed the course of a mission. "He told me that I had the heart, and that could make up for a lot of things," Dornhoefer recalls. "He told me that if I kept trying, I'd make it someday."

By the summer of 1977, when he decided that the next NHL season (his eleventh with the Flyers) would be his last, Dornhoefer had discovered what the Dream was all about: black bullets rising from the point, lumber in the small of the back, slashes across his ankles, sticks between his thighs, elbows in his face. "I've been hit and I've hit back," he said. "I've had sticks in my back and I've given them. Sometimes it smarts for a while, but it's worth it."

That's because it is the code of the game. If one fails to abuse when the opportunity arises, others will soon take advantage; if one does not retaliate when abused, others lose respect. During so many seasons in professional hockey, however, there were countless nights when Dornhoefer did not think there was anything left to give. Strains here, sprains there; assorted aches and bruises; lacerations still in the process of healing; sickness; fatigue. "Those are the nights," he told me, "when you've really got to work to get yourself 'up.' Maybe you don't feel like you can put one skate in front of the other, but that's the wonderful thing about this game. Maybe you really feel miserable, but all of a sudden somebody gives you a shot with his stick or elbow. You take his number and you say to yourself, 'OK, you want to play that way? Fine.'"

Dornhoefer also was one of those extremely rare players who performed on two Stanley Cup champion teams, although for the first—against the Bruins in 1974—the shoulder he separated in the second game of the finals sidelined him for the duration of the series. "It was very disappointing," he recalls. "There's no greater feeling than your first Stanley Cup, but I was all drugged up and really didn't feel part of it. In the second one [against the Buffalo Sabres in 1975], it was my first Cup. But by then it was old hat to everybody else; it just wasn't the same for the other guys as it was for me."

As he spoke, the veteran's face was faintly scarred, laced with the marks of hundreds of games and thousands of pitched battles in the corners and in front of nets at both ends of the ice. "It's really kind of a shame," he continued, "but until you play for a winner you're never going to fully appreciate the sacrifices that have to be made. It's actually something you can't communicate to someone who's never been on a champion. Unfortunately, there are a lot of hockey players who'll never know that feeling, simply because they'll never get the chance."

When Gerhardt Otto Dornhoefer ("Gary" for short, "Dorny" by trade) realized that it was time to quit living the Dream, he was 34 years old. Bone chips in his right knee had required surgery, followed by a cast, then two months of intense rehabilitation. He had found that the usual complement of bruises and contusions, muscle pulls and tears that comprise a typical NHL season were healing more slowly, if they did at all. "You love playing the games, but because of all the travel you get so tired it seems like you never catch up," he said. "I know, the last few years were particularly tough, because I'd lost a step. I wasn't fast enough to get out of the way. I took a lot of punishment, and there never was enough time to recover."

In anticipation of his final season in the NHL, all the veteran wished was that he might go out in style: skate a regular shift, score 20 goals, and hopefully contribute to a fifth-straight division title and one more Stanley Cup. In the fall of 1977, he reported to training camp in the finest physical condition of his career, but the fates were ominous from the start.

First came an exhibition game in which an errant stick left a nasty gash in his eyebrow. That was stitched and bandaged, but the following night a slap shot ricocheted off another stick into his face, reopening the wound. Five games into the regular-season schedule, he was blind-sided in the corner and collapsed with strained ligaments in his left knee.

A month later, Dornhoefer rejoined the Flyers, but because he was no longer playing regularly and was becoming increasingly concerned over what awaited him after hockey, he found he could not sleep

The handwritten sign added onto the bottom of the door of the Washington Capitals' locker room emphasizes what it takes to be a winner in the National Hockey League—discipline, commitment, and a sense of humor.

NO SMOKING
HOCKEY
LOCKER
ROOM

CAPITAL PLAYERS
AND STAFF
ONLY

Are you ready to
sacrifice to win?
IF NOT,
TURN AROUND!

at night. On the team's first West Coast trip, in December, he twice blacked out in practice. He was returned to Philadelphia, where tests revealed he was suffering from a mild case of exhaustion. After a week of rest, he returned to the club again, but did not dress for the games. Late one rainswept evening in Atlanta, as we walked through the deserted airport to catch the Flyers' chartered flight home, Dornhoefer told me, "Sometimes I wish somebody would break my leg and get this over with. I feel like I'm in a straitjacket."

Dornhoefer didn't break a leg on Christmas Day, as the Flyers practiced for an exhibition game the following night against a touring team from Czechoslovakia. Instead, he suffered a hip pointer. More rest; more therapy; more games from the press box. In January he was playing in his second-straight game for the Flyers when, in one of the corners again, his skate found a rut and he fell heavily to the ice, twisting his left knee again. A half hour later, word came from the team's clubhouse that Dornhoefer would be out for three more weeks.

"Cheryl [Gary's wife] really felt bad that night," he would recall. "She knew how much it meant to me to play in two straight games, and she almost cried on the way home. That would have been a first for her, too, because she's a very strong person."

In his first year as a professional hockey player, Dornhoefer earned $3,250 at Minneapolis. By the time he retired, after the 1977–78 NHL season, he was making $115,000 with the Flyers, which was not so much a remnant of the league's seven-year price war with the WHA as it was the fruits of playing for two Stanley Cup champions. "It wasn't until the last three or four years that I made really good money," he said. "Until you're number one, and we were when we won those Cups, you never have quite the leverage you need when you're negotiating with management."

As a result, for their last five years in the Philadelphia area, Dornhoefer, his wife, and their two children, Stephanie and Steven, lived in a handsome, Spanish-style home in suburban Berlin, New Jersey. The exterior was yellow stucco, immersed in an impressive spray of shrubbery, and it was situated on a half-acre lot covered with oak and pine trees. Off the redwood deck was a 16-foot by 39-foot swimming pool; in the driveway, a 1971 and a 1976 Mercedes. The

Opposite: *Los Angeles Kings' superstar Marcel Dionne gives a postgame interview. Win, lose, or draw, the players must answer to the press and fans.* Top: *The tools of Bill Barber's trade.* Above: *Hung in readiness are the sticks of the New York Rangers team.*

interior was tastefully furnished from the second-floor bedrooms to the den beneath the main level, where a lush orange rug with the black Flyer logo covered the floor, gleaming trophies were on the shelves, and framed photographs from Dornhoefer's career adorned the walls. Clearly, professional hockey had been as good to Dornhoefer as he had been to it; but when his career was over, what next?

"Did I want to coach?" he asked. "There, I'd only be an assistant, you know, shooting pucks out of the corner in practice, 'cause there can be only one boss. Did I want to scout? Work in broadcasting? Almost any meaningful job in hockey entails traveling, and I wanted to get away from that. My children are at an age [then 13 and 10, respectively] where they're going to have to have their father around. They're going to have questions, problems, and they can't keep turning to their mother, who was both their mother and their father when I was away so much. So if traveling was what you wanted to eliminate, and I did, you could eliminate most any job in hockey. So I just made a clean break and got involved in something else."

As it developed, that "something else" was at Sherwood Leasing Company in Trenton, New Jersey, where the former hockey player was no longer a mini-celebrity with the Philadelphia Flyers but a sales executive whose job it was to lease automobiles. It was a job, a good job, with the potential for advancement, but despite all the planning that he and his wife had done preceding his retirement, the transition was something that Dornhoefer had never before experienced in his life.

For as long as he could remember, the former hockey player had been insulated by the game's "system." Whether it had been in Junior A, the minor leagues, or the NHL, the game had fed, clothed, and housed him. It had told him where to be, at precisely what time, and once he was there his only responsibilities were to follow the instructions of his coaches and to perform to the best of his ability. Yet three months after his retirement, Dornhoefer was commuting an hour each way from his home, in the height of rush-hour traffic. For the first time in his life, he was immersed in the "real world," so to speak, as a bona fide member of the eight-to-five society.

Now his "office" was no longer The Spectrum, where on Thursday and Sunday nights in the winter the red seats rising steadily toward the rafters were occupied by 17,077 of the most rabid fans in the NHL. Instead, it was in a gray, corrugated steel building that was not unlike a quonset hut with a round roof, surrounded by a parking lot embraced by a tall wire fence. Inside, there was no orange-and-black uniform hung neatly in his dressing cubicle, no trainers bustling about, no whine of skates being sharpened, no smell of linament, no teammates in various stages of undress anticipating the excitement of another crowd and another game.

No, what there was was a desk with a telephone on it, surrounded by other desks with telephones on them—desks occupied not by friends who filled the room with lighthearted profanity and an occasional practical joke, but by associates who worked amid the clamor of everybody else's business.

"Sometimes I'm stuck in that office all day and I get so depressed I feel like a caged lion," Dornhoefer said. "Ten, fifteen desks thrown together, people talking on the telephone, phones ringing, typewriters going. Believe me, sometimes I've wanted to run out of that office and jump off the nearest bridge."

That was 15 months after he had retired from professional hockey, and I was sitting on Dornhoefer's redwood deck in Berlin. During the last hockey season, his first away from the game, Dornhoefer had combined his work at the leasing company with that for the Flyers' cable television network and, for $375 per game plus expenses, some 25 games for "Hockey Night in Canada." After she returned with a large pizza for us and the children, who were watching television in the den, Dornhoefer's wife joined us on the deck.

Cheryl Dornhoefer is an attractive woman—blonde, fit, athletic, and she was as tan as her husband. She is also a woman of considerable strength, sensitivity, and community involvement, and among her outside interests at that time was volunteer work for the cardiac evaluation unit at West Jersey Hospital.

"Through my volunteer work I became aware of what stress can do," she said. "At first, Dorny was really excited about his new business. As a teenager, his whole scope had been limited. He wasn't interested in automobiles or anything else; it was hockey and golf, and that was it. Until he began making his own contacts in the leasing business, he was in that office five days a week, day after day in that office, and there were nights when he'd come home with headaches from all the noise and the confusion.

"But Dorny's background is not that of a quitter. He's very much like his parents; strong, stoic people who will persevere. It was those nights when he'd come home so depressed that, I admit, the possibility of a heart attack crossed my mind. I don't think Dorny ever contemplated what the Average Joe does. At twenty, you have a chance to grow into it, but at thirty-six, I don't really know."

It was, indeed, a time when Dornhoefer was able to reflect upon what he missed most being away from the game he had played for 26 years. "You figure, you had June, July, and August off, scott free," he said. "You could go out and play golf every day if you wanted to. In that way, hockey was like no other occupation. I know, there are still days when I'll be driving to work and my car, it keeps trying to make a left-hand turn into the golf course.

"Also, you're used to living a high life-style. Expensive house, expensive cars, you go out to eat a lot, you entertain a lot. This all costs a lot of money. Now all of a sudden you go from that salary to something, maybe twenty-five thousand dollars, and you still have the same bills every month. Those bills aren't coming down either, mostly they're going up, but your salary certainly has come down. And if you can't adjust to that, you've got a lot of problems.

"I was used to the good things in life, and the reason was that the money was always there. When you're making it, you overlook how much it really is. You think nothing of spending seventy-five dollars for dinner. But now all of a sudden you can't afford a new suit this week, we couldn't eat steak three times a week, and all the time I'm thinking, 'How do I get my income back up?'"

As it turned out, "Hockey Night in Canada" was so impressed with Dornhoefer's work during the 1978-79 regular season and the Stanley Cup playoffs that he ultimately was hired on a fulltime basis. And one night in September 1979, as he prepared to move his family back to Canada, Dornhoefer told me, "I really don't miss playing the game at all. I feel very strongly about that. I spent twenty years putting skates on, and I've had enough.

"When I look back at all the great things I was involved in, sometimes I've thought, 'Was it really worth it?' Now, I have a very bad right knee. I can't even walk eighteen holes of golf anymore but what it fills up with fluid. I can't play tennis; I can't play racquetball. As the doctors have told me, I have the knees of a seventy-year-old man, so my knee certainly won't improve, it's only going to get worse.

"But when I look back, that's the only thing I regret, that I can't get involved in some activities other people my age do. After all, I'm really a very lucky man. I realized a dream by playing the National Hockey League, then on a Stanley Cup champion. Hockey was very good to me and my family, and then, just when I thought I was out of it for good, the game opened up an entirely new career field for me."

So far as a career in the NHL is concerned, one will hear few complaints from Gerhardt Otto Dornhoefer. For he lived the Dream, and, in hindsight, would have had it no other way.

Since Gary Dornhoefer first broke into professional hockey almost 20 years ago, the Dream has undergone a series of sweeping changes. Wayne Gretzky will live a different kind of Dream. A league of 6 teams numbers 21; their rosters, once exclusively Canadian, are now liberally sprinkled with Americans and Swedes, even with Czechoslovakians, and the salaries they earn are among the highest in professional sports. Hockey continues to demand an uncommon breed, for it remains an uncommon blend of speed and beauty, of risk and danger. But, as hockey moves into the eighties, to live the Dream has never been so appealing to so many in so many parts of the world.

And it all began with the cold.

2
Skill, Speed, and Something Extra
NHL Strategy
by Frank Orr

Like worried widows clutching small annuities, for more than 60 years the men who made the decisions in North American professional hockey cleaved to the shaky notion that the care and nurturing of the game was their exclusive property.

The game was invented and developed in Canada, and through approximately seven decades, Canadians dominated hockey and guarded it carefully. Their view was a narrow one, their horizons very close. Most Canadians who played, coached, and administered the sport insisted that hockey had such speed, skill, creativity, and beauty that to tamper with it would be the same as retouching a Rembrandt or meddling with Mozart.

That outlook came from a narrow base. For 30 years before 1967, North American major-league hockey, the National Hockey League, was restricted to a tiny, six-city pocket in the northeast portion of the continent—Montreal, Toronto, Boston, New York, Detroit, and Chicago. Any change in the way hockey was played or coached was regarded with supreme suspicion; innovators were treated as heretics to be exiled to some other line of work. Alterations in hockey, even minute ones that made immense good sense, never were adopted willingly. As an example, hockey goaltenders never wore protective face masks until 1959. It was just that way in hockey—the surface was ice, the puck was rubber, and goalies were barefaced.

When Jacques Plante, the brilliant goalie of the Montreal Canadiens, fed up with cuts and stitches in his face from errant pucks, first donned a crude face mask for protection in 1959, the team management strongly opposed the move. Plante's use of the mask was viewed as a sign that he had lost his nerve, that he lacked the courage to play effectively in perhaps the most demanding and hazardous position in all of sport.

Plante was a strong skater and skilled puckhandler even when wearing his bulky goaltending equipment. When he started to skate away from his net to field loose pucks and guarantee possession by his team, it was regarded as a radical departure from a tradition that held goalkeepers close to their goal creases like dogs chained to a kennel.

Again the Canadiens' management objected. Plante's ventures afield were passed off as mere

showboating, although it made good sense that a goalie who could skate 20 feet to pass the puck to a mate or clear it out of danger was an advantage for his team.

Pro hockey had a monkey-see, monkey-do attitude to new ideas. When a pioneer like Plante added a new wrinkle that was successful, especially if he were a prominent player on a strong team, other players quickly used it. After Plante weathered the opposition to his new tricks, face masks and puckhandling safaris became standard parts of the goalies' repertoires. But the coaches and management of most teams accepted the fairly simple changes with reluctance.

Another sound idea that the NHL was extremely

tardy in accepting was the deployment of more than one coach per team. When Fred Shero, coach of the Philadelphia Flyers at the time, hired an assistant coach, Mike Nykoluk, in 1972, the move was regarded as downright radical. The expected guffaws were heard from the traditionalists.

"Can't understand why the Flyers would spend the money for a second coach when there's nothing for him to do?" said an NHL team owner.

"Maybe Freddie the Fog wants someone to have a beer with on the road. There can't be any other reasons for a head coach having an assistant."

44

Preceding pages: Gilles Gilbert of the Detroit Red Wings leans into the save on an approaching shot. Above: Montreal's Jacques Plante initiated two goaltending innovations—wearing a mask and playing out from the net. Opposite: Dave Schultz was the toughest of the 1970s' Philadelphia Flyers.

When the Flyers won the Stanley Cup in 1974 and 1975, the swing started to the coaching staff approach. There were some stubborn holdouts, of course, those who stuck to the one-coach, one-team philosophy. But in the 1980–81 NHL season, the 21 teams employed a total of 48 fulltime coaches.

Although some renovations to the NHL's elderly traditions came from inside the lodge, the largest evolution perhaps the game has ever seen was not inspired by some creative, inventive Canadian or U.S. thinker but by the rapid ascent to the top of the global hockey hill by the Soviet Union, followed closely by Czechoslovakia and Sweden.

The first hints that the USSR was up to something in hockey came back in 1954, when the Soviets won their first world amateur championship, defeating an ordinary senior amateur team from Toronto in the final. Up to that time, Canada could send its weakest amateur team to the world tournament and win easily. Canada regained the title in the late 1950s with teams of a top minor pro caliber, but in the 1960s, the Soviets simply were too strong and the Canadian amateurs had problems beating the Czechs and Swedes, too.

The NHL scoffed at the Soviets and the other European countries, claiming that Canada's top 500 players were too busy playing pro hockey to be bothered with some dinky world amateur tournament. But, the barriers between the two schools of hockey—the amateurs of Europe and the pros of North America—finally fell in 1972, when an eight-game series was arranged between the national team of the USSR and Team Canada, an NHL all-star side.

Among the surprise attacks of history, the night of September 2, 1972, ranks right up there with Pearl Harbor and the iceberg's collision with the Titanic. The NHL and everyone involved in Canadian hockey smugly predicted a sweep of the series by Team Canada. But on that sweltering evening in the Montreal Forum, the Soviet team initiated a large metamorphosis in hockey and the way it is played by whipping the all-stars, 7–3. Team Canada did rally to win the series by the slimmest possible margin—a goal 36 seconds away from the conclusion of the eighth game.

Although the proud in the NHL claimed that the

46

Opposite top: *Dave Christian, who led the Winnipeg Jets in scoring his first year in the NHL, was a key member of the U.S. Olympic team in 1980.* Opposite bottom: *U.S. Olympic player Phil Verchota celebrates a goal scored against the Soviet team.* Above: *Now playing in the NHL are former Olympians Mark Johnson (left), United States; Peter Stastny, Czechoslovakia; and Ken Morrow, United States.*

"Summit Series" was staged in September when the NHL players were not in top playing condition was the only reason for its closeness, the thinkers in the league knew that the NHL's arrogantly held spot at the top of the world hockey ladder was a tenuous one. Through the 1970s, as the exchanges between the NHL and Soviets continued and increasing numbers of European players, notably a sizable group of Swedes and a few Czech defectors, were recruited by NHL teams, the reality of the situation slowly was driven home to the NHL: the Europeans and Soviets simply played better hockey than the pros.

Not that NHL hockey didn't have many superbly skilled players, the equal of any on the globe, or that the quality of NHL play and its entertainment value wasn't high. But in basic hockey skills, notably skating, making a pass, and, especially, taking a pass, team strategy, coaching methods, and the conditioning of players, the foreigners had moved ahead while the pros were spinning their wheels.

The second NHL-Team Canada downed an inferior Soviet national team in the 1976 Canada Cup tournament. However, the USSR didn't use many fine but aging players, breaking in a batch of skilled youngsters. Several of those young players were on the Soviet club that ended forever all NHL notions of superiority. In the 1979 Challenge Cup series of three games in New York between the NHL all-star team and the USSR nationals, the comrades lost the first match but won the next two, including a 6–0 triumph in the third game. The NHL stars didn't score a goal in the concluding 94 minutes, 54 seconds of the series.

The skill, speed, and teamwork of the Soviets drilled some points home to the NHL: their game was stagnant, even the best NHL players had weaknesses in fundamental skills, and the league's coaching had lagged far behind and, in some cases, was just plain inferior.

Of course, more than a few hockey people incorrectly viewed the amazing gold-medal triumph of the U.S. Olympic team at the Lake Placid games as something that took North American hockey off the hook after the Challenge Cup debacle. If anything, that gold medal represented the antithesis of the "off-the-hook" viewpoint. For many years, the NHL, a league in which teams are managed, coached, and staffed almost entirely by Canadians, had the same outlook toward American college hockey as it did toward the Europeans and the Soviets. That outlook was: they're nice folks doing some interesting little things that have no value to pro hockey.

Masterminded by coach Herb Brooks, the U.S. team used an approach that was perhaps 20 percent NHL (tenacious checking), 80 percent European (speed, movement, puck control, teamwork) in its influence. The splendid success of several members of the U.S. team in their post-Olympic whirls with NHL teams—Jim Craig, Mike Ramsey, Rob McClanahan, Ken Morrow, Steve Christoff, Dave Christian, and Mark Johnson—emphasized a point very strongly: U.S. college hockey had pulled even with Canadian junior hockey, the traditional source of most NHL players, as a development area.

Although the NHL has not made gigantic alterations in its way of doing things, as the league heads into the 1980s, the signs are there that the men who run it at least are cognizant of the need for changes in several areas—player development, coaching, conditioning, skill teaching, and team play.

Really, the 1970s were a lost period for the NHL, although when the decade opened, the seventies were hailed as bonanza time for hockey, a period when the game would move into the very front ranks of team sport in the United States and rank with baseball, football, and basketball. The NHL had expanded from 6 to 12 teams in 1967, then to 18 clubs by 1974. That proliferation itself greatly diluted the available talent, but when the World Hockey Association was born in 1972 with a dozen teams, the qualified players were spread as shallow as a starlet's smile.

The battle between the two leagues was costly in two areas—financially, as the gigantic escalation in salaries placed many teams on the verge of fiscal ruin, and artistically, as survival, not any improvement of the game, became the focal point for the majority of teams.

Because in the 1970s assembling a team of skilled players was close to impossible for just about every club but the Montreal Canadiens, some teams took a different approach. Instead of skaters, they recruited musclemen, players who had belligerence as their main skill, and attempted to intimidate their foes into

Above: *Mark Johnson,
leading Olympic scorer,
plays for the Pittsburgh
Penguins.* Left: *Jim
Craig's Olympic
goaltending earned him
jobs with Atlanta and
Boston.*

Above: *Islander coach Al Arbour holds team practice.* Right: *John A. Ziegler, Jr., NHL president, succeeded Clarence Campbell in 1977.* Far right: *Claude Ruel operated Montreal's "finishing school."*

50

submission. The word "goon" became part of hockey's language.

The Philadelphia Flyers were the team that carried the muscle approach to its extreme. They became the "Broad Street Bullies," a rollicking team of large-sized, ultra-aggressive workers who established team penalty records and made what the purists called "the science of intimidation" part of their tactics.

Fisticuffs and bench-clearing scraps became a way of life for the Flyers, but they also won the Stanley Cup in both 1974 and 1975. While the team seemed much more proficient with its fists than its hockey skills, the Flyers also became a large contradiction because they combined the best and the worst factors of hockey. The two sides of the Flyers exerted large influences on the overall game.

Fred Shero was the Flyer coach in that era and he was regarded by many as some sort of evil genius who added new dimensions to the game at both ends of the spectrum. An admitted admirer of the Soviet approach to hockey and an apostle of Anatoli Tarasov, the man who choreographed the USSR ascent to the hockey summit, Shero was not only the first head coach in the NHL to have a fulltime assistant coach, but the first to employ Soviet-oriented practice methods and the man who produced the "Shero system," a disciplined style of play that resulted in a very effective team when it stuck to hockey.

But Shero didn't discourage the total bellicosity of his players, the all-for-one brawling approach. Often, the fights in which the Flyer roughnecks, notably winger Dave ("The Hammer") Schultz, were involved seemed to be started deliberately, not the spontaneous flare-ups.

The NHL did make some mild efforts to reduce the violence in the sport with changes in the rules, such as the "third-man-in" law in which a player who interfered in a fight received a game misconduct. An added incentive for the NHL to crack down on its most flagrant offenders came from outside the game—the government of the Province of Ontario.

Concerned about increasing violence in amateur hockey in the province, the Ontario government first ordered an investigation in which all aspects of the game came under close scrutiny. The NHL was scorched badly by the report from that examination of hockey because of the "emulation factor," the bad example pros set for the youngsters. In 1976, Ontario's attorney general, Roy McMurtry, decreed that acts of extreme violence on the ice would be treated no differently than if they had happened on the street. Four NHL players—Don Maloney, then with the Detroit Red Wings, Dave ("Tiger") Williams of the Toronto Maple Leafs and four Flyers (Joe Watson, Mel Bridgman, Don Saleski, and Bob Kelly) were charged with criminal offenses for incidents in games at Maple Leaf Gardens in Toronto. Two Flyers (Kelly, Watson) were fined for incidents involving fans; the others were acquitted.

McMurtry's action produced the expected reaction from the NHL brass: We can run our own operation and don't need any help from government. But the Ontario happenings did emphasize the point that hockey had deteriorated to the point where some aspects of the game were socially unacceptable.

An even more important event than the crackdown on violence in getting hockey back on the rails was the regaining of the Stanley Cup by the Montreal Canadiens for four consecutive years from 1976, when they blew off the Flyers in a four-game final, to 1979. While assorted NHL teams became second-rate imitations of the Flyers by building their own goon packs, the Canadiens had reconstructed their roster with superbly talented young players.

The Montreal club never joined the swing to muggers. The Canadiens' game was pure hockey with an emphasis on skating speed, passing skill, and teamwork. They had enough big, strong players to supply the required protection for their small, swift attackers. However, the Canadiens, always at or near the bottom of the team penalty list, seemed to feel that goon hockey simply was far below their dignity.

Through their illustrious history, the Canadiens never had wavered from their "firewagon hockey" approach, and when they started the goon era on its slide to oblivion, their opponents quickly realized that a change in style from muscle to speed was necessary if they were to have any chance of being competitive with the classy Montrealers.

Interestingly, the team that ended the Canadiens' playoff domination—the Minnesota North Stars, who ousted the Montreal club in an exceptional seven-game quarterfinal series in 1980—is constructed in the Canadiens' mold. The Stars have assembled a group of skilled, very fast forwards and mobile defensemen, and the team is one of the NHL's bright hopes for the 1980s.

The final block in the restored foundation of intelligence upon which pro hockey can be reconstructed in the 1980s was the merger of the NHL and the remnants of the WHA in 1979. Serious negotiations on a joining of the two leagues had been in progress for three years before the finalization of the arrangements in which four surviving WHA teams—the Winnipeg Jets, Quebec Nordiques, Hartford Whalers, and Edmonton Oilers—were taken into the NHL fold to form a 21-team league.

Thus, after an eight-year war that threatened to do irreparable damage to the pro game, peace was restored to major-league hockey and the attention of those in the sport could be devoted to improving it, instead of merely trying to keep some breath in its lungs.

The man who played a major role in the restoration of hockey peace, NHL president John Ziegler, summed it up best. "For the past eight years, just about the only subject discussed in our board of governors' meetings has been survival," said Ziegler on the day the war ended.

"We've talked on and on and on about lawsuits against us, our legal actions against the other league, the collective bargaining agreement with the players' association, the financial problems of many of our teams, and the gigantic escalation in salaries. One thing we just haven't found the time to discuss very often is the caliber of play on the ice and what we might do to improve it."

Well, the war is over now and, all of a sudden, a great many chaps in the NHL are devoting large amounts of time and energy to the way the game is played and improving it. The changes in the game as it heads into the 1980s are sizable. Here are a few of them.

Coaching. The almost universal swing to coaching staffs for NHL teams indicates that clubs now feel that a coach can do much more for the team than open the bench gate and make certain there are six players on the ice.

52

Top: *Fred Shero, shown coaching the Rangers, influenced the grind-it-out style of play.* Above: *Chicago center Terry Ruskowski (left) practices under the eyes of coach Keith Magnuson.* Opposite: *Bernie Parent won the Conn Smythe Award for his Stanley Cup performances in 1974 and 1975.*

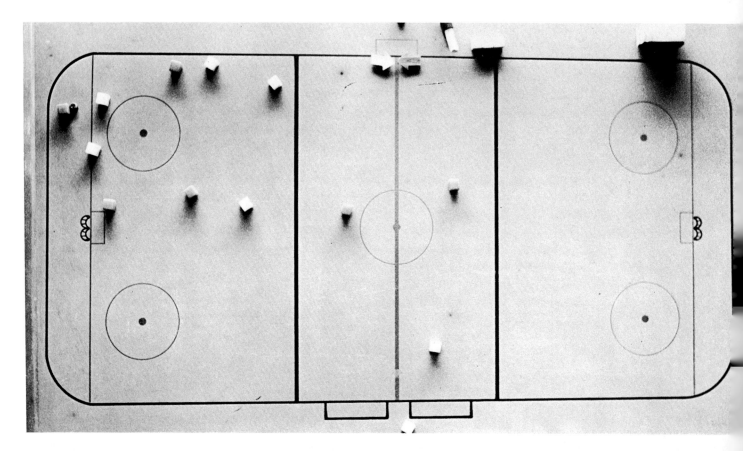

Top: *With more emphasis being placed on strategy and total team play, strategy boards are helpful teaching tools.* Above left: *Red Kelly, former Toronto coach, hoped to "whip" his players into shape.* Above right: *On the road, ex-Winnipeg coach, Tom McVie, has pregame lecture on the team's opponent.*

Although two NHL clubs, the Boston Bruins and St. Louis Blues, employed only one fulltime coach for the 1980–81 season, the 21 NHL teams had a total of 48 coaches. Several teams had three-man staffs. Eleven of those coaches had college degrees in a variety of disciplines ranging from physical education to psychology. Ten didn't play as much as one game in the NHL.

That represented a noteworthy change. Team owners once regarded with suspicion coaches or players who had completed high school, and the only qualification a coach needed was NHL playing experience.

Style of play. Speed and motion! Quickness and movement! Those phrases were tossed around freely by NHL coaches to describe the style of play they wanted their teams to employ heading into the 1980s, the approach the Montreal Canadiens always have used.

Gone is the stop-and-start, up-and-down-the-wings, static style used by the "grinder" teams of the 1970s. Replacing it is a puck-control, everyone-in-motion, total-team approach.

Conditioning. Preparation for an NHL season once consisted of an hour's skating per day and a few scrimmages through a two-week training camp. Off-ice training activities were scorned and physical fitness experts were regarded as weirdos. Now most NHL teams have a conditioning expert on their staff, almost all players are involved in sophisticated off-season training programs, and, after the discovery that the Soviets could control the majority of NHL players with one arm, upper-body strength is being stressed.

The result is that hockey now is played by better athletes in better condition than ever before.

Skill upgrading. Through much of its history, the NHL operated on a simple axiom: the fact that a hockey player was good enough to be considered for a big-league team meant that he knew all there was to know about how to play the game. Any teaching of skills was done at the junior level and, in the six-team NHL days, very few players escaped an apprenticeship of several seasons in the minor pro leagues where they learned a limited amount by osmosis.

The expansion of the NHL means that players are rushed to the big league very quickly, many of them

before they have used up their junior eligibility. It took a long time for NHL teams to realize that young players needed large amounts of upgrading in specific skills.

Of course, the Canadiens realized it a long time ago. That's why they had the Claude Ruel Finishing School. Now head coach of the club, Ruel was an assistant for several years and his main job was to teach specific skills to the young talent. Few players, even the mighty Guy Lafleur, became regulars until they graduated with honors from Ruel's classes.

Technology. NHL management and coaches long made jokes about football's devotion to game films, claiming that a football coach couldn't tell you the score of the game until he studied the films of it. Hockey was viewed as a game of emotion, reflexes, and creativity that could be enjoyed on film but not dissected and analyzed.

Some coaches in the NHL retain a reluctance to use videotapes for analysis, as a teaching aid, or a method of advance scouting of an upcoming opponent. Other clubs, notably the Buffalo Sabres under coach Roger ("Captain Video") Neilson, rely heavily on video.

The Sabres also produce many sheets of statistics to evaluate players' performances and, in the 1979–80 season, became the first hockey team to use electronic communication between the bench and a spotter high above the ice during games.

Player development. Once, production of hockey players was simple. Every Canadian boy wanted to play in the NHL. He learned to skate on a pond or river, joined his local team where, if he had any talent, was spotted by the "bird dog" for an NHL club, funneled through a junior hockey system sponsored by a big-league team and, if he survived the severe talent distillation process, eventually made it to the NHL.

The NHL no longer sponsors junior teams and, anyway, the proliferation of big-league hockey made it impossible for the Canadian junior system to supply enough talent. To meet the large demand, the NHL was forced to mollify its strange view that Europeans, especially Swedes, were too cowardly and U.S. college players simply weren't good enough to play big-league hockey.

Now, being good enough is the only qualification a player needs. NHL teams scout European hockey very closely and U.S. players are very high selections in the NHL entry draft, an area once the exclusive property of Canadian juniors. The NHL also is taking a close look at Canadian junior hockey, where many teams face financial problems and the long schedules make adequate skill teaching almost impossible.

The Men Behind the Bench

Because the NHL operated almost as a closed shop for almost 70 years, a tight little lodge into which outsiders seldom gained entry, fresh ideas were as rare as a pork chop at a bar mitzvah. In fact, any innovation was regarded with maximum suspicion and with such narrow statements as "Hockey's a great game, so why would anyone want to change it?"

With very few exceptions, coaches were recruited from one source—the ranks of former players. Thus, a man who had played the game for a coach who had prepared for the job by playing the game for a coach who had prepared the same way became a coach. The same stale philosophies, the same dull approaches, were passed on and the cycle seldom was broken because few coaches with new ideas from outside the lodge were hired for an NHL coaching job.

Many players who became coaches when their careers were finished never had a chance for success were because they thrust into a job for which they were unprepared. Men with no knowledge of the teaching arts, no idea of motivation except shouting, were given what, basically, is a teaching and motivation job.

"I can remember once going to my coach, who had been a great player himself, and asking him to help me to be a better passer," a former NHL player said. "He told me just to work hard and everything would be okay, because he didn't have the faintest idea how to go about teaching one of hockey's most simple skills."

The archaic system, however, did produce some outstanding coaches—Toe Blake, who guided the Canadiens to eight Stanley Cup victories, including five consecutive triumphs from 1956 to 1960; Hap Day (in the 1940s) with the Toronto Maple Leafs; and Scotty Bowman, who had great successes with the St. Louis Blues, the Canadiens, and the Buffalo Sabres.

In other team sports, notably football and baseball, where coaching staffs with a head man and several assistants were used, a good coaching prospect had the opportunity to serve an apprenticeship and learn the coach's craft. After a few years as an assistant, he would be well-prepared for a head-coaching post. Football and baseball teams, needing a head man, often canvassed the assistants' staffs of other clubs looking for good candidates.

Because hockey had no assistant coaches, there was no way anyone could learn the profession at the major-league level and gain the experience necessary to make an easy transition to a head-coaching post. All too often a man went from player to coach with no intermediate steps in between. One day he was drinking beer with his mates; the next day he was their boss.

Hockey had the same problems in finding qualified front-office personnel. Most NHL teams were operated by one man—the general manager. There were no assistant GMs learning how to eventually head up an organization.

When the coaching-staff approach finally was used by NHL teams in the late 1970s, little time was needed for teams to look to other clubs' assistants when they required a leader. When the Colorado Rockies needed a head coach for the 1980–81 season, they hired Billy MacMillan, assistant coach under the brilliant Al Arbour with the 1980 Stanley Cup champion New York Islanders.

Appropriately, the men who coached the Stanley Cup winners for seven consecutive years from 1973 to 1979—Bowman, who took the Canadiens to five triumphs, and Shero, who won the other two with the Flyers—were the men who pioneered the coaching-staff approach. Although Shero had served a long, successful apprenticeship in the minor leagues, NHL teams overlooked him because he was thought to have a few radical ideas about the way the job should be done. But after they had floundered through their first five seasons as one of the original 1967 expansion teams, the Flyers hired Shero as coach for the 1971–72 season. A year later, Shero hired Mike Nykoluk as the NHL's first fulltime assistant coach. Nykoluk had had a 15-year career as a player with the Hershey Bears of the American League.

"I found that to do the coaching of an NHL team properly was just too much for one man," Shero said. "I wanted to try some new things and that was very difficult by myself.

"For instance, when one coach had to conduct a workout and do some specific drills with, say, the team's specialty units—the power-play and penalty-killers—it meant the other players were left on their own to waste time. Having an assistant made our practices much more productive, and the players didn't become bored."

"I didn't look on myself as any trailblazer for hiring an assistant coach. I can't understand why some team hadn't done it long ago."

When the late Barry Ashbee had his playing career ended by an eye injury in 1974, he was added to the Flyers coaching staff. Claude Ruel was a splendid young Canadien defense prospect in the 1950s, but his career hopes were ended when he lost the sight of an eye. Ruel worked as a scout for the Canadiens, then was named coach of the team in 1968, when Toe Blake retired.

Ruel lasted for two and a half seasons on that job, but when he recognized the toll of mental strain, he went back to the scouting staff. When Scotty Bowman, who had guided the St. Louis Blues to considerable success as an expansion franchise, returned to the Canadiens as head coach in 1971, he slowly worked Ruel into the assistant's role, although Ruel never held that title officially. Ruel's main job was the operation of his "finishing school" for young prospects. After each workout, Ruel would drill the youngsters in basic skills.

"At the time, I didn't like Ruel a great deal because I didn't do much for two years except work with him on what seemed to be trivial little things," said Steve Shutt, Canadiens' all-star left winger. "But there were big holes in my game and he filled them in with daily repetition of his drills. For instance, I'd been a big shooter in junior hockey so I hadn't worked on my passing game, both in giving and taking a pass. Every day, Claude would pass the puck to me dozens of times. Finally, I got it right.

"When I look back now, I realize that I owe him a great deal, because Claude really taught me how to play the game."

One of the game's shrewdest, brightest men, Bowman was another innovator in coaching at the NHL level. Perhaps some of the credit he deserved was siphoned off because his team always had excellent talent with which he could work. But several players who became all-stars with the Montreal club were, simply, very raw material when they arrived. Under Bowman and Ruel, they developed into front-line stars.

When the Canadiens refused to give Bowman the job he really wanted in their organization—the general manager's post—when the game's best executive, Sam Pollock, retired in 1978, he used an escape clause in his contract to move to the Buffalo Sabres as director of hockey operations, general manager, and, for the 1979–80 season, head coach. "There are many ideas I want to try in the operation and coaching of an NHL team," Bowman said. "Now that I'm in charge of an organization, I'll be able to try them.

"They're not far out, revolutionary things. It's more a matter of using everything that's available as coaching and teaching aids, such as videotape, statistical breakdowns, and electronic communications."

To execute his plans for the Sabres, Bowman found the perfect accomplice in Roger Neilson, the team's associate coach in the 1979–80 season who was promoted to the head coaching post when Bowman concentrated on the general manager's chores in 1980–81. From 1968 to 1977, Neilson coached the Peterborough Petes of the Ontario Major Junior league, where he earned a reputation as one of the game's most advanced thinkers. A few of the NHL's traditionalists figured he was slightly mad.

Possessor of degrees in physical education and education, Neilson was the first coach to make heavy use of videotapes of games and their breakdown into statistics. He worked with fitness experts on conditioning programs for his players and his practice methods were based on structured learning processes. Neilson once used his dog, Jacques, to help teach proper fore-checking techniques to his junior players. When an opponent was in possession of the puck behind his team's net, the Pete centers were having problems staying in front of the net until the opposition made its move to clear the puck. During a workout, Neilson stationed Jacques in front of the net,

went behind with the puck himself, and Jacques wouldn't move from his post until his master crossed the goal line with the puck.

"I don't think the players liked the inference, but they got the message," Neilson laughed.

In his time with the Petes, Neilson produced some of the NHL's best technical players—Bob Gainey and Doug Jarvis of the Canadiens, Craig Ramsay of the Sabres.

Neilson spent one season in the Central League before he was named coach of the Toronto Maple Leafs in 1977. At last, Neilson had the chance to test his theories at the big-league level, and in the 1977-78 season, he engineered a big improvement in the Leafs and the team advanced to the Stanley Cup semifinal for the first time in a decade.

When the Leafs spluttered in 1978-79, more because of a lack of talent than Neilson's coaching, team owner Harold Ballard, the most traditional of NHL moguls, had no problems finding the man to blame. Late in the season, Ballard fired Neilson and rehired him the next day, then did it permanently at the end of the term.

Ballard made a 180-degree turn in his views on Neilson in those two hectic years. When he hired Neilson in 1977, Ballard said: "We have a young team and Roger is a bright young guy with a lot of new ideas who can relate well to the young players." When he sacked Neilson in 1979, Ballard said: "If you want a guy to write a book full of high falutin' hockey ideas, Neilson is perfect, but all that schoolboy stuff doesn't work with NHL players."

When pucks fly and competitive energies flow, passions often flair. Above: *Some members of the Philadelphia Flyers and the New York Rangers mix it up at Madison Square Garden.* Opposite: *The Rangers again square off, this time against the Toronto Maple Leafs during a playoff series.*

Obviously, Bowman didn't agree because he quickly hired Neilson as associate coach and added Jim Roberts, who had played on Bowman's teams in St. Louis and Montreal, as an assistant coach. Then, when Neilson moved up to the number-one spot in 1980–81, Ron Smith, who had headed the very successful coaching certification program for the Ontario Hockey Association, joined the Sabre staff as an assistant.

"In the use of video and statistics, Neilson is the most knowledgeable man in hockey," Bowman said.

In technology and its application as a coaching aid in hockey, the Sabres were in a class by themselves. Of course, there have been many jokes cracked about the Sabres' coaching staff and the addiction to electronic gizmos, but several other NHL coaches have studied their approach closely.

Neilson does much more with videotapes of games than a simple overview. He breaks them down carefully into a statistical rating of the Sabre players' performances and retapes from them highlights in specific areas. "For instance, we have an accumulative tape of our penalty-killing unit taken from the game tapes," he said. "That means a player who's on that unit can very quickly analyze his work in recent games."

As pregame preparation, Neilson produces a written report on the Sabres' opponent, analyzing that team's style of play in several areas—fore-checking patterns, penalty-killing and power-play techniques, or the way they work their breakout plays from their zone. If a tape of a recent game of that team is

Morris Lukowich, who led the Winnipeg Jets in scoring during their first year in the NHL, is attended to by Jets' trainer Bill Bozak and concerned teammates, after he sustained an injury.

available, Neilson will prepare a short highlight film to illustrate each point on the written sheet. "It's one thing to give the players a written report on the way a team is moving the puck from its own zone," Neilson said. "But if we have a short tape sequence to show the club doing it, it's much more effective."

The use of two coaches behind the bench, one in communication with a spotter in the press box, was Bowman's idea. The Sabres had a small two-way radio setup developed for their use. "Changing lines and trying to get the right match ups on the ice takes all the attention of one coach," Bowman said. "That coach has little opportunity to study the play of the other team and make adjustments.

"Sure, a coach can receive a report from his spotter between periods, but if the other team throws something new at you, your club can be down a couple of goals by the end of the period. The spotter can pass the information along to the second coach at the bench right away and you can make adjustments immediately."

"Probably seventy-five percent of the information the spotter sends down that is passed on to the players on the bench by the other coach is positive reinforcement," Neilson said. "If a player has a good shift or makes a good play, then we tell him right away."

The Sabre players admit that they were skeptical about the system at first. "It was all so new to us that I suppose we were suspicious," said Sabre defenseman Jim Schoenfeld. "But before long, I found that I was telling Jim Roberts things to ask the coach upstairs. If the other team say, had fore-checked us well on a shift, I wanted to know why and would get Roberts to ask the man in the press box."

Although coaching techniques in the NHL and, because of the major-league influence, in Canadian junior hockey as well, had remained stagnant for many years, large advances were made in coaching at other levels of the game, notably Canadian and U.S. college hockey. "I feel that the coaching in U.S. college hockey always has been extremely competent," said Minnesota North Stars' head coach Glen Sonmor, who started his coaching career at the University of Minnesota after an eye injury ended *his* playing days.

"For one thing, working in the university milieu is entirely different than coaching a Canadian junior or a pro team," Sonmor added. "The athletes are in an educational setting, involved in the learning process all the time and, therefore, are very open to learning new things in hockey.

"The college schedule of approximately thirty-five games in a season is very conducive to skill teaching because the practice-to-game ratio is so good. Most college teams play a couple of games each weekend and have the remainder of the week for workouts. Most have their own arenas and all the ice time the players want and need is available.

"Because of the sports programs in most colleges, the facilities are complete in all areas. Conditioning experts, kiniseologists, sports medicine and psychology specialists, experts in video and films are available for a coach's use."

However, the NHL has been very reluctant to hire coaches from the U.S. colleges. Of the 48 coaches working in the 1980–81 NHL season, only 2 have U.S. backgrounds—Sonmor and Andre Beaulieu, assistant coach of the New York Rangers. Five coaches from Canadian colleges were added to NHL staffs in 1980–81—Smith (Buffalo Sabres), Pierre Page (Calgary Flames), Bob Boucher (Philadelphia Flyers), Bill Mahoney (Washington Capitals), and Tom Watt (Vancouver Canucks).

"Skill teaching has become such an important part of coaching at the NHL level that a man like Tom Watt, an educator who taught on the University of Toronto phys-ed faculty in addition to coaching hockey, is ideal for an NHL team," said Canucks' coach Harry Neale.

Perhaps the most interesting coach to enter the NHL in recent years is Gary Green of the Capitals. Green was only 26 when early in the 1979–80 season, after great success with Peterborough juniors, he took over the job as the youngest coach in NHL history. The scoffers claimed that Green simply was too young to gain any respect from pro players.

"If I'm able to do the job intelligently and make the players believe that my way is the way for the team to accomplish some good things, then I'll get the respect," Green said. "I don't really see what my age has to do with it. I worked hard to learn the coaching profession from all angles."

The Way the Game Is Played

Scotty Bowman never stopped saying it and never stopped winning, either. Pat Quinn of the Philadelphia Flyers said it often during the 1979-80 NHL season and the Flyers were unbeaten in 35 games during one stretch and advanced to the Stanley Cup final.

Al Arbour of the New York Islanders started saying it partway through 1979-80 and his team listened all the way to the Stanley Cup championship. Glen Sonmor said it often that season, too, and his Minnesota North Stars were one of the most entertaining teams in the league. Joe Crozier said it from the start when he was named coach of the Toronto Maple Leafs for the 1980-81 campaign.

It? That the best way to play the game of ice hockey was with speed, motion, and skill.

"When we saw the way the Soviet national team played the game in the Challenge Cup, their beautiful passing plays with the puck always going to a player who was on the move, and the way all players on the ice were involved in their plays, it was drilled home to us that our game needed some changes," said Calgary Flames' general manager Cliff Fletcher.

"The Europeans and the Soviets play such an entertaining brand of hockey with so much skating and passing skill that it was natural NHL teams wanted to play that way," said Fred Shero, late of the New York Rangers.

"They showed us that total team play is the easiest way to do it, that by passing the puck and being on the move all the time a team can get up the ice much more easily than by individual rushes.

"I see a great many NHL players still trying to beat opponents one-on-one. You never see a Soviet player trying to do that, because instead of trying to deke a man, he'll pass off, break into the clear, and get the puck back."

Shero exerted as much influence as any coach on the popularity of the slow-it-down, grind-it-out style of play that infested the NHL through much of the 1970s. Because the playing talent was spread very thinly by the explosion in the number of teams, finding a full roster of players who could skate and pass well enough to play the speed-and-movement

game was almost impossible. Instead of a team that could dominate play with quickness and skill in open ice, Shero built the Flyers to boss the show along the boards, in the corners of the rink, and in front of the net, the "pits" of hockey, with muscle and aggressiveness.

The Flyers carried to its zenith a style of play that had long been in vogue in the NHL and had a large hand in its production of dull entertainment. It's called "shoot-and-chase" hockey. When an NHL team carried the puck across the center red line, it didn't try to pass or carry the puck across the opposition's blue line. The puck was shot into the attacking zone. Instead of attempting to retain possession of the puck, the attacking team gave it up, then attempted to regain it by forcing opponents into mistakes through fore-checking.

A negative approach, really! NHL teams didn't try to produce goals through their own good plays on original rushes. They attempted to produce their scores from the opposition's mistakes.

The Flyers of the 1970s were very successful with that approach. Big and belligerent, they would fire the puck into the other team's zone, then bust in after it with their malevolence in high gear. The Canadiens countered the Flyers approach by arranging a very quick exit for the puck from their zone. That nullified the Flyers' strong fore-checking tactics.

When the New York Rangers played the Canadiens in the 1979 Stanley Cup final and won the first game by firing the puck into the Montreal team's zone, then harassing the Canadiens into mistakes, the Canadiens quickly adjusted. When the Rangers fired the puck in, the Canadiens very quickly moved it out into the neutral zone, often just lobbing it across their blue line with no particular target. That placed the puck up for grabs and, with their quickness, the Canadiens won 75 percent of the battles for possession.

An interested spectator at the finals that spring was Victor Tikhonov, the coach of the USSR national team. Tikhonov admitted that he was very puzzled by the Rangers' tactics. "Why do the Rangers keep on trying a tactic that isn't working for them?" Tikhonov asked. "Why do they continue to give up the puck by shooting it into the Canadiens' zone when the Canadiens are moving it out so quickly?"

In contrast to the shoot-and-chase style of the NHL, the Czechoslovakian national team produced more than 80 percent of its goals on original rushes in six world-championship tournaments in the late 1970s.

In the NHL's grind-it-out style, the wingers, especially, concentrated on defensive play, moving up and down the flanks as if on rails. On the attack, one winger always stayed near the blue line, instead of making a deep penetration into the attacking zone, ready to back-check if the opposition launched an attack. In their own zone, the wingers skated near the top of the face-off circles and stopped.

"Some teams in this league have played defense all the time, even when they had the puck," Bowman said. "Those teams kept their players under a strict system all the time and allowed little room for spontaneous, creative play.

"Of course, there are some specific things players must do when the other team has the puck. But a coach can reduce their effectiveness offensively by placing such tight limits on them.

"If a team checks strongly, everyone says that it's a good defensive team. But if a club plays a strong puck control game and attacks well, no one ever says it's a good defensive team. But the more a team has the puck under its control the less time there is for the other team to do damage with it. To me, that's the best form of defense."

The speed-and-motion game isn't all that complicated. Its major ingredient is consistent movement by the forwards, who don't stand around waiting for something to happen but stay on the move to make it happen. Speed in moving the puck also is important.

"Many hockey games are decided by which

Ice hockey is more than a game played on ice.
It involves the poise and discipline of
a dancer and the speed and agility of a well-trained athlete.

team's end of the rink is the site for the most play," said Crozier, former Maple Leafs' coach. "If we spend more time in the other team's zone than they spend in ours, then we'll win the majority of those games. If you don't want the other team in your end, then you make certain the puck isn't there, because that's what attracts them.

"The best way to avoid that is to get the puck on the move very quickly when it goes into your end, to get it up and out over the blue line before our opponents can get in to fore-check us into mistakes.

"There are two main ingredients in that—the defensemen or whoever gets the puck in our end getting it on the move very quickly and the forwards on the move to receive a pass.

"Too many times the fans will boo a defenseman when he's having trouble moving the puck, and it's not his fault. He'll pick up the puck deep in our zone but, because no forward is moving into the hole for a pass, the defenseman must hang on to it or just bang it out into the neutral zone—and that's when we get into trouble."

"Tempo! That's a big word in our plans for the North Stars," Sonmor said. "We have a team that skates well and has excellent quickness. We want our team to keep the pace of the game, the tempo of the play, as high as possible. We want the puck on the move all the time when we have it and we want our team to 'counter-punch' well, to go from defense to offense very quickly when we get the puck.

"That always has been a great asset of the Canadiens, their ability to break up your attack and mount one of their own all in one motion. A club that can do that keeps opponents on edge all the time."

Bowman has been a top student of the Soviet approach and he finds Tikhonov's ideas on the game refreshing and sound. "I read the translation of an article Tikhonov had written containing some of his ideas and I like what he says, especially his views on how the ice surface should be used," Bowman said. "The NHL approach always has been that a team operates in three zones—its defensive zone, the center or neutral zone, and the attacking zone, defined by the two blue lines.

"Under Tikhonov's approach, the Soviets have changed that to two zones, divided by the center red line. That idea has a great influence on the way the Soviets play the game, especially when they move to our rinks from the larger rinks of Europe.

"In our three-zone style, we restrict our defensemen on the attack very often and our wingers in backchecking by using the blue line as a boundary. The Soviets consider only the center line. Their blue line is for use only by the other team.

"Our wingers usually come back to the blue line or farther when the puck is in our zone. The Soviets keep their wingers out in the neutral zone, on the move and ready for a pass. When the Soviet defensemen pass the puck back and forth between them, one of the forwards can break for the long pass, which opens up their attack."

Bowman's view is that the application of the two-zone plan in the NHL would open up the game and cut down on the jamming-up of players in the attacking zone. "Tikhonov has written about the way the NHL squeezes ten skaters into one zone that is approximately sixty-five feet by eighty-five feet," Bowman added. "In the Soviet style, that zone with the central line as the boundary becomes eighty-five feet by one-hundred feet. That creates all sorts of new situations.

"When play is in your zone, your wingers stay outside your blue line and the other team's defensemen can't move up tight to your blue line. The game is more spread out and the opportunities for quick breaks, long passes, and wide-open play increase.

"I feel the two-zone approach would create more entertaining, exciting hockey for the fans in the NHL. People have talked about how exciting the Soviets were in the Challenge Cup [Bowman was coach of the NHL all-stars] with their great skating and passing. Well, their basic approach with the two-zone system plus, of course, their speed and skill in fundamentals, is the big reason for it."

A problem the NHL has is in the size of its ice surfaces. Most rinks are 200 feet long and 85 feet wide. Most European rinks are 210 feet to 215 feet long and 100 feet wide. "Our players are much bigger now than when that size of ice was established," Shero observed. "They skate faster now than ever before. But they just don't have enough room. If we could give them four more feet of ice all the way around the rink, the game would be that much better."

The Islanders have been an excellent team for several seasons, masters of the tight, disciplined, defensively oriented hockey. They played the dump-and-chase style extremely well because of their size and speed. But that wasn't enough. The Islanders were a bomb in the Stanley Cup playoffs. After two superb seasons in 1977-78 and 1978-79, the Islanders were eliminated by the Maple Leafs and Rangers.

The Islanders upgraded their muscle in 1979-80, but they also changed their approach. "Perhaps we had become a bit static in our play, lacking some flexibility," Coach Arbour said. "We loosened up a fair amount during the 1979-80 season and improved our work in the neutral zone. We made far more plays in that area than we ever had before, allowing our players to try more things.

"I don't think our changes were that great. We have some players who skate very well and who are very strong in fundamentals, especially in passing the puck. We just harnessed their creativity a little more than perhaps we had in the past."

The 1980 U.S. Olympic team's victory is difficult to analyze precisely because it was achieved through a combination of factors—sound tactical strategy, excellent basic skills, good team speed, and an incredible amount of ambition. The Olympic kids simply outworked some opponents.

The intense Brooks, who had achieved great success in college hockey at the University of Minnesota, drove the team relentlessly. Some players regarded him as cold and aloof. Brooks drilled the team hard in a possession style of game, tossing out the NHL's dump-and-chase. "I didn't want the team throwing the puck away with no reason," Brooks said. "That's stupid! It's the same as punting on first down.

"There was no way I was ready to concede that the Europeans and Soviets had better hockey players or athletes than we did. Thus, the success we could have came down to our conditioning, the style of hockey we played, and the level we could attain at playing it.

"The style I wanted combined the best features of the two schools of hockey: the determined checking of the North American game and the good features of the European style—speed, good tactics, puck control, and possession."

Brooks concedes that the transition to his approach wasn't easy for his players. "When we had the puck, our players had a great deal of freedom to be creative, to play with it," Brooks said. "But that freedom was countered by a responsibility when we didn't have it—the need for our team to check tenaciously to get it back.

"The two things dovetailed together quite well. If our players wanted to have that offensive freedom—and that style of hockey is great fun to play—then they had to be strong in the other area. How much freedom I was willing to give them on the attack depended directly on how well they played defensively, because I didn't want the team engaging in shooting matches.

"Our players responded beautifully to that approach. I think in the Olympics the fact that we were more aggressive defensively than the European teams was a big thing in our favor."

Producing Better Players

Because a situation existed for so long in North American hockey in which the entire Canadian hockey system produced players for only six big-league teams, the NHL devoted very little time or money to the development of talent. A simple distillation process up through the ranks of boys' hockey to junior leagues to minor pro play sent the cream of the crop to the NHL and, because the league was the best in the world, there was no standard of excellence to which the talent could be compared.

But when big-league hockey expanded suddenly into 34 teams in the early 1970s, the game discovered the facts of life very quickly: staffing 6 teams was one thing; staffing 34 clubs was something else.

To fill out their rosters, NHL and WHA clubs were forced to employ workers of lesser skills, and just about every hacker and chopper who could stand up on skates and hold a hockey stick in his hands was earning a major-league salary. Then along came the European and Soviets with their superbly conditioned, excellent skating, thoroughly skilled players to drill home the point that North American hockey had been doing a bad job of training players.

Thus, as the game enters the 1980s, the people involved in all levels of hockey from peewee to pro are taking a close look at the methods being used to prepare players.

Calgary's Fletcher has the view that the NHL must take a long, careful look at the entire system that produces talent for the pros. Until the NHL expanded from 6 to 12 teams in 1967, the NHL teams operated their own development system, sponsoring junior teams and spreading financial aid as far down into minor hockey as the bantam (14 years) level.

The Canadian government at the time was quite strong in its view that the NHL's influence in amateur hockey should be ended. The NHL withdrew its sponsorship and the entry (amateur) draft was established to divide the graduating crop of junior players. Now Fletcher wonders if the NHL should regain some influence in the pre-professional development of players.

"Since the NHL sponsorship of junior teams ended, the skill level of junior players the system has produced has decreased steadily, not a gigantic amount, but enough to be noticeable," Fletcher said. "When an NHL team sponsored a junior club, it didn't have winning championships or making a profit on that club's operation as the number-one concern. The NHL teams were willing to lose a sizable amount on the sponsorship if the junior team produced some quality talent.

"Now the junior teams are all operated as independent businesses and the men who operate those teams are more interested in not losing money than in the skill level of the players they produce."

The NHL contributes substantially to the coffers of the major junior leagues. But, in order to influence the current situation, junior teams will have to shorten their schedules and improve their game-to-practice ratio. "The U.S. colleges are doing a better job of skill teaching than the juniors are," Fletcher said. "The reasons are rather obvious. The colleges play a much shorter schedule than the juniors and have much more time for practice to work on skills. If we can help the juniors reduce their schedules and devote more time to instruction, it would help."

Many NHL teams, however, realize that skill improvement also must be done at the big-league level. "Our schedule and travel make it difficult to find the time for working on specific skills, but we simply must do it," said Ted Lindsay, former coach of the Detroit Red Wings.

"Because teams can make only small improvements through trades, the way up the ladder is through wise claims in the entry draft and then developing these young players as much as possible. The teams that do the best jobs in the skill-improvement area will be the most successful ones in the future."

Max McNab, general manager of the Washington Capitals, feels hockey should consider the example of major-league baseball and operate instructional leagues in which younger prospects are prepared thoroughly in the basic fundamentals.

"Baseball draws much of its talent from the colleges, which do a good job of preparing the players up to a certain skill level, just as the junior hockey leagues used to do for the NHL," McNab said. "But to take those players closer to the major-league skill level, baseball has the rookie or instructional league in Florida in the off-season. The best skill teachers are big-league teams who work with the young players.

"Perhaps it's time the NHL took a serious look at a similar arrangement, a development program for players between junior and pro hockey. The emphasis in it would be on the teaching and improving of basic hockey skills."

McNab summed up the NHL's outlook for the 1980s well. "We can produce some mighty exciting hockey with the level of skill we have now in the NHL," he said "But after watching the Soviets and seeing the way the Swedes and Czechs in the NHL play the game, just think how exciting our hockey would be if we added their level in basic skills to the good things our game has now."

The excellent skating ability and skillful stickhandling of center Bob Bourne (14) are among the reasons the 1979–80 New York Islanders were able to add flexibility to their attack. Coach Al Arbour feels this versatility was crucial to their success in the Stanley Cup playoffs.

3
"Never Saw Anything Like It"
Great Games
by Gary Ronberg

Bill Barilko, April 21, 1951

With that curly brown hair, clear blue eyes, even white teeth, and look of perpetual innocence, his appearance was that of an altar boy. But what he really was, was a hero for the common man, a professional hockey player who could be found laughing with the fans over a few ales at a local tavern or, before he got there, playing with the kids on a Toronto street corner at dusk.

A crude product of a minor-league team called the Hollywood Wolves, Bill Barilko crashed into the defense of the Toronto Maple Leafs during the 1946–47 season on desire alone. Certainly it wasn't his skating ability (he had to advance several strides on the tips of his blades to catch up with everyone else), nor was it his shot (he never scored more than seven goals in a National Hockey League season). His best moves? Snapping his hips into an onrushing opponent, or dropping to his knees in the face of a shot aimed at the Toronto net.

Even as the Maple Leafs marched to Stanley Cup titles in 1947, 1948, and 1949, Barilko never attained the notoriety of such Toronto stars as Max Bentley, Tod Sloan, Ted Kennedy, Cal Gardner, and goaltenders Walter ("Turk") Broda and Al Rollins, a youngster who would win the Vezina Trophy in 1951. In fact, Barilko's most noteworthy statistic was the league-leading 147 minutes in penalties he accumulated during his rookie year, and continued to embellish with numerous fights thereafter.

Then came the spring of 1951. The Leafs' streak of Cups had been snapped 12 months earlier by the eventual Cup-champion Detroit Red Wings in the first round of the playoffs; but now they were in the finals once more, against a Montreal contingent that had upset the powerhouse Red Wings to get there.

In the first game, at Maple Leaf Gardens, Barilko preserved a 2–2 tie by sprawling to deflect Maurice Richard's drive at an open net with only minutes left in regulation play. Sid Smith then rewarded Toronto with victory 5:51 into sudden death. But in the second game, Richard make no mistake, scoring for a 3–2 Montreal triumph 2:55 into overtime.

At the Forum, Toronto coach Joe Primeau opted

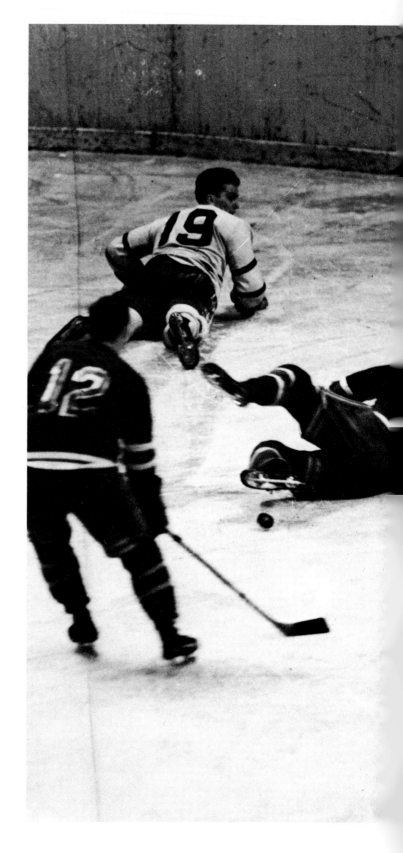

Preceding pages: *A playoff-winning goal by Montreal Canadiens' Jean Beliveau (4) during the second sudden-death overtime eliminated the Boston Bruins from the Eastern Division playoffs in 1969. Above: The Maple Leafs' Bill Barilko (19) earned a reputation for aggressive play that often found him down on the ice.*

for Rollins in place of the veteran Broda, and the Leafs prevailed, 2-1, on Kennedy's strike 4:47 into overtime. Three straight sudden-death games? Try four, with Harry Watson giving the Leafs a 3-1 advantage in games with his goal at 5:15 of sudden death.

The Canadiens were not about to die, however, and going into the final minute of the fifth game at Maple Leaf Gardens, they led, 2-1. But then Primeau pulled Rollins for a sixth attacker, and Sloan scored with only 32 seconds left, sending the fifth game into overtime.

By now, Primeau was debating whether to continue to employ the rambunctious Barilko on defense. "Bill had been committing himself too much, going on offense," Primeau would say later. "He would get caught out of position, which was dangerous with Rocket Richard on the ice. I finally told him I'd fine him if he didn't lay back and concentrate on defense."

Barilko promised that he would, indeed, play defensively. Except that there he was, 2:50 into sudden death, with the puck skittering toward him—inside a blue line he had just vowed not to cross. Back onto the tips of his skates he vaulted, churned toward the puck, and, in one motion, flailed away. "He looked like Dagwood catching a bus," Toronto owner Conn Smythe would say later.

It was a moment that deserved to be frozen in time—Barilko, floating headfirst through the air, as his shot eluded goaltender Gerry McNeil's frantic glove and billowed in the net. Indeed, for one long moment, 14,577 people in Maple Leaf Gardens were frozen in their seats until they finally realized what had happened, and saw Barilko buried beneath his delirious teammates.

"I won't fine you for charging that one!" Primeau screamed.

"I told you the slap shot was a deadly shot!" yelled Barilko, referring to what had been considered a fad around the NHL.

"At times Bill was such a problem I wanted to send him down to Pittsburgh," said Smythe, "but thank God we kept him."

Bill Barilko finally was a national hero. And a few months later, in August, he was still basking in Stanley Cup glory when he took off in a private plane on a fishing trip into northern Ontario...

He was never heard from again.

Bill Mosienko, March 23, 1952

There was very little interest in the final game of the 1951–52 season between the Chicago Black Hawks and the New York Rangers. It was already etched in stone that neither team was playoff bound; the Hawks were doomed to sixth place, the Rangers to fifth, and as a result only 3,254 die-hard hockey fans paid their way into Madison Square Garden the night of March 23, 1952.

So far as the Rangers were concerned, in fact, games of far more importance were being played in the American Hockey League, where Cincinnati, their AHL affiliate, still was pursuing a playoff berth. Consequently, New York's regular goaltender, Emile ("The Cat") Francis had been sent to Cincinnati; his replacement was Lorne Anderson, 20, most recently of the amateur New York Rovers. As the fates would have it, though, Anderson had a date with National Hockey League history. So did Chicago's Bill Mosienko, 30, who only a few days earlier had been leafing through an NHL record book when he remarked to some friends, "Gee, it would be nice to have my name in there with some of the hockey greats."

The game itself was to be the tamest of affairs. With nothing at stake, neither team threw a check all night, and referee George Gravel did not call a single penalty for the entire 60 minutes. But before long, the wide-open affair had the cheers of the meager crowd rattling throughout the 15,000-seat arena.

First, the Hawks scored. Then the Rangers replied with three unanswered goals. The Hawks cut their deficit to 3–2, but then New York scored twice for a 5–2 advantage after the first period.

Early in the second period, New York's Ed Slowinski scored his third goal of the night for a 6–2 lead. But then Mosienko, a fleet, 5-foot-6-inch right wing, took a pass from center Gus Bodnar and beat Anderson at 6:09 of the third period.

Following that seemingly inconsequential goal, Gravel dropped the puck at center ice. Bodnar controlled it immediately and saw Mosienko alone at the Ranger blue line. Bodnar's pass was perfect; Mosienko flitted in on Anderson and scored again. The time was 6:20, only 11 seconds between goals. "That was my thirtieth goal of the season," said Mosienko, who had already grabbed his twenty-ninth for a souvenir. "So again I went into the net and got the puck."

Another face-off at center ice. And again, Bodnar won the draw. Except that this time he fed George Gee in left wing. Gee broke down the left boards, lured a Ranger defender toward him, then feathered a pretty pass into the slot, where Mosienko was in full flight.

As he whirred in on Anderson, Mosienko felt that the rookie would be anticipating another shot low to the stick side. So, hesitating an instant to draw Anderson from his crease, he put his shot on the top shelf, the red light burned, and the scoreboard clock was frozen at 6:30. Three goals in 21 seconds, and all at once Mosienko was part of NHL history. Indeed, not only had he scored the fastest three goals in the annals of the game, breaking the previous mark by 43 seconds, but no *team* had ever scored three as quickly.

Three years later, Mosienko would retire after scoring 258 goals in his NHL career. But he would never forget the three in particular that he scored during that leisurely game in Madison Square Garden won by the Hawks, 7–6.

Lorne Anderson? After giving up 17 goals while starting the Rangers' final three games of the season, he never played another game in the NHL.

Rocket Richard, March 17, 1955

Of the many distinctions that he owns, Maurice ("Rocket") Richard's most distinctive is that he is the only professional athlete ever to have had a riot tossed in his honor. It could be argued that the $100,000 debacle was thrown more in an effort to *dis*honor National Hockey League president Clarence Campbell, of course, but had Richard not been the passionate hero that he was throughout French Canada, the ugly scene never would have unfolded at all.

Throughout his career, Richard had had his share of conflicts with the NHL president—primarily as a result of his fiery temper, which for various assaults, both on the ice and off, had cost him $2,500 in 13 years, more than any other player in the history of the league. But the stage for what would become known as *L'affaire Richard* was set during the final weeks of the

1954–55 season, when Richard was seeking his first NHL scoring title at the same time the Montreal Canadiens were trying to break a chain of six regular-season championships in a row by the Detroit Red Wings.

Going into a Sunday-night game against the Bruins in Boston Garden on March 13, the Canadiens were in first place by two points over runner-up Detroit, and Richard was two points ahead of team-mate Bernie ("Boom Boom") Geoffrion in the scoring race. But with the Bruins leading 4–2 with only six minutes remaining, Richard was in no mood to be high-sticked by Boston defenseman Hal Laycoe, and when the Canadiens' pepper pot discovered that he was bleeding from the wound, he went beserk. Repeatedly, he slashed back at Laycoe with his stick, and,

Maurice ("Rocket") Richard is the only professional athlete ever to have had a riot tossed in his honor. It was his suspension from play in all remaining league and playoff games late in the 1954-55 season that brought on L'affaire Richard *on March 17, 1955.*

when linesman Cliff Thompson intervened, Richard threw a flurry of punches at the official, blackening his eye. Richard was quickly ejected from the game by referee Frank Udvari, but everyone knew he would be on Campbell's carpet within 48 hours.

After interviewing all the parties involved, Campbell issued his decision: "Richard is suspended from playing in the remaining league *and* playoff games."

"No sports decision ever hit the Montreal public with such impact," the Canadian magazine *MacLean's* would comment later. "It seemed to strike at the very heart and soul of the city."

Indeed, no sooner was Campbell's decision made public than the NHL office was besieged with enraged telephone calls, including some that threatened the very life of Campbell. Even Mayor Jean Drapeau was incensed. "It would not be necessary," he said, "to give too many such decisions to kill hockey in Montreal."

The ultimate irony, however, was that the Canadiens were hosting the Red Wings the following night, March 17, at the Forum. With the championship at stake, how would the team react without Richard? Would the Rocket attend? Would Campbell, as was his custom?

By the opening face-off, almost 1,000 demonstrators were parading outside the Forum, Richard was already inside, and Campbell was en route. And by the end of the first period, with Montreal trailing 4–1, more than 16,000 pairs of eyes were fixed on Campbell, who was sitting with his secretary behind a goal at one end of the Forum.

Soda cups, popcorn sacks, and programs began to descend on Campbell's party from the balcony. Then came the fruit, and a youth raced down the aisle to

Above: *NHL president Clarence Campbell adjusts his hat after fans at the Forum let loose a barrage of eggs, overripe tomatoes, and water-filled bags. The game was called after a tear-gas bomb exploded inside the arena.* Opposite: *One of the estimated 10,000 fans who went on a spree of looting and violence is hauled off by Montreal constables.*

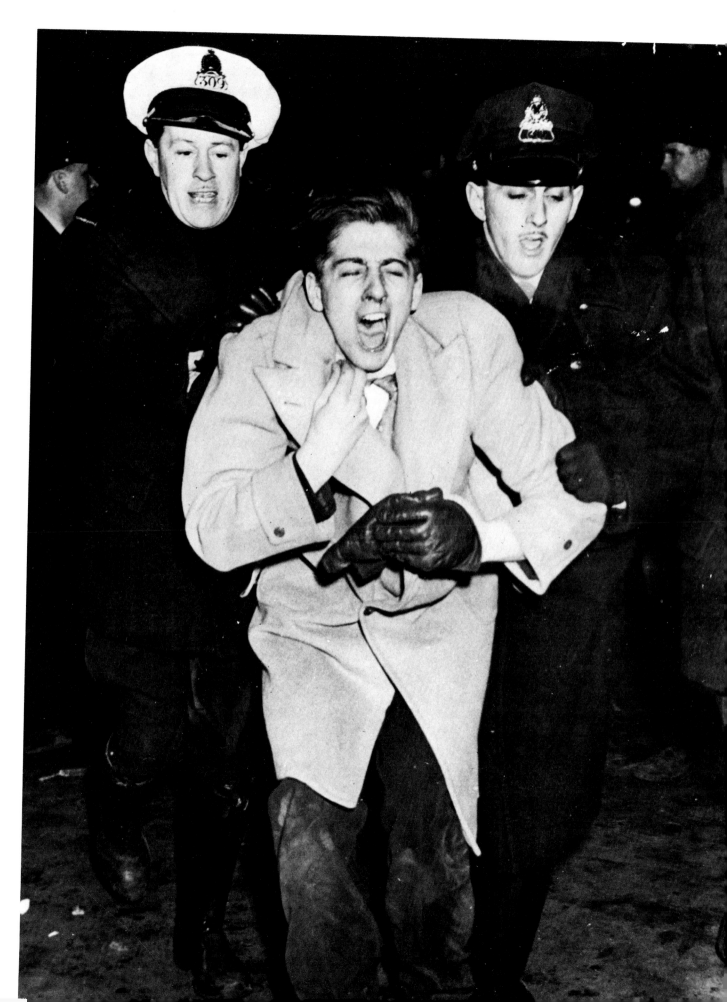

hurl several punches at the NHL president's face. Another man walked up to Campbell and squashed several tomatoes on the vest of his blue suit.

What may well have saved Campbell from serious injury, however, was a tear-gas bomb that suddenly went off in the huge arena. As he seized the hand of his secretary and departed into the bowels of the Forum, the crowd swirled out the doors and into the cold night air. But there, the riot ensued. A crowd estimated at 10,000 went on a looting spree in the blocks immediately surrounding the Forum, smashing windows, overturning newstands and setting them afire, hurling bottles and mugging taxicab drivers. By the wee hours of the morning, 37 people had been injured and more than 70 arrested.

The next afternoon, Richard went on radio and television to appeal for "law and order" and ask that "no further harm be done." He also asked the community to unite behind the team to outlast Detroit.

As it was, however, the Red Wings won their seventh consecutive championship, Richard lost the scoring title by a point to Geoffrion, and Detroit defeated the Canadiens in the Stanley Cup finals.

Clarence Campbell? A few years later, he married his secretary, Phyllis King, who had sat with him through one of the most frightening nights in hockey history.

Jacques Plante, November 1, 1959

From the beginning, his face had been a target for missiles of frozen rubber; missiles that, as the decades passed, would only increase in velocity and lethal potential. Yet despite all the blood he may have shed, for any National Hockey League goaltender to wear any sort of facial protection remained taboo. Even though the rest of his body would eventually resemble that of a mummy, encased in pads from shoulder to toe, to protect his face was to sacrifice too much vision—or, worse yet, suggest that he was afraid.

But Jacques Plante wasn't just any NHL goaltender: by the night of November 1, 1959, in New York's old Madison Square Garden, he had already led the Montreal Canadiens to four consecutive Stanley Cup championships (and ultimately would achieve a record fifth). Moreover, Plante was an innovator, who, while elevating his professional duties to an art form, also had been experimenting with a fiberglass mask in practice. And so it was that, moments after the Canadiens took the ice against the Rangers that night, a new, imminently safer world for NHL goaltenders began to unfold.

As he skated across the blue line, New York's Andy Bathgate unleashed a rising 30-foot shot, and all at once Plante was sprawled facedown in an ever-widening pool of blood, an ugly gash extending from his left nostril to his upper lip. Even Bathgate, after racing to his opponent's side, nodded helplessly as the

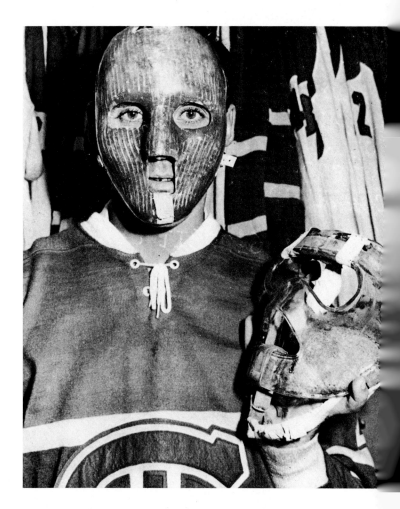

Montreal goalie Jacques Plante demonstrates the semi-finished fiberglass mask he designed for use in regular-season action. He holds an older mask he wore only for practice sessions because, "My range of vision wasn't good enough."

Montreal trainer arrived.

A hush fell over the capacity crowd of 15,925 as Plante was assisted from the ice and into the Montreal clubhouse for emergency treatment. But as he entered the room, Plante, who only a week earlier in Chicago had been severely cut on the right side of his face, clomped past the waiting doctor and went directly to a mirror. "Before you do anything," he snapped, "I want to see what this one looks like."

Finally, Plante laid down on a table and the physician, working without anesthetics, stitched up the wound. Twenty-five minutes later, Plante returned to the Montreal bench. "Why don't you use your mask for the rest of the game?" suggested the Canadiens' coach, Toe Blake.

"I don't think I can go back in without it," Plante replied.

When Plante skated back onto the ice wearing his crude, homemade mask, cheers rolled from the crowd and the organist played, "For He's a Jolly Good Fellow." By the time the game was over, only 1 of 29 shots had eluded Plante in a 3-1 triumph. And that one, off a rebound by Camile Henry, had not been due to his mask. Asked if he planned to continue wearing his mask, Plante nodded to Blake, who was standing nearby. "He's the boss. Ask him."

Blake said the decision was Plante's to make, on one condition: "The first time he cracks wearing that mask, he takes it off."

But Plante did not crack, spurring the Canadiens to a record fifth Stanley Cup and further enhancing his status as the league's premier goaltender. And today, of course, a goaltender's mask is as much a part of his regular equipment as his stick and glove.

"You still can't convince me that a goaltender can see as well with a mask as without," says Blake, who is now a vice-president with the Canadiens. "Even if there's a bump on your nose, you can't see as well as you can without one. But it had to come. Sooner or later a goalkeeper would have been killed."

Bobby Hull, March 12, 1966

After the 1944-45 season, during which the Montreal Canadiens' Maurice ("Rocket") Richard scored 50 goals in 50 games, there were those who were convinced that the record never would be equaled. That was the era, of course, when to score 20 goals in a single season was comparable to hitting .300 in baseball. In fact, even after the National Hockey League schedule was increased to 70 games five years after Richard set the record, it wasn't until the 1960-61 season that Montreal's Bernie ("Boom Boom") Geoffrion managed to score 50 goals.

By then, however, a muscular left wing for the Chicago Black Hawks named Bobby Hull was already filling NHL nets with his blazing slap shots; and after *he* scored 50 in 1961-62, Hull became the odds-on choice to become the first to reach 51.

It wasn't until the 1965-66 season, however, that Hull got off to the searing start the he needed, and even though he missed five games with a knee injury, he scored his fiftieth goal of the year with 13 games remaining. By now even casual hockey fans were following Hull's progress, much as millions had in 1961 when Roger Maris was closing in on Babe Ruth's record of 60 home runs in a single baseball season.

But as the tension mounted with every unsuccessful attempt by Hull, and his teammates abandoned their usual style of play in an attempt to provide him additional shots, the Hawks suffered. In fact, they were shut out by Toronto, then Montreal, and even the lowly New York Rangers. Headlined one Chicago newspaper: "Will Any Hawk Score?"

Then, on the night of March 12, 1966, the Hawks took the ice of Chicago Stadium for a game against the Rangers. More than 20,000 fans turned out to watch Hull's latest assault on the new record. But after a scoreless first period, thoughts of that newspaper headline were creeping into the minds of many in the huge audience.

In the second period, it was the Rangers who, with the Hawks still working feverishly to set up Hull, seized a 2-0 lead. But early in the third, Hull set up teammate Chico Maki to cut the New York lead to 2-1, and at the 4:05 mark, Ranger defenseman Harry Howell was penalized for slashing.

Their manpower advantage was almost over, though—only 30 seconds remained in Howell's penalty—when Chicago's Bill Hay passed to Lou Angotti, who quickly fed Hull and headed for the Black Hawk bench on a line change. Hull cruised over the Rangers' blue line and, as Eric Nesterenko steamed toward goaltender Cesare Maniago, pulled up short about 30 feet from the net. It was from there that he unloaded a low wrist shot, instead of slapping at the puck with his stick.

As Maniago split to make the save, Hull's shot and Nesterenko arrived at precisely the same instant —and when Nesterenko tipped Maniago's stick, Hull's fifty-first goal clanked into the back of the net. As a mighty roar split the expectant air and hats, programs, and paper streamers descended onto the ice, Hull picked up one of the hats and dropped it on his head.

Before the season was over, Hull would score three more times for a record 54 goals, and three years later he would set another mark with 58. None, however, were quite as difficult—or so welcome—as that prized 51.

Chicago Black Hawks' famous number 9, Bobby Hull.

Punch Imlach, May 2, 1967

Abrasive, stubborn, incorrigible, egomaniacal. Those are a few of the words that have been used to describe George ("Punch") Imlach through the years, and they're the nice ones.

Nevertheless, it's indisputable that a cunning hockey mind whirs in the bald head beneath the omnipresent fedora of one of the most colorful coaches and general managers in the game's history. After leading the Toronto Maple Leafs to 10 playoff berths and 4 Stanley Cups in 11 years, Imlach had the Buffalo Sabres in the Cup finals in only their fifth year of existence. And now Imlach is back in Toronto, trying to work another miracle like . . . well, like the one he worked with the Maple Leafs in the spring of 1967.

"Punch's Old Folks Home" is what Toronto was called that season, for in addition to grizzled goaltenders Terry Sawchuck (38) and Johnny Bower (42), the Leafs flaunted the likes of Allan Stanley (41), Red Kelly (39), and the mid-30ish looks of Tim Horton, Marcel Pronovost, Bobby Baun, and George Armstrong. After off-season back surgery had enabled Sawchuck to stand erect for the first time in years, he collapsed while taking a shower in early December and would not return until months later. At one stage, the Leafs lost 10 games in a row; and even Imlach himself was hospitalized for three weeks with stomach problems. Clearly, the team that had won three straight Stanley Cups from 1962 through 1964 was on the dark side of the mountain (some said "over the hill") now.

The Leafs opened the playoffs against the Chicago Black Hawks of Bobby Hull, Stan Mikita, et al, who had scored a record 264 goals while breezing to the regular-season championship 17 points ahead of second-place Montreal. After managing to win two of the first four games, Imlach nominated Bower to start the fifth in Chicago; but with the Leafs leading 2–1, Bower was injured late in the first period and

Sawchuck took over.

Early in the second period Sawchuck was felled by a searing slap shot off the stick of Hull ("I thought at first that I'd been stabbed by a red-hot poker," he said later), only to return to the Toronto nets and play what Imlach would call "the finest two periods in the history of goaltending." Indeed, he turned away no fewer than 36 drives the rest of the way—3 of which were certain goals by Hull—and the Leafs prevailed, 4-2. "Only time I ever scored three goals and the light didn't go on once," Hull lamented afterward.

Toronto went on to eliminate the Hawks in the sixth game by a 3-1 score, and their reward was an appointment with the Canadiens, who had vanquished the New York Rangers in a 4-game semifinal and brought a 10-game winning streak into the finals. Still, Imlach, always looking for the psychological edge, made an issue of the fact that the experienced Canadiens were employing goaltender Rogatien Vachon, 22, who only a few months earlier had been toiling in a Junior B league. "You can tell that Junior B goaltender he won't be playing against a bunch of pea shooters," Imlach warned. "When he plays against the Leafs, we'll take his head off with our first shot."

It was Sawchuck who got burned in that first game, however, as Montreal swept to a 6-2 victory. Bower salvaged the second contest in the Forum with a 3-0 shutout, and, at Maple Leaf Gardens, he stopped an incredible 60 shots—20 in 28 minutes of overtime—and the Leafs survived, 3-2. But then Bower pulled a muscle warming up for the fourth game and once more Sawchuck was strafed, 6-2.

Early in the fifth, however, Sawchuck produced a sensational save on Ralph Backstrom, recaptured his magic, and the Leafs cruised to a 4-1 triumph that set the stage for May 2, 1967. In a stirring goaltenders' duel which would see Sawchuck turn away 46 shots and the veteran Gump Worsley, 36, the Leafs carried a 2-1 advantage into the final minute of play.

And alas, when the Canadiens pulled Worsley in favor of a sixth attacker, who did Imlach respond with? Old folks Stanley, Kelly, Armstrong, and Horton (with Bob Pulford representing Toronto's "youth"). Stanley then shoveled the puck to Kelly, who fed up-ice to Armstrong, who sealed Toronto's fourth Cup in six years—and the most unexpected of all—by scoring into the empty net.

"That was my most satisfying Cup," Imlach recalls. "Everybody said I'd never win another Cup with those old guys. A lot of people thought that I was being sentimental, putting those old guys out there, but I went with the guys I thought could do the job. When you get down to that stage of the game, you're not going to be sentimental—although I admit it's kind of nice now to look back and remember who was out there in the end."

Red Berenson, November 7, 1968

"Just watch him," said Glenn Hall, the all-star goaltender who had played 10 years with Stan Mikita and Bobby Hull as a member of the Chicago Black Hawks. "He seems to combine the skills of both Stan and Bobby. There isn't anything he can't do. He's a great playmaker and his shot—well, the only trouble with his shot is that sometimes he shoots *too* hard."

The object of Hall's amazement was teammate Gordon ("Red") Berenson of the St. Louis Blues, which in the late 1960s would become the most successful of the National Hockey League's six expansion teams. And although Berenson would never attain quite the notoriety of Hall of Famers Mikita and Hull, he enjoyed a night on November 7, 1968, that only one other player in NHL history had equaled—scoring six goals in a single game. (Seven years later Toronto's Darryl Sittler exploded for six goals and a record 10 points against Boston, but Berenson's feat was particularly noteworthy because it signaled the arrival of the NHL's expansion's first superstar.)

"It's just like planting trees," Berenson, now coach of the Blues, said afterward. "Some years you plant twelve and five or six come up. Some years you plant twelve and none come up. This time, everything just went right."

And how. Late in the first period, with the Blues

and the Philadelphia Flyers locked in a scoreless duel in The Spectrum, Berenson hopped on a loose puck at his own blue line, skated around a retreating Flyer defenseman, and beat goaltender Doug Favell high into the left corner. And midway through the second period, he outraced another Philadelphia defender to a loose puck and went in to score on a breakaway. Then, in the space of 32 seconds, linemate Camile Henry twice set up Berenson for scores, all but putting the Flyers out of the game.

That Berenson was carrying a hot stick was really no surprise to Scotty Bowman, who a year earlier had taken over as the St. Louis coach. In fact, days after his promotion, Bowman had urged general manager Lynn Patrick to trade forward Ron Stewart to the New York Rangers for Berenson.

"The fact that Stewart was leading our club in scoring at the time didn't mean a thing," said Bowman. "We couldn't score anyway. Stewart is a checker—a defensive forward—and that's what [New York general manager] Emile Francis wanted all along. But Berenson, now *there's* an offensive player."

Indeed, before the second period was over, The Red Baron—as he would become known in St. Louis—would take a pass from Bill McCreary and score again, his fourth goal of the period, tying a record set by Toronto's Harvey Jackson in 1934 and matched by Chicago's Max Bentley nine years later. It also gave Berenson five goals on five consecutive shots, and he would finish 6-for-10 for the game.

By the 14-minute mark of the third period, the Blues were on top, 7–0, when Berenson eluded a check by Flyer defenseman Ed Van Impe and scorched a 40-foot slap shot over Favell's shoulder. This tied the modern NHL record of six goals in one game, set February 3, 1944, by the Detroit Red Wings' Syd Howe (no relation to Gordie) in a 12–2 romp over the Rangers.

As the game entered its final five minutes, The Spectrum crowd of 9,164 was chanting, "We Want Red!...Go Red, Go!" And Bowman responded by rewarding his red-headed center with additional ice time. However, Berenson failed to score a seventh goal, which would have tied the all-time pro hockey mark set in 1920 by Joe Malone, of the old Quebec Bulldogs.

"Six goals," said St. Louis' other goaltender

headed for the Hall of Fame, Jacques Plante. "Even The Rocket [Maurice Richard] never did that."

"Van Impe almost cut my legs off on the last one," said Berenson, "but somehow I got by him."

"He's the best forward in the Western Division," said Bowman, referring to the NHL's expanded framework. "He showed moves like this in practice for years, and now he's getting free in the games."

For one night, at least, freer than any other forward in modern hockey history—except Syd Howe.

The hot stick of St. Louis' Red Berenson flips the puck behind Philadelphia's goalie Doug Favell to score the first goal of the night. By the third period, Berenson had scored five more and tied the modern NHL record.

Jean Beliveau, April 24, 1969

By the late 1960s, the National Hockey League had taken the boldest step forward in its long and often-controversial history. Having doubled in size, from its original six teams to a dozen which included such far-flung areas as Los Angeles and San Francisco, the NHL was making its long-awaited pitch for acceptance in communities where many could not distinguish a hockey puck from a piece of coal.

Alas, if only such people could have been given a crash course as to what was unfolding between the Montreal Canadiens and the Boston Bruins, the task of expansion might have been more immediately successful. For with the Canadiens scrambling to fill holes left by such legends as Richard, Harvey, Moore, Geoffrion, and Plante, their traditions of speed and elegance on the ice were the target of a brash, pugnacious band of Boston Bruins, who were led by the game's most charismatic performer of the time—Bobby Orr.

The signal for what was coming had occurred in the spring of 1968, when the Canadiens defeated the Bruins in a quarterfinal series that was much closer than Montreal's four-game sweep suggested. Indeed, it only set the scene for the 1969 semifinals between the two teams, which may well have been the most stirring series played since then.

In the regular season, the Canadiens had finished first in the NHL's East Division by 103 points, only 2 in front of the second-place Bruins, who scored a league-leading 303 goals. The teams were so evenly matched in fact that twice Boston carried a one-goal lead into the final minute of the first two games at the Forum, only to have the Canadiens rally for ties and victories in sudden-death overtime. After the Bruins prevailed with relative ease in the third and fourth games at the Boston Garden, the series returned to the Forum deadlocked at two games apiece.

The fifth game, back at the Forum, was an absolute spellbinder, but when it was over the Bruins looked up at the scoreboard, saw that they had outshot the Canadiens, 42–25, in their own building—and still had lost, 4–2. In the second period alone, the Bruins had fired a record 26 shots at Rogatien Vachon, but only two—by Ken Hodge—eluded Montreal's sideburned goaltender. In fact, no fewer than six times Vachon denied Phil Esposito, who during the regular season had scored 49 goals and set NHL records for that time with 77 assists and 126 points.

"Every time I looked up, there he was, standing in front of me," said Vachon.

"Look, I don't want to downgrade Vachon," said Esposito. "He was great. But half the time I was standing there in front of the net. All I had to do was shoot. So what do I do? Fire wide or straight into his pads, that's what. I wish I knew what was wrong."

The series shifted back to Boston, where the Canadiens had not won all year, and where the Bruins had not lost a game since Christmas. The Bruins seized an early 1–0 lead and kept it throughout a stirring first period of action. In the second, the Bruins only gained momentum, pouring 22 shots at Vachon compared to Montreal's 8 on Gerry Cheevers. However, the turning point of the game, and the series, came halfway through the period, when at 9:21 Montreal's John Ferguson was penalized for elbowing and, 36 seconds later, when Canadiens' coach Claude Ruel drew a two-minute bench minor for verbally abusing referee Art Skov.

This left Montreal two men short for the next minute and 24 seconds, yet with the Bruins rolling into the attacking zone in waves, the Canadiens' penalty killers were outstanding. Led by Jacques Laperriere, Ted Harris, and Claude Provost, and more stellar goaltending by Vachon, Montreal still trailed only 1–0 when the penalties expired.

Early in the third period, with Boston's Don Awrey off for charging, Jean Beliveau won a face-off to defenseman Serge Savard, who drove a 40-foot slap shot behind Cheevers to tie the game. After that, both goaltenders were unbeatable in the face of golden opportunities by gunners from both teams, particularly Orr.

The game remained tied, 1–1, through the tension and excitement of the first sudden-death overtime period, with Boston again dominating play. The same was true through the initial seven minutes of double overtime—until Beliveau, the Canadiens' only link with their storied past but who had not had a good series—finally got *his* chance.

Boston's Awrey broke out of his own end and aimed a pass at teammate Ron Murphy, who was starting up the left side. But Provost intercepted for Montreal and passed to Beliveau at the rim of the right face-off circle. "I gave Claude a little yell and he gave me the puck," Beliveau would recall. "I saw a lot of net over the left shoulder. It was a wrist shot. Twenty feet. I shot and hoped."

"As soon as the puck hit Beliveau's stick it was gone," Cheevers said. "By the time I got organized the puck was going over my shoulder and into the net."

The Bruins, after outplaying the eventual Stanley Cup champions by a wide margin in most of the six games, had somehow—incredibly—lost. But as Beliveau said, "We are always lucky . . . in the playoffs."

Montreal captain Jean Beliveau proudly displays Cup won when his team defeated the St. Louis Blues in 1969. Had it not been for Beliveau's sensational overtime goal in the playoffs, the Canadiens might not have been in the finals at all.

Season's End, April 5, 1970

Never in the history of the National Hockey League had there been a 24-hour period quite like it. April 4 and 5, 1970: a weekend when so much pride, hope, destiny, and, yes, money, were riding on every shot, save, and shift from Detroit to New York and Montreal to Chicago, with Boston right there in the maddening clutter of it all. In point of fact, the only certainties were that the Toronto Maple Leafs were going to finish last in the NHL's East Division, and that the league's rules for determining final standings were going to be pushed to the ultimate.

The situation was this: going into the Saturday- and Sunday-night games of the final weekend of the 1970 season, the Chicago Black Hawks and Boston Bruins were deadlocked for first place in the NHL East with 95 points. Next came the Detroit Red Wings with 93 points, the Montreal Canadiens with 92, and the New York Rangers with 90.

Clearly, only four of the five teams would make the Stanley Cup playoffs by the wee hours of Monday morning, April 6, and to make it all the more intriguing, every contender was involved in a home-and-home series: Chicago versus the Canadiens in Montreal Saturday night, in Chicago Sunday night; the same was true for Boston versus Toronto and Detroit versus New York. And when somebody ran the possibilities through a computer, no fewer than 125 combinations of finishes were conceivable.

The basic reason was the NHL rules for determining final standings at the time. The were: two teams ending the season tied in points would have the team with the most victories finishing higher; if those teams had the same number of victories, the most goals scored would break the tie; and if the teams were still tied after that, the club permitting the fewest total goals would gain the higher rung in the standings.

So, on Saturday afternoon, the first puck was dropped in Detroit's Olympia Stadium, where the Red Wings went on to clinch a playoff berth with a 6–2 victory over the Rangers. That night came the games in Montreal and Toronto, where the Black Hawks upset the Canadiens, 4–1, and the Bruins defeated the

Maple Leafs, 4–2. That left Chicago and Boston still tied for first with 97 points each, followed by the Red Wings with 95, and the Rangers, with 90, still trailing the Canadiens, with 92, by two.

As they took the ice against the Red Wings on Sunday afternoon in Madison Square Garden, the Rangers' mission was obvious: since a New York victory and a Montreal loss would still leave both tied for the fourth and final playoff spot with records of 38–22–16, and New York led in goals-against totals by 184 to Montreal's 191, their deadlock would be broken by total goals (New York trailed in that category 237 to 242). In other words, the Rangers not only had to defeat the Red Wings and hope the Black Hawks bested the Canadiens in Chicago, they also had to score at least five more goals than Montreal did.

Consequently, Rangers' coach Emile Francis sent a fore-checking forward into each corner and ordered his defensemen to play within 35 feet of the Detroit net. This super-offensive strategy, combined with the aftereffects of the Red Wings' champagne charter to New York the night before ("I didn't think we could make second place because I couldn't see Boston losing to Toronto," explained Detroit coach Sid Abel), produced a 9–5 New York victory and exerted extreme pressure on the Canadiens later in the day in Chicago.

Deadlocked at 92 points apiece, the Canadiens needed either a tie or five goals in Chicago to make the playoffs. But as the Hawks burst to an early lead and led 5–2 with eight minutes remaining, Montreal coach Claude Ruel pulled goaltender Rogatien Vachon in an attempt to score at least three more goals.

The Hawks, however, gleefully fired five more goals into Montreal's empty net, Chicago went on to win 10–2, and the Canadiens missed the playoffs for the first time in 22 years.

"Never saw anything like it," said Bobby Hull.

Neither did the NHL. Within months the rules concerning ties in the standings were changed to when two teams are tied in wins as well as points at season end the situation is resolved by the results of the season series between the tied clubs.

Bobby Orr, May 10, 1970

It is a wire-service photograph, and for all it represents, especially in hindsight, it has become a classic. For there is Bobby Orr, still the boy wonder of the National Hockey League, soaring through the smoke-filled air of Boston Garden the afternoon of May 10, 1970, one skate hooked in the crook of Noel Picard's stick, as the puck Orr fired an instant earlier has nestled in the net behind goaltender Glenn Hall.

When he finally reached the Boston Bruins in September 1966, at the tender age of 18, Bobby Orr was already hailed as the one player who would lead Boston out of its forest of hockey futility. And, perhaps, even to the Stanley Cup, which the Bruins had not won since 1929. "He's the best player for his age I've ever seen in my thirty years in the NHL," observed the late Lynn Patrick, then general manager of the St. Louis Blues. "And he's still getting better."

"Orr can do everything," agreed Boston general manager Milt Schmidt, an all-star for the Bruins in the 1940s. "The fact is, we have yet to find anything he *can't* do. You watch him every game and you say, 'That's the best play he's ever made.' Then you look again, and he's doing something better."

And so far as the NHL was concerned, Orr was—despite a series of knee operations which eventually would terminate his career after only one brief, glorious decade—the one player who packed the house everywhere the Bruins traveled, be it the

A joyful Bobby Orr, skate hooked in the crook of St. Louis' Noel Picard's stick, celebrates his winning goal in the overtime period. Orr's goal gave the Boston Bruins their first Stanley Cup victory in 29 years.

Montreal Forum or the Oakland-Alameda Coliseum Arena. "I've never seen him when he isn't trying to live up to his reputation," noted Boston coach Harry Sinden. "He won't tell anyone when he's injured, if he's able to keep going. He just says, 'I'm all right.' But every coach needs a player like him. When the team is in trouble on the ice, you say, 'Bob, get out there.' And suddenly you've changed the entire flow of the game."

But for all the individual records he would accumulate, for the charismatic appeal of his bold rushes and cracking slap shots that jerked even novice hockey fans from their seats in appreciation, Orr was the consummate team player. A player who, in fact, would seek the refuge of the training room so that writers, faced with impending deadlines, would have to talk to teammates instead.

And so it is that wire-service photograph, snapped the instant Orr's goal in sudden-death overtime gave the Bruins a 4–3 victory over the Blues and brought the Stanley Cup to Boston after 31 years, probably represents the greatest moment in Orr's career. The Blues clearly were no match for the high-octane Bruins in that series; after Boston swept the first two games in St. Louis, then the third at home, everyone knew it was only a matter of days until the Cup came to "Beantown."

But Scotty Bowman, coach of the Blues, had assigned Jimmy Roberts to ignore the puck and follow Orr everywhere he skated, hoping to neutralize the superstar's myriad talents. "Every great player in the league has had that kind of attention," Bowman explained after the Blues' first loss in St. Louis. "But really, how do you practice something like that? We worked on it for six hours, but we don't have Bobby Orr to practice against."

"If they watch me like that in the next game, I won't even have to take a shower afterward," Orr said. "I expected to be watched, but not like that. I could have gone out for lunch for all the chances I had to get in the play. So I just stayed out of things."

Two nights later, Roberts was again assigned to shadow Orr; but after the Bruins broke out to a 3–0 lead, Bowman gave up the idea. The Bruins won, 6–2, and went back to Boston to seal the Cup in four straight games—with Orr scoring the winner moments into sudden-death overtime of the fourth game.

Why had Bowman pulled his shadow from Orr? "I did the same thing when I was coaching the Montreal Junior Canadiens and Orr was playing for Oshawa," he replied, looking up from a sheet of statistics. "The only difference was that Bobby was playing sixty minutes then instead of forty.... We lost that night too."

Phil Esposito, March 12, 1971

It was unavoidable that, while en route to the greatest season ever enjoyed by a National Hockey League shotmaker, Phil Esposito would pass the milestone established by his good friend and former teammate with the Chicago Black Hawks, Bobby Hull. In fact, after it was over, after he had shattered Hull's 1969 record of 58 goals in the first period—then become the first player in NHL history to score 60 in a single season in the second period—Esposito was insisting, "Bobby Hull's still the greatest."

Going into the latter stages of the 1970–71 season, Esposito had already scored 50 goals with almost ridiculous ease; and despite the incredible scoring totals he was bound to accumulate before the regular season was completed, die-hard hockey fans were lamenting that Esposito's feats were little more than the residue of a league that had been weakened by expansion. There were, they fumed, simply too many goaltenders and defensemen in the NHL that would never have sipped even a cup of coffee in the pre-expansion league.

Nevertheless, on March 11, 1971, there was Esposito, in the Oakland–Alameda Coliseum Arena triumphantly tying Hull's mark of 58 goals. Esposito scored numbers 59 and 60 the following night in Los Angeles in relative complacency. Had he been at home in Boston, surely there would have been celebrating afterward.

At the 7:03 mark of the first period, Esposito tipped Ted Green's shot from the point behind Los Angeles goaltender Denis Dejordy. And at 15:40 of the second, Dallas Smith and Ken Hodge set him up for number 60, sending the Bruins winging to a 7–2 triumph.

"To be honest, I felt more pressure two years ago when I was the first to score more than a hundred points in a season," Esposito said afterward. "No one else had ever done it, and I wanted to be the first. But I'm glad it's over. With eleven games left, I knew that I'd get the record sooner or later, but I still wanted to get number 59 in seventy games, so there wouldn't be any asterisk after it in the record books."

Indeed, Esposito's two goals and an assist had given him 128 points for the season, breaking the record of 126 he had established two years earlier. And his sixtieth goal had also broken a record set by the Montreal Canadiens' Jean Beliveau in 1955, when he finished with 59—47 in 70 regular-season games and 12 in the playoffs.

With that out of the way, Esposito charged down the stretch with a flourish that left him with one record that still stands today—most goals (76)—and another that held until 1981—most total points (152) of any player over a regular season.

In fact, he saved the icing for the final game of the regular season, against the Canadiens in Boston Garden, where he scored his seventh hat trick of the season for numbers 74, 75, and 76. Afterward, after 15,000 of the most knowledgeable fans in the game had given him a minute-long standing ovation for a truly remarkable scoring feat, Esposito said, "For the first time in my life I was shy. During that ovation I just didn't know how to react."

Phil Esposito (7) watches as the puck he has just hit heads for the Oakland Seal goal guarded by Gary Smith. Once inside the net, the goal became Espo's fifty-eighth and broke the all-time goal-scoring record set by Bobby Hull.

Team Canada versus Soviets, September 1972

Finally, in September 1972, Canada and the Soviet Union had gotten together. Finally, after 15 years of waiting, it was our best against your best, a no-strings-attached confrontation between the two most powerful forces in the sport. Four games on Canadian ice, four on Russian, with the victor emerging with bragging rights to world hockey superiority. "Eight straight," a lot of Canadians boasted before the series even started. "We've finally got those Russians where we want them."

"Eight straight," a lot more figured after Phil Esposito scored against the USSR only 30 seconds into game one at the Montreal Forum. And still more agreed six minutes later, when Paul Henderson gave Team Canada a 2-0 lead against the finest product the Soviets had put on ice since vodka. But Coach Harry Sinden, pacing the bench behind Canada's heroes, wasn't all that euphoric. In fact, he was scared.

"The Russians tore up and down the ice making beautiful passes, getting their men into position, outskating us to loose pucks, and doing everything but put it into the net," Sinden wrote after the series was over. "It was right then that I knew the Russians were everything I didn't want them to be."

Before the period was over, the Russians had tied the game, 2-2, one of their goals coming shorthanded. In the second period Valeri Kharlamov gave the invaders a 4-2 advantage, and, after Bobby Clarke made it 4-3, scored three times in the final seven minutes to win 7-3. The Soviets were ecstatic; an entire nation went numb—and the scene was set for the most memorable series of hockey games ever played.

Two nights later in Toronto's Maple Leaf Gardens, Team Canada rode some stellar netminding by Tony Esposito and goals by Phil Esposito, Yvan Cournoyer, Pete Mahovlich (shorthanded), and his brother Frank, to a 4-1 victory that sent a swoon of relief throughout the entire nation. Then, at Winnepeg, the Canadians blew leads of 1-0, 3-1, and 4-2 as the Soviets struck twice in the final five minutes for a 4-4 deadlock. Gloom swept the country again after the

Soviets left Vancouver with a 5-3 triumph and a 2-1-1 lead in the Series.

By the time Team Canada arrived in Moscow for game five, three players—Vic Hadfield, Richard Martin, and Jocelyn Guevremont—had returned to Canada because of their lack of ice time. Goals by J.P. Parise, Clarke, and Paul Henderson gave Team Canada a 3-0 lead going into the third period; but after the Soviets exploded for five in the final 20 minutes to prevail 5-4, the visitors were faced with the unlikely prospect of sweeping the final three games on foreign ice to win the series.

As sometimes happens, seemingly insurmountable odds bring a team closer together, which is precisely what happened with Team Canada. Despite playing shorthanded for six minutes of the first period, the Canadians escaped with a scoreless deadlock. The Soviets struck first in the second period, but then Dennis Hull, Cournoyer, and Henderson scored three times in 83 seconds. Late in the period, the Russians drew within 3-2, but despite a rash of penalties—including one period in which they played two men short for a full two minutes—Team Canada hung on for victory.

The seventh game was another thriller, with Phil Esposito asserting himself as the Canadians' unofficial leader. Esposito scored first, and, after the Soviets replied twice, pulled Team Canada even at 2-2. The second period was scoreless. After Rod Gilbert made it 3-2, the Soviets tied it on a power play—but with only 2:06 remaining, Henderson scored his second-straight winner for a 4-3 triumph. To the amazement of the watching world, the series was tied.

The eighth and deciding game, on September 28, was the most exciting and tension packed of all. With Team Canada two men short, the Soviets scored. Esposito tied it, and, after the Russians scored again, Brad Park provided a 2-2 deadlock at the end of one. In the second period, the Soviets again seized a one-goal lead, only to have Bill White take Gilbert's pass and tie it again. But at the end of the period, the Soviets were leading, 5-3.

Still, after once trailing in the series 3-1-1, the Canadians had come from too far back to quit. At the 2:27 mark of the third period, Esposito whittled the deficit to 5-4. Now, for the first time in the series, the Soviets went into a defensive shell, trying to protect their lead. This, of course, only allowed Team Canada to roll into the attacking zone in waves, and at the 12:56 mark Cournoyer shocked the Soviets with the tying goal.

Going into the final minute, the score was still 5-5. If it stayed that way, there would be bragging rights for neither team. Then, as the clock ticked inside 40 seconds, Henderson took a pass from Esposito and had two chances at the winner. Vladislav Tretiak, then the finest goaltender in the world, stopped his first shot, but Henderson hopped on his own rebound, drove it into the net for his third-straight winning goal—and Team Canada and millions of followers throughout North America went bonkers.

Kate Smith, May 19, 1974

By the time the lights were turned down and a red carpet had been rolled to center ice of The Spectrum on the afternoon of May 19, 1974, the Philadelphia Flyers and Boston Bruins had already set the stage for a hockey match of classic proportions.

In game one of the Stanley Cup finals at Boston Garden, Bobby Orr's goal had given the Bruins a 3-2 victory with only 22 seconds remaining in regulation play; two nights later, a goal by Philadelphia's Andre Dupont with 52 seconds left in regulation had sent the game into sudden death, and Bobby Clarke's strike at 12:01 of overtime had lifted the Flyers to a 3-2 triumph—their first win on Boston ice in seven years.

The series then shifted to Philadelphia, where the Flyers seized a 3-1 advantage in games with 4-1 and 4-2 victories. But the fifth, back in Boston, belonged to Orr, who set up a shorthanded goal by Gregg Sheppard, then scored twice himself to send the Bruins winging to a 5-1 triumph. Afterward, Boston coach Armand ("Bep") Guidolin nodded in the direction of the Flyers' clubhouse and chortled, "Tell the Flyers they don't have to take all that champagne back

to Philadelphia. They can leave it here and we'll drink it Tuesday."

Guidolin's message was clear: if the Flyers did not capture the Cup on Sunday afternoon, against a team loaded with the four top scorers in the league (Phil Esposito, Orr, Ken Hodge, and Wayne Cashman), the Bruins most certainly would in the seventh and deciding game at the Boston Garden.

Although the Flyers had some firepower of their own in the likes of Bobby Clarke, Rick MacLeish, and Bill Barber, it was obvious that what the Flyers needed was an impeccable performance from Bernie Parent, the league's premier goaltender at the time, and something else...

Over the years, the 17,077 Spectrum faithful had come to relish a recording of "God Bless America," which Philadelphia management occasionally substituted for the national anthem prior to home games. And the Flyers seemed to enjoy it, too, since on those nights they had forged a rather impressive record of 36 wins, 1 tie, and only 3 defeats. So on this particular afternoon, with the stakes as high as they could possibly be, there came Kate Smith, *in person*, sweeping onto that red carpet in a glittering gown, blowing kisses to the delirious crowd and clasping her hands above her head. After she thundered out "God Bless America" as only she could, even the Bruins were impressed.

"Super song, Kate," said Esposito as he and Orr, perhaps to counteract whatever blessing she had given the Flyers, presented her with a dozen roses. "Bless you," Miss Smith replied, placing a hand on Orr's shoulders.

Those words seemed prophetic in the early minutes of the game as the Bruins drove the tentative Flyers into their own zone and kept them there as they strafed Parent from every angle. Indeed, halfway through the first period Boston had outshot Philadelphia by 13-4.

But then the Flyers began to test Gilles Gilbert at the other end of the ice, and in the fifteenth minute of play it happened. MacLeish won a power-play face-off back to Andre Dupont and darted toward the net. From 35 feet, Dupont lofted what appeared to be a routine drive at Gilbert, but at the last instant MacLeish put his stick on it. "I knew it was off the ice and I had my stick up," MacLeish would say later. "It brushed my leg and hit my stick about two feet in front of the crease."

"I had a clear view from the point but lost it as it came across," recalled Gilbert. "It hit his stick and went *whoosh!* That was it. It was over for us."

Certainly it did not appear to be that way at the time, for what followed were 45 minutes of stirring, end-to-end action. But Parent and Gilbert were unbeatable the rest of the way. With three minutes to play, and the Flyers still clinging to a 1-0 lead, Hodge broke in alone on the wing. "I couldn't look," recalls Terry Crisp, who was trailing the play at center ice. "I put my glove over my eyes and just turned away. Then I heard this unbelievable roar—Bernie had stoned him —and three minutes later I was drinking champagne from the Stanley Cup."

Philadelphia Flyers versus Soviets, January 11, 1976

"The scouts came back and they told us, 'None of 'em can shoot the puck, their goaltending is bad,' "Bobby Clarke was saying. "Then the games started and they were shooting it by our ears twice as hard as we can shoot. And their goaltender turns out to be one of the best in the world. You hear scouting reports like that and you think it's gonna be a cakewalk."

It was early January 1976, and the captain of the Philadelphia Flyers was recalling how overconfident Team Canada had required a series of desperate rallies in Moscow in 1972 to finally subdue a band of Soviets who had so embarrassed the Canadians on the ice of their homeland. But on this, the eve of Philadelphia's January 11, 1976, confrontation with the Soviet Red Army team in The Spectrum, there was no hint of overconfidence: two Soviet teams had already won five, lost one and tied one of seven games while on a simultaneous tour of North America (the Red Army was unbeaten—2-0-1—in three), and National Hockey League prestige was in tatters. Warned Flyers' coach Fred Shero, "If they win, their players won't brag; their coaches do all the talking. But if they lose, you can be sure as hell, they'll blame it on somebody on the team. That's the way they are."

With the NHL's fleeting hopes pinned on its reigning Stanley Cup champions, and a worldwide audience watching on television, The Spectrum was rocking with the roars of 17,077 as both teams took the ice. When Kate Smith's recording of "God Bless America" was played, the throng almost blew the roof off the building. "My knees were shaking," Flyers defenseman Tom Bladon would recall later. "I'll never forget that moment for as long as I live. That song—and the crowd—just gave me shivers up and down the spine."

The Russians seized the opening face-off and immediately launched a series of sharp, 20-foot passes in their own zone; the problem was, every time they approached the Flyers' blue line, where Shero had strung his players alongside one another in something of a Berlin wall, the Soviet attack disappeared. "They could pass the puck all they wanted in their zone," the Flyers' Gary Dornhoefer would explain afterward. "We wouldn't chase them like they wanted."

Philadelphia was also prepared to hit every red shirt in sight, however, and at 11:21 of the first period, one of the strangest scenes in hockey history unfolded. Ed Van Impe, the Flyers' heavy-hitting defenseman, left the penalty box after serving a two-minute minor, skated directly to Valeri Kharlamov, and flattened the Soviet with—depending upon the observer—a clean check, a charge, or an elbow.

As for Kharlamov, he did not get up. As he lay on the ice, and referee Lloyd Gilmour not only refused to call a penalty on Van Impe, but gave the Soviets a two-minute bench minor for delaying the game, coach Konstatin Loktev called his players off the ice and bench and sent them back into their dressing room.

"I guess they thought they'd upset us," said Orest Kindrachuk. "Well, we took a few shots, then came in here [the clubhouse], took off our skates, and relaxed. We weren't going anywhere. We live here."

NHL president Clarence Campbell, NHL Players Association president Alan Eagleson, and referee-in-chief Scotty Morrison went straight to the door of the Soviets' clubhouse, where a heated discussion occurred. "Their coach said he didn't want to take home

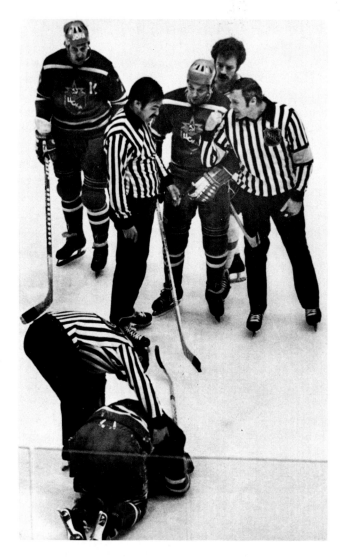

An official checks the condition of Soviet Army's Valeri Kharlamov, who fell after a check by Flyers' Ed van Impe. As other officials and the Soviets argued over the incident, play was disrupted and the Soviets threatened to withdraw from the series.

any injured players," Morrison said afterward. "He feared his players would be injured for the Olympics. We told him that good, clean body-checking is part of the game, and we're not gonna take it out. The high-sticking, spearing, elbowing, we guaranteed him we'd call that.

"You know, they hadn't received any of their money from this tour yet. When Clarence Campbell started talking about the money end of it, their attitude changed."

"Never!" insisted Campbell just down the hallway. "Never did I mention the money angle. I told them this was no way to terminate a series. Their reason for leaving was the alleged injury to Kharlamov. They were never satisfied in leaving the ice. It was the only unfortunate incident in the whole series."

Sixteen minutes after they had departed, the Soviets returned to the ice. And 17 seconds later the Flyers scored when, with the Soviets a man short for the delay-of-game penalty, Reggie Leach deflected Bill Barber's drive behind goaltender Vladislav Tretiak.

Even as the crowd chanted "Hit 'em again, harder, harder!" the Flyers concentrated on hockey the rest of the way and prevailed without further incident by a 4–1 score. "I've never been so happy," beamed defenseman Jimmy Watson after the Flyers had salvaged at least a measure of NHL prestige. "This compares with winning the Stanley Cup."

Referring to the reigning champions of the USSR, who had entered the game with victories over the New York Rangers and the Boston Bruins, and a 3–3 tie with Montreal in The Forum, Bob Kelly said, "The fact that they had [already] won the series didn't mean anything unless they beat us. After all, we're the best team in the NHL, aren't we?"

Philadelphia Flyers versus Toronto Maple Leafs, April 17, 1977

To fully appreciate how swiftly it transpired, one probably should have been a bug on the wall of the visitors' clubhouse in Toronto's Maple Leaf Gardens on the night of April 17, 1977. For it was there, in their dressing room, that Ross Lonsberry and Gary Dornhoefer of the Philadelphia Flyers were able to measure in the time required to take a *shower* the most dramatic comeback in Stanley Cup playoff history.

After capturing the Cup in 1974 and 1975, then losing it to Montreal in 1976, the Flyers were expected to seek retribution against the Canadiens in the 1977 finals. However, after dropping the first two games of the quarterfinals to Toronto at The Spectrum, the Flyers had dodged the bullet of an 0–3 deficit in games only when Rick MacLeish tied the third contest with 38 seconds left in regulation play, then stunned the 14,685 people in Maple Leaf Gardens with the winner 2:55 into sudden-death overtime.

But now, in the fourth game, the Flyers were once again in deep trouble. With only 14 minutes left in regulation play, Toronto's Lanny McDonald had already scored four goals, the Leafs led 5–2, and both Lonsberry and Dornhoefer had been ejected from the game for burning the ears of referee Bruce Hood. And even after Mel Bridgman scored a shorthanded goal, the Flyers trailed 5–3 as the game entered the final two minutes of regulation play.

But then, with 1:49 remaining, Tom Bladon's drive from the right point darted over goaltender Mike Palmateer's shoulder and just under the crossbar. Down in the Philadelphia dressing quarters, Lonsberry and Dornhoefer were heading for the showers in disgust when trainer Frank Lewis came through the door and said, "Would you believe it's five to four?"

Moments later, both players were emerging from the showers when Lewis walked through the door again. "Would you believe," he said, "that it's five-five?"

It *was* hard to believe, but only 16 seconds after he had scored, another drive by Bladon had demanded a sprawling save from Palmateer. The rebound flew directly to Bobby Clarke, who, after waiting an agonizing second "just to make sure," flipped the rebound into the net to tie the game. Only 1:33 remained on the clock high above center ice.

"Before the third period," Philadelphia coach Fred Shero recalled later, "I told them that there are moments that live forever, and that that third period was going to live forever." But alas, even Shero, for all his flair for the dramatic, could not have envisioned how phophetic his words would be.

The Leafs, of course, never recovered. Only 50 seconds into sudden-death overtime, Reggie Leach's 50-foot slap shot brought victory to the Flyers, who went on to win the series in six games.

Actually, the only other comeback to rival this

one had occurred 33 years earlier, during the 1944 finals at the Forum, where the Canadiens trailed the Chicago Black Hawks 4–1 going into the final 10 minutes of game four. "The fans were booing, yelling that it was fixed, because the Canadiens led 3–0 in the series and should have been winning easily," recalls Ron Andrews, the NHL's resident statistician-historian. "The Hawks had finished fourth that year, the Canadiens first, and the Canadiens hadn't lost a game in the Forum all season."

But then, at the 10:02 mark, Elmer Lach scored for Montreal. With only 3:45 remaining, Rocket Richard cut Chicago's lead to 4–3, and with 2:40 left, Richard tied the game. Then, 9:12 into sudden death,

Toe Blake, who had assisted on all four of Montreal's previous goals, won the game, the Stanley Cup, and the Canadiens became the only team ever to complete an entire season undefeated at home.

"But to my knowledge, nothing like what the Flyers did has ever happened," says Andrews. "I can't recall a team scoring two goals in the final two minutes, three in the final six, to force sudden death. Especially a shorthanded goal."

"I was twenty-six years old before the game began and now I'm thirty," Philadelphia's Orest Kindrachuck said after it was over. "I think it's just a very good lesson to be learned: never give up, regardless of what it is."

Guy Lafleur, May 11, 1979

The burning rivalry between the Boston Bruins and the Montreal Canadiens, born during the Stanley Cup playoffs of 1968 and 1969 and nurtured in the decade that followed, became a raging fire in this playoff series. By May 11, 1979, there they were, two old foes going at each other's scar tissue, one with grit, the other with *élan*, deadlocked at three games apiece, with the victor headed for a date with the New York Rangers in the Cup finals.

The Boston coach, Don Cherry, had made no secret that his contract dispute with the Bruins would most likely leave him somewhere else in the months to come (it turned out to be Colorado). And Scotty Bowman, the Canadiens' coach, wanted to make it four straight Cups (five in his eight years in Montreal), then become a general manager (it turned out to be Buffalo). As a result, their teams played one of the truly spellbinding games in Stanley Cup history.

The Bruins' Rick Middleton opened the scoring midway through the first period, and Montreal's Jacques Lemaire tied it shortly thereafter. In the second period, two strikes by Wayne Cashman gave the Bruins a 3–1 advantage going into the third. Despite outgunning Boston 27–20 over the first 40 minutes, the Canadiens appeared doomed: except for Lemaire's shot, everything they threw at the hot hand of Boston goaltender Gilles Gilbert he had somehow

stopped.

"There were some very discouraging moments," said Montreal goaltender Ken Dryden, who retired after the playoffs to pursue a career in law. "But you have four months to feel the discouragement if you eventually lose and there's no sense starting twenty minutes earlier."

So the Canadiens glanced up at those portraits of Montreal's Hall of Fame players staring down from the walls of their dressing room, reached back into their storied past, and fought back. Six minutes into the third period, Guy Lafleur fed Mark Napier, who rifled a 20-footer behind Gilbert—and the Forum exploded. And only two minutes and four seconds later, there was Lafleur again, feathering a pass to Guy Lapointe, who drilled a screen shot behind Gilbert to tie it up. As 17,500 shook the house with cheers, surely the Canadiens wouldn't be denied now.

But then Lapointe was blasted into the boards by Mike Milbury, carried from the ice on a stretcher with injured knee ligaments, and Montreal's three-men defensive force had been shaved to Larry Robinson and Serge Savard. A minute later, Middleton grabbed Jean Ratelle's pass, swept from behind the net and put a shot off Dryden's glove and into the far corner. With only 3:59 remaining, the Forum fell silent.

"I thought it was over," said Bowman. "It gets

that late in a game, it looked like the goalie was going to beat us. It's happened before, it will happen again. I don't think we could have done it if it wasn't for that last power play."

Power play? "It was my fault," Cherry would say later, choking back the tears. "It's always the coach's fault when there's too many men on the ice. Hell, we were so close to it, and so excited, I had to pull back two other guys or we would have had eight guys on the ice."

With just over two minutes left, and the Bruins in the midst of a line change, a whistle blew and Boston was caught with too many men on the ice. And now Lafleur, having accepted the torch from Beliveau and Richard and Canadien heroes past, made them pay. "What developed were the kind of situations that Guy Lafleur thrives on," noted Dryden. "It was going to be his game to decide."

Having already set up the goals that had pulled Montreal into the 3–3 tie, Lafleur tied it again, this time by flying down the right wing and scorching a 35-foot shot past Gilbert with only 1:14 remaining in regulation time.

Overtime. And instead of cautious, tentative hockey, it was wide open, end-to-end, with lots of shots (there would be 14 in all, 11 by Montreal)—and one that would win it. Dryden blanked Don Marcotte and Terry O'Reilly at his doorstep; Gilbert stoned Steve Shutt. But then, in the ninth minute, Savard frisked the puck from Middleton and sent Rejean Houle wheeling up ice. Houle gave it to Mario Tremblay on right wing, and Tremblay put it on the stick of Yvon Lambert driving to the net. Gilbert never had a chance.

"It's a masochistic kind of game anyway," said Robinson of the Canadiens, who would go on to win the Cup from New York in five games. "It comes down to twenty minutes, even less in overtime, for ten months of work. It seems unfair, but that's the way the playoffs are arranged and we were lucky."

"What the heck, I'm not going to spoil a great effort like that by complaining about the [late penalty] call," said Cherry. "I'm just as proud of my players as I'm sure Scotty is of his. I don't know what else to say."

Indeed, after a game such as this one, both teams had already said it all.

Someday the portraits of Montreal's Hall of Famers will be joined by that of Guy Lafleur, a player who consistently manages to turn "situations" into victories.

Gordie Howe, June 4, 1980

His hair, once dark brown, was wispy and almost white. His face, though still handsome in a rugged sort of way, had been laced together with countless yards of catgut. Four of his front teeth had been false since his rookie year, which was 1946. He was still six feet tall and weighed 205 pounds, as he did back then, but his stomach, once hard and ribbed as a washboard, had the subtle slope of a bowling pin.

"It's nights like this that make you think, 'Has the time come?'" said Gordie Howe, then 51 years old. "They say you can play tennis when you're seventy, and I guess you can. But in tennis, your opponent puts one down the line, you say, 'Nice shot,' and start over again.

"It doesn't work that way in this game, and I really don't know why I go on. It's not the money, and I've certainly had my share of glory. The thing is, this isn't a job to me. It's a way of life, and nobody teaches you how to give it up."

Ironically, when Gordie Howe first signed a contract with the Detroit Red Wings, his sole ambition was to last one year in the National Hockey League; that first season, he clipped every article that mentioned his name and every photograph of himself in a Detroit uniform, "just to *prove* that I had played." By his tenth year, however, he was the finest player the game had ever known; by his fifteenth, he wanted to become only the second man in NHL history to play 20. Only after a quarter-century with Detroit, however, did he retire. And by that time, moments both memorable and historic had followed him around like no other player in history. For example:

*the night in the Detroit Olympia in April 1948, when he sustained a severe concussion that almost claimed his life. "In the hospital, they opened up Gordie's skull to relieve the pressure on his brain," recalls former teammate and coach Sid Abel, "and the blood shot to the ceiling like a geyser."

* the night in February 1959, when he cemented his reputation as the most feared player in the game by pummeling Lou Fontinato, the New York Rangers' enforcer, in Madison Square Garden. "Never in my life had I heard anything like it, except maybe the sound of someone chopping wood," recalls Frank Udvari, the referee that night. "*Thwack!* And all of a sudden Louie's breathing out of his cheekbone."

* the night in November 1963, when he broke Maurice ("Rocket") Richard's NHL record of 544 career goals by scoring number 545 against—of all teams—the Montreal Canadiens, for whom Richard had played.

* the night in December 1968, when against the Pittsburgh Penguins he scored goal 700 of his career, a mark that at that time rivaled Babe Ruth's lifetime record of 714 home runs in baseball.

*and, incredibly, the night of December 7, 1977, when, after two years of retirement in the Detroit organization, he had come back to star for the Houston Aeros of the World Hockey Association and scored his one-thousandth goal in professional hockey against the Birmingham Bulls.

Ironically, the most significant moment in Howe's career may well have been the saddest: June 4, 1980, when he announced that, after 32 seasons in major league hockey, he was retiring permanently.

Then 52 and a grandfather, he said, "I probably have another half-year in me, but I'd rather retire now than try again and tire halfway through next season."

In all, Howe played in a record 2,421 major league games and scored 1,071 goals, 801 of them in the NHL, the league's all-time record. He was the NHL's most valuable player six times, won the scoring championships six times, and played in 22 all-star games. "There have been so many years and so many exciting moments that they all blend into one," Howe explained.

Yet the greatest, he had to say, was against the Bruins in Boston Garden, March 9, 1980, when he realized what had become a dream of the last decade—playing on the same line in an NHL game with two of his three sons, Marty and Mark.

"That was the ultimate," he says. "There were times when I had my doubts whether it would ever happen, but it did. And I'll never forget it."

Gordie Howe, whose career spanned five decades, once clipped every article about himself just to prove that he had once played in the NHL. In fact, he played so many years that one season two of his three sons played on the same team with him. When he ended his career with the Hartford Whalers, he had scored 1,071 goals, 801 in the NHL.

4
Goal!
Action Portfolio

Preceding pages: *Islander Bob Bourne camouflages his shot with a spray of ice in the face of former Boston goalie Gerry Cheevers.*
Right: *On the road and off the ice often means restaurant game meals.*
Opposite top: *Chicago's Peter Marsh prepares stick for play.* Below: *Player is taped by Bill Bozak, ex-Winnipeg trainer.*
Opposite left: *Traveling bags of Gordie (9) and Mark (5) Howe.*

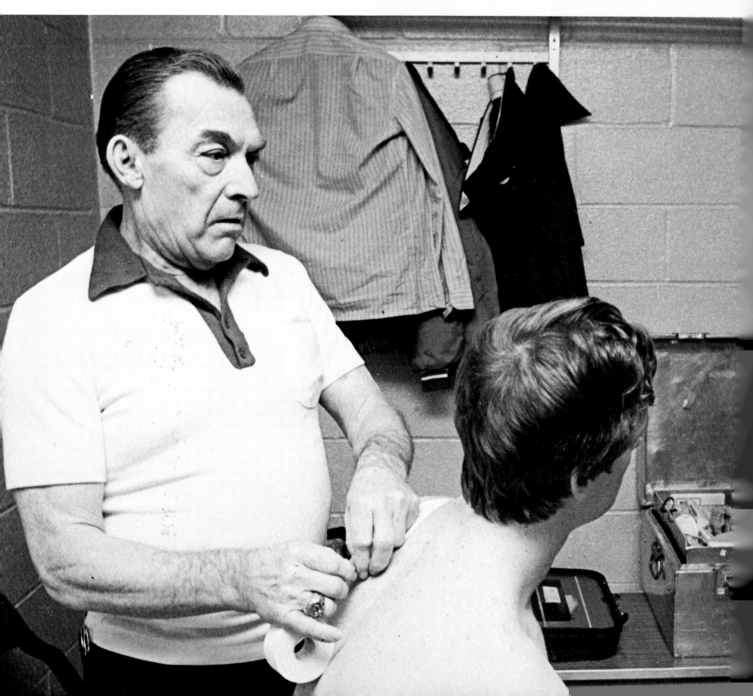

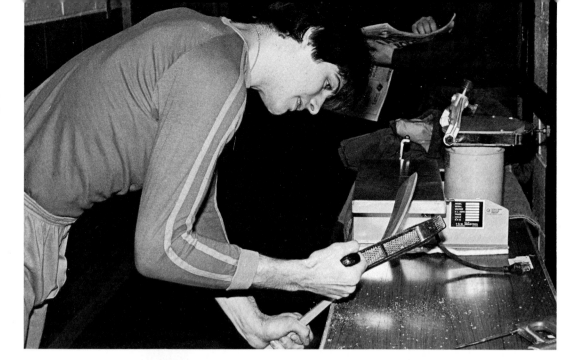

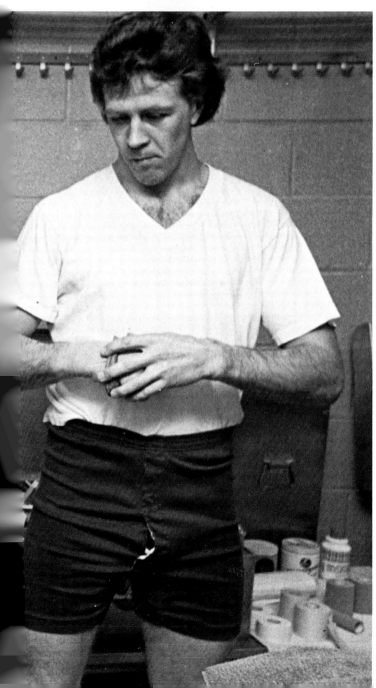

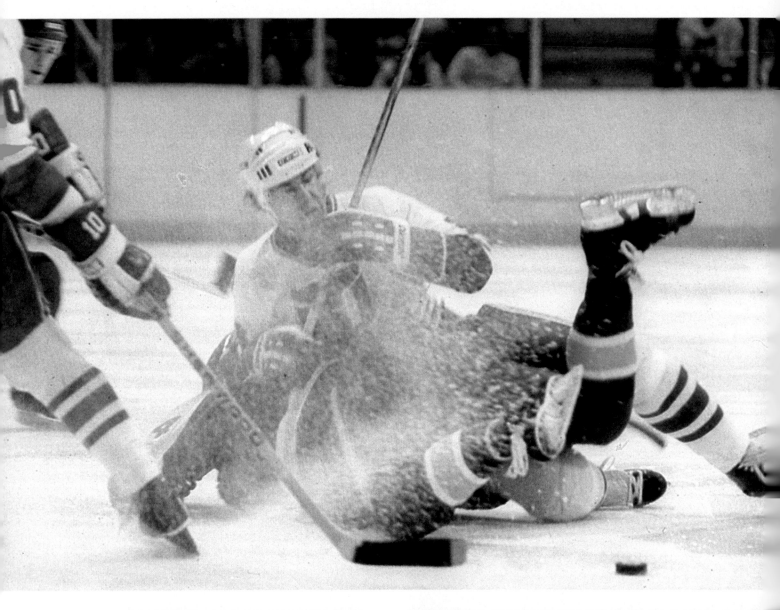

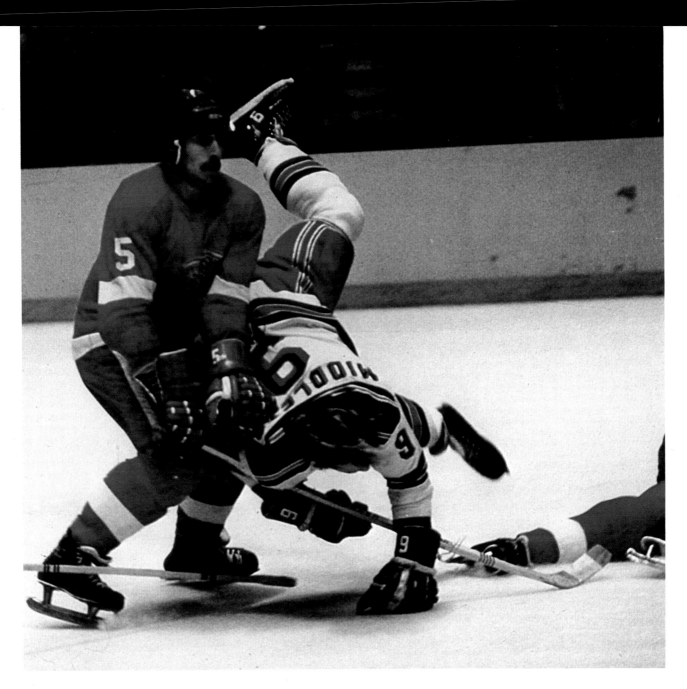

Although proficient skating is the basic skill required in hockey, it is not always easy for a player to keep his skates on the ice. Opposite top: *The puck squirts free from Hartford Whaler and Los Angeles King pileup.* Opposite left: *Philadelphia Flyer Gary Morrison is upended by Washington Capital Howard Walker.* Opposite right: *Ex-New York Ranger Pat Hickey sails high over the hip check of former Flyer Kevin McCarthy.* Above: *Unceremoniously dumped by Detroit Red Wing defenseman Jean Hamel is former Ranger Rick Middleton.*

Hockey has an intimacy that allows brothers to play side by side or even as opponents. Above: Defenseman Dave (left) and winger Don Maloney were two of the leaders in the New York Rangers' drive to the 1979 Stanley Cup finals. Opposite: Although sometimes overlooked in the public eye as a result of his brother's leadership role for the New York Islanders, Jean Potvin plays defense along with his brother Denis. In fact, they sometimes share even their penalties together.

Above: *Bill Barber has been a key player for the Philadelphia Flyers ever since their two consecutive Stanley Cup–winning seasons in 1973 and 1974. Here he goes to battle for position with ex-New York Islander Billy Harris.* Right: *Los Angeles Kings' outstanding goaltender Mario Lessard waves his glove teasingly at a shot as it goes wide of the net.*

Above: *Bruins' Wayne Cashman, whose superb corner work aided in Phil Esposito's scoring records when they played on the same line, is upended by Rick Lapointe.* Right: *Former Capital Robert Picard (left) is pulled down by Chicago's Keith Brown.* Opposite: *Two former Calder Trophy winners, Eric Vail (left) and Steve Vickers, tangle at center ice.*

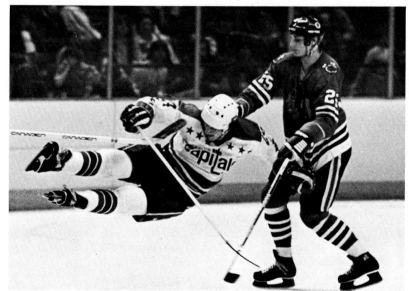

Opposite: *Powerful New York Ranger forward Nick Fotiu sits out the action from the penalty box at Madison Square Garden.* Above: *Ken ("Rat") Linseman, the Philadelphia center who has a propensity for getting under the skins of his opponents, prepares to return to the ice as his penalty ticks off.* Left: *Ron Grahame, mask in hand, glances up to the crowd before skating onto the ice.*

111

Anatomy of a slap shot. Rick Martin of the Buffalo Sabres displays the motions that make up one of hockey's basic maneuvers. From left to right, Martin winds up for the shot, getting behind the puck. He follows through and shoots. He continues the follow through as the shot heads out toward the goal.

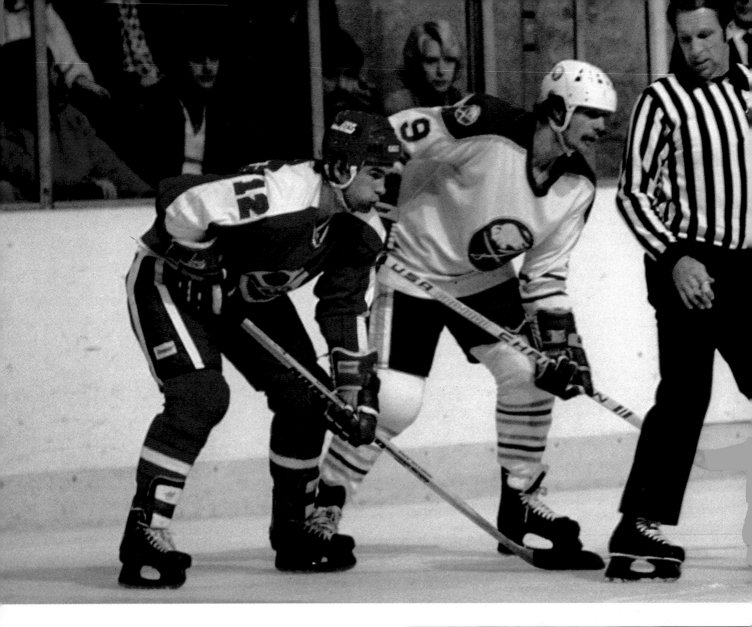

Winning face-offs is a crucial part of hockey strategy, especially when the game is close. Who wins the face-off determines which team takes possession of the puck. Above: Buffalo's Don Luce wins the face-off from Winnipeg's Dave Christian while the ref keeps Jean Sauve (9) and Morris Lukowich (12) at bay. Right: Anticipating the drop of the puck by linesman Gordy Broseker, Boston's Peter McNab musters his strength to grab the face-off. Opposite: Quebec Nordique Robbie Ftorek (left) and Buffalo's Derek Smith go one-on-one for the puck.

114

Above: *The Zamboni driver
cleans and refreshes the ice
between periods at Madison
Square Garden.* Right: *Linesman
Ray Scapinello refreshes himself
while doing some patch work on
the ice.* Opposite top: *An
emptying Madison Square
Garden.* Opposite bottom:
*Maintenance crew uses Zamboni
shavings to fix large soft spot in
the ice.*

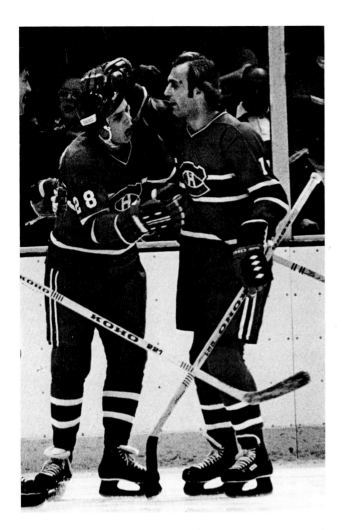

Preceding pages: *Vancouver goalie Gary Bromley pounces on a loose puck in the crease while Tom Gradin (left) ties up an opponent and Dave Logan makes sure the puck doesn't get away.* Opposite: *Former Philadelphia teammates Ross Lonsberry (left), Mel Bridgman, and Rick Lapointe celebrate a goal.* Above left: *Congratulating each other are Canadiens Pierre Larouche (left) and Guy Lafleur.* Above: *Buffalo defenseman Bill Hajt (right) and former teammate Don Luce talk strategy.* Left: *Hartford forwards Don Nachbauer (left) and Jeff Brubaker demonstrate youthful exuberance.*

Above: *Flyers' Rick MacLeish is "hooked" by Ranger Don Maloney.* Right: *Defensemen Vitezslav Duris (right) and goalie Jiri Crha, both of Czechoslovakia, now play for Toronto.* Opposite: *Unleashing a vicious slap shot, Philadelphia's Behn Wilson grimaces.*

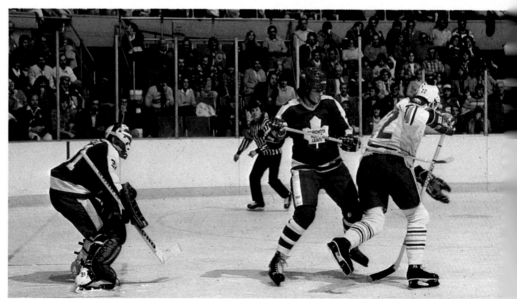

122

Above: *Wayne Babych was the St. Louis Blues' leading scorer during the 1980–81 season.* Right: *Captain Brian Sutter, who has five brothers playing pro hockey, inspires his St. Louis teammates with his hard-nosed, hustling style of play.* Opposite: *Shouts of "Eddie, Eddie" resound approvingly from Ranger fans who recognize Eddie Johnstone's consistent, all-out efforts on the ice.*

124

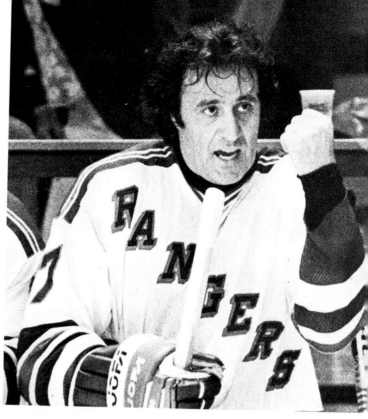

Preceding pages: *Action in front of the net is usually fast and furious. Page 126: Philadelphia's Ken Linseman and Blake Wesley are entangled in the Buffalo goal. Page 127: Colorado Rockies' goalie Hardy Astrom and teammates try to keep the puck out of the net. Opposite: Referee John McCauley renders a guilty decision on a penalty. New York Islander Dave Langevin* (above left), *Ranger Phil Esposito* (above right), *coach Harry Sinden* (left), *and Quebec's Marc Tardif* (above) *disagree.*

Before November 1, 1959, when Jacques Plante skated onto the Madison Square Garden ice wearing a crude, homemade mask to protect him from reinjuring a face wound, it was considered taboo for an NHL goalie to wear such contrivances. Today, each goalie dons an individually designed and decorated mask. Opposite: Jim Rutherford, Detroit Red Wings. Top (left to right): Jiri Crha, Toronto Maple Leafs; Paul Harrison, Toronto Maple Leafs, Gilles Gilbert, Detroit Red Wings. Above (left to right): Ed Staniowski, St. Louis Blues; Wayne Thomas, New York Rangers; Glenn Hanlon, Vancouver Canucks.

131

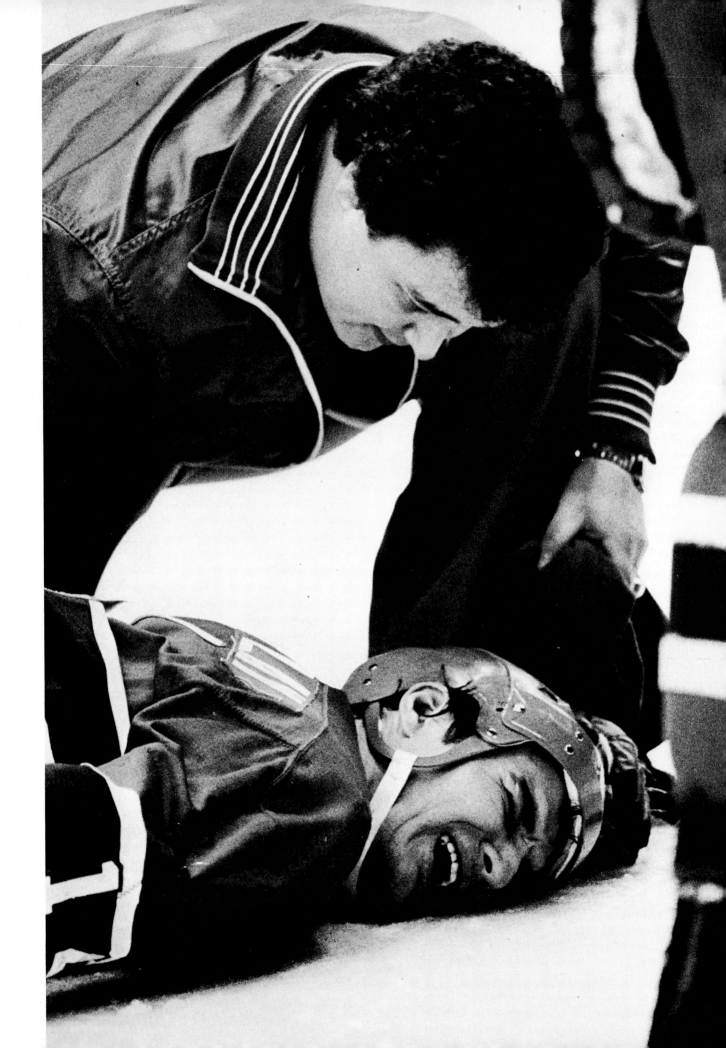

Opposite: *The pained grimace of Montreal's Mario Tremblay shows he was bumped just a little harder than usual.* Top: *New York Islander Steve Tambellini wraps up ex-Vancouver Canuck Jere Gillis with his stick as he rides him into the boards.* Above: *Philadelphia's Ken Linseman goes around Whaler defenseman Rick Ley, trying to distract him as much as outmaneuver him.*

Above: *Montreal Canadien Bob Gainey, regarded as the best defensive forward in hockey, is helpless as he slides past the often-elusive puck.*
Opposite top: *Referee Andy van Hellemond does his best to recover after having the wind knocked out of him.* Opposite right: *New York Islander Billy Smith gets an icy view of his loose-puck recovery.*

Preceding pages: *Although Carol Vadnais gets control of the puck on a Ranger power play, the Los Angeles Kings are in the defensive "box" formation trying to kill off a penalty.* Left: *During the early and mid-1970s, aggressiveness and intimidation became more predominant in hockey play. This sometimes led to brawls, but recent NHL rules changes such as the "third man in" rule and the fisticuffs rule, forbidding players from dropping their gloves in a fight, have attempted to curb this type of incident. Below: The New York Rangers and the St. Louis Blues fail to agree to disagree. Opposite: Toronto's Rocky Saganiuk is drawn out of an altercation by linesman Ron Asselstine.*

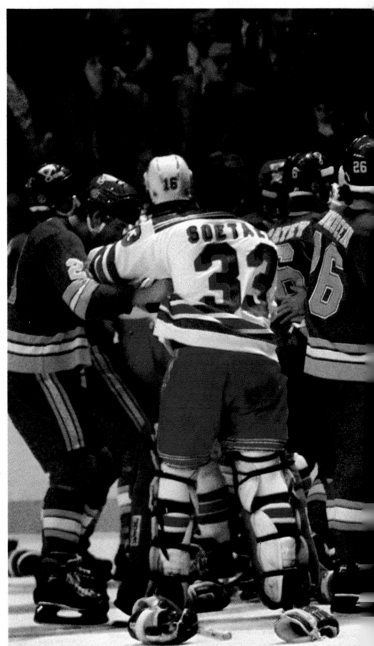

Right: *Sticks up, Philadelphia's Bill Barber glares menacingly at Islander Gordie Lane.*
Opposite: *Toronto captain Darryl Sittler scored six goals in one game in 1976.*
Below: *Edmonton's Stan Weir tries to slow down Islanders' Anders Kallur.*

5
The
Ice Houses
Arenas
by Jay
Greenberg

The Forum

If an arena is just a place to watch sporting events, a city is only a collection of buildings. And if hockey is just a game to the people of Montreal, the Olympics were merely a track-and-field meet to the Greeks.

Hockey's Olympus sits on St. Catherine Street between Atwater and Closse. Only the players are asked to remove their shoes upon entering, and that's because the game is played on ice skates. But if it was considered appropriate that the 16,074 persons who attend every game enter in stocking feet, there would be no arguments.

This is not just the home of the most successful team in the league's 63-year history, but a shrine. Other franchises have heroes, this one has a martyr. When Howie Morenz, the first Canadien superstar, died of complications five weeks after suffering a broken leg in a 1937 game at the Forum, 15,000 people came to the building to view his body.

Other teams had triumphs, the Canadiens had a cause. After NHL president Clarence Campbell suspended Maurice ("Rocket") Richard in 1955 for inadvertently punching a linesman, 5,000 fans rioted at the next game.

There are a lot of places where hockey is played, very few where it is lived. Ten of the 21 buildings the National Hockey League calls home are featured in this chapter. Obviously the six hallowed, pre-expansion halls belong, but also included are a few of the post-1967 arenas that have been the sites of landmark games. Each building has its own feeling, but only at the Forum, hockey's temple, do fans go to worship.

"You grow up with it," said Jean Beliveau, the Canadiens' great, "from the time you start playing until you are lucky enough to become part of it, like I was."

The Forum is not just a historical landmark. The Canadiens still live there and it continues to exert a less-than-subtle influence on their success. From the locker room wall, the faces of Richard, Morenz, and now Beliveau overlook the dressing players, not as ghosts but as inspiration. Their eyes are unrelenting, and so are the city's. Playing for the Canadiens has

never been a job or an obligation. It is a privilege.

An open-air ice-skating rink, where such legends as Art Ross, and Lester and Frank Patrick cavorted, had been located at the corner of Atwater and St. Catherine Streets for 20 years before a group of sportsmen approached a Montreal insurance company about building the biggest hockey arena in the world. However, the company, convinced the project for a 9,000-seat palace was on too grand a scale, backed out before ground was broken. Then local financiers Donat Raymond and H. L. Timmins came to the rescue. The arena cost $1.5 million and opened on November 29, 1924, with the Canadiens, one of two Montreal entries in the National Hockey League, defeating the Toronto St. Pat's, 7-1.

Montreal's other team, the Maroons, was created that same year by the three businessmen who owned the Forum to provide an English rival to the French Canadiens. Leo Dandurand, the Canadiens' owner, rented the Forum until 1935, when he sold the Canadiens to the Canadian Arena Corporation, still the owners of the Maroons. The merger complete, the corporation then began to phase the Maroons out.

The Maroons had won their second and final Stanley Cup that year, but sagging Depression attendance made two teams impractical. In 1938, the Maroons were folded and the Canadiens became the Forum's sole major-league hockey attraction.

Canadiens' attendance, after the death of Morenz, floundered until Maurice Richard joined the club in 1942. The following season, the team won its first Stanley Cup in 14 years, and by 1949, the demand for tickets was so great that two 1,750-seat balconies were constructed on the sides of the arena.

The progression of heroes was orderly. As Richard's career went into twilight, Beliveau arrived in 1953. Jean retired the same year Guy Lafleur broke in. But it was Richard, then the most exciting player in the game, who first hallowed the Forum halls. And also, by his enforced absence from the ice that night in 1955, almost tore them down.

Today, some amateur sociologists refer to the

Preceding pages: *The New York Islanders won their first Stanley Cup ever at the Nassau Veterans Memorial Coliseum on May 24, 1980, in a playoff series with the Philadelphia Flyers.*

Richard riot as the first stirring of French nationalism. An English bureaucrat, Clarence Campbell, had suspended the French national hero. If it was nationalism, not hockey, that drove the angry mob that night, it was an isolated instance. French or English has never been a consideration in who plays for the Canadiens and, once the puck is dropped, such issues are forgotten in the grandstand, too.

"You may have the odd French-English fight," said Red Fisher, who has covered the Canadiens for 26 years for the late Montreal *Star and Gazette*. "But there were only two times I sensed that kind of tension through the whole building. One was the night of the 1976 elections. They started flashing the results on the scoreboard and the Parti Quebecois was winning in a big upset. Nobody was watching the game, they were cheering the returns.

"The other time was the Richard riot. You could feel that building up all day long."

Richard, the greatest hockey player of his era, was battling for the league scoring title in the closing days of the 1955 season when Boston's Hal Laycoe's stickwork cut him for six stitches near the temple. Richard quickly punched Laycoe to the ice, and linesman Cliff Thompson, trying to pull the Rocket away, also took a few shots of his wrath.

It was two days later when Campbell announced a suspension that would carry into the upcoming playoffs. The Red Wings were at the Forum the next night and by noon a handful of picketers, carrying anti-Campbell signs, appeared in the park across the street. They were mostly kids in leather jackets, but by game time, their numbers were sizable and their rage growing.

A few forced their way inside and waited to see whether Campbell would appear in his customary seat. By the time he did, the Red Wings, who had won five straight regular-season titles and were trying to hold the Canadiens off for a sixth, had jumped to a 3–0 lead.

At first only insults were hurled at the league president, but by the end of the first period, it had become a steady stream of garbage. One youth approached Campbell pretending to offer help, and then took a swing. An usher grabbed him before he could make contact. A second youngster then slapped Campbell twice in the face before being hauled away.

Richard said the boy told him later that the plan was to strip Campbell to his shorts and parade him around the ice.

A tear-gas bomb, which landed just a foot from where Richard was seated, filled the Forum with smoke, driving the fans still seated for the intermission into the hallways. Campbell and his fiancée were hustled into the first-aid room, where the Montreal fire chief had just finished telling general manager Frank Selke that he was closing the building.

Campbell wrote a note to Detroit coach Jack Adams, declaring the Red Wings the winner, which was fine with Adams so long as the four goals that Detroit scored went into the record book. Campbell and his escort were then smuggled, with covered heads, to the fire chief's car for the ride home. Although new battalions of rioters were coming in from the street, the public address announcement that the game had been canceled miraculously caused no greater panic.

Though the entrance on the St. Catherine Street side was jammed with incoming rabble-rousers, 15,000 spectators left peacefully by side doors. Those who chose to riot stayed for the parade up and down St. Catherine, smashing windows and phone booths. By 2 A.M. it was over, with 52 arrests but no serious injuries.

The Forum windows, it could be said, underwent their first remodeling that night. In 1968, the same evening that Toe Blake won his eighth Stanley Cup and announced his retirement as coach, workmen moved in for a demolition that, this time, was contracted.

After 44 years, the Forum was being rebuilt. The roof was raised and all the outer walls were torn down. Except for the removal of view-blocking posts that supported the old roof and the building of a second level at the ends, the seating itself was left intact.

The Canadiens played their first eight games of the 1968–69 season on the road, while workmen feverishly raced the calendar. When the Forum reopened on November 2, the people who had left their old friend to $10.5 million worth of progress five months before were convinced they had just walked into the world's eighth wonder.

The Forum was virtually the same building, minus only the inconveniences and plus almost 5,000

new seats. The other 12,000, replaced two years before, remained. Though these seats were without armrests and a bit narrow, the dollars generated and the intimacy saved were probably worth it.

"It was pretty well the same Forum we always had," said Beliveau. "We did not feel at all like we were coming back to a strange place. This is, first of all, a hockey arena, like Dodger Stadium is a baseball stadium, and none of that feeling was lost."

Of course the 15 Stanley Cup banners were back in the rafters, retaining a homey touch. Beliveau scored the first goal when the building reopened, and tradition, which would bring 6 more Cups in the next 10 years, was left intact.

Today, the Forum is not only hallowed, but vibrant and spotless. The Metro stops across the street, and four different bars and restaurants are scattered around the building's three levels, which are accessible by escalators on both sides. The visiting players say there is no faster ice surface and no place as inspiring to their performance. Roger Doucet's renditions of the Canadian and U.S. anthems bring chills, even if *le match de ce soir* usually brings defeat.

There are louder and more partisan crowds in other league buildings, but none are more appreciative of the game itself or more demanding of the home team. "They have always given the visiting team a break," said Fisher. "It has been a point of irritation sometimes with the Canadiens' management and players, but they have always applauded good plays by the other team."

But they also know a bad one by the Canadiens when they see it. "There is pressure, yes," said Beliveau, smiling. "But that is what makes you perform."

146

Opposite: *The old Montreal Forum, hockey's Olympus on St. Catherine Street between Atwater and Closse, was the home of both the Montreal Canadiens and the Maroons, until the Maroons failed in 1938.* Below: *After 44 years, the Forum was rebuilt for the 1968–69 season.* Bottom: *Montreal's Hall of Famers decorate and inspire the Canadiens' locker room.*

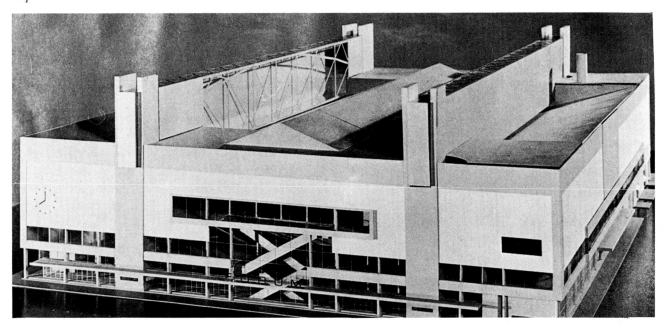

Boston Garden

Roger Naples has missed three Bruins games at Boston Garden in 42 years. If that wrecking ball ever comes through Section 127, he will probably be sitting in his seat taking it, like a medicine ball, in the belly.

"Not that it couldn't stand improvements," said Roger, "but I hope they never tear this place down. The Celtics are talking about a new building out here in Revere [where he works for the recreation department]. It would be about a thirty second walk from my desk, but I wouldn't want to see it. The Garden is, well, chummy. That's the best way I can put it. It's a chummy little place."

And after 52 years, it's a little crummy around the edges, too. Periodic paint jobs can't hide its age, and grown men swinging hockey sticks can't scare away the mice. One, which periodically ventures by the visiting players' bench, has been facilitating line changes for years. But the truth is he doesn't bite, and chances are he's lived at the Garden as long as Roger.

If the Bruins ever move out, they might as well switch leagues and become an indoor soccer team. The Garden is as inarguably Boston as it is hockey. "Of course, any building of its age is going to have its problems," said Steve Nazro, the Garden's director of sales. "But I don't think any of the new buildings I've seen compare for bringing you close to the action."

And though the Celtics, the griping basketball tenants, point out that 1,200 of the 14,673 seats put you behind posts, the fact remains that if the Garden wasn't such a damn good place to watch a hockey game from behind a pole, nobody would come. They would have torched it decades ago.

It's only the first-nighters who are put off by the inconveniences. And this is not a first-night crowd. Even though most of the Bruin home games are on TV, and the Jets come in now just as often as the Canadiens, Naples doesn't care. It's the Bruins he wants to see, not the visiting team. And certainly not some miniature facsimiles on a 19-inch screen.

"I believe," said Roger, "that you gotta be there. I don't know of a better way to put it. There is just nothing like it."

Naples could have an armchair and instant replays, but chooses instead to climb eight sets of stairs to get to his wooden seat. There are places in the Garden that are easier to get to and closer to the ice, but in 1975, Roger declined the chance to relocate.

When the Garden ownership changed hands for the sixth time, the new management wanted to install private boxes for corporate clients at the top of the building up where Naples and his friend sat. They called themselves "Gallery Gods," and 42 years ago founded what was, in effect, the world's first arena club. There were no waiters, no private rooms, and no bar, but long before a night at a hockey game became a way to sell mutual funds, these guys had the idea.

Roger was vice-president for 35 years, acceding to the presidency in 1972. At one time there were 1,047 members, lined up in the six rows of seats hanging, literally, from the Garden rafters along both sides of the rink. They did not buy their tickets from the box office. The Bruins sold them collectively to the Gods, and each section's leader was in charge of distributing them for the next game. "When it was a three-dollar seat," said Naples , "we'd charge an extra fifteen cents for dues."

"When the Jacobs brothers [Max and Jeremy] bought the team [in 1975] and wanted to build the private boxes, they promised to relocate us. Which they did. They also asked if they could handle the tickets and that was okay with us, too. Frankly it was sort of becoming a pain in the butt."

The new luxury boxes were to be on one side only, which meant half of the Gallery Gods' seats would remain. "Everyone else moved around," said Roger. "Some moved downstairs, or in the balcony behind the goal—anywhere there were seats available.

"We're down to about four-hundred seventy members, so they were able to take care of everybody. The management kept all their promises. I stayed up top. I've sat downstairs for three games in forty-two years and can't take it. I like the whole thing in front of me. Down there you have to get up, lean forward... aw, it just wasn't for me."

Gerry Cheevers, former Boston goalie who led the Bruins to Stanley Cup triumphs in 1970 and 1971, probably has the best seat in the house at the Boston Garden. His seat may be "warmer" now, though, since he has taken over the Bruins as their coach.

Demolition of the property above North Station began on December 3, 1927. The Boston-Madison Square Garden opened on November 17, 1928. The building was constructed by Tex Rickard, who had already developed its namesake in New York. Rickard had envisioned a chain of six huge sports palaces, and Boston looked like the logical place for number two.

The Boston-Madison Square Garden opened with an American Legion boxing carnival, the highlight bout matching French featherweight champion Andre Routis and Dorchester's Dick ("Honeyboy") Finnegan. The opening-night crowd literally broke down the doors, leaving posterity with only an estimated attendance of 17,000. The Bruins, who had played their first four NHL seasons in the Boston Arena across town, moved in three nights later.

The Canadiens beat the Bruins that evening, 3–2, after a late goal by Dit Clapper was disallowed, and the crowd littered the ice with paper. But their disappointment did not last long. The team, managed by the legendary Art Ross and led by goalie Tiny Thompson, won its first Stanley Cup in the Garden's inaugural year, allowing only three goals in two series against the Rangers and Canadiens.

Rickard died five years later, passing on his interest to two New York associates, Major Dibley and Dick Dynn. But the Depression cut into the standard 20,000 Friday-night fight crowds, so they soon sold the building to Bostonian Henry Lapham.

A contest was held to rename it, and the panel of judges was overwhelmed with the ingenuity of Ruth Fasano, of Dorchester, who came up with "Boston Garden." Lapham had turned the management over to George V. Brown, whose son, Walter, ran the building and later bought it. It took ten years for Ross to rebuild to another championship team in 1939. Anchored by Thompson's replacement, Frankie Brimsek, and the high-scoring Kraut Line, the team repeated its victory in 1941. But it was to be 29 years, including 8 straight during the fifties and sixties in which the Bruins did not even make the playoffs, before Bobby Orr would lead them to another Cup in 1970.

Still, except for a slump in the late 1940s and early 1950s, the Bruin tradition was so well established that the attendance held up. With Walter Brown's death in 1963, the Garden passed to Weston Adams, the grandson of the original Bruins' owner.

The 52-year-old Boston Garden, its ceiling decorated with numerous championship banners, underwent a major face-lift in 1976. The "Gallery Gods," founded 42 years ago, sit in the six rows of seats that hang from the Garden rafters.

When Adams died in 1973, Storer Broadcasting bought both the team and building, and then sold them to the Jacobs brothers (of Buffalo) in 1975.

The Coconut Grove Nightclub fire in 1940 brought stricter fire laws to the Garden, banning its standing room and shrinking its seat capacity to 13,909. Upholstered seats were put into the loge level, increasing the total to 15,500, but this was lessened by 800 with the removal of half of the Gallery Gods' domain.

"I always said," said Tom Fitzgerald, who covered the Bruins for the Boston *Globe* for over 35 years,

The Boston-Madison Square Garden, opened on November 17, 1928, was constructed by Tex Rickard, who had envisioned a chain of six huge sports palaces like the Garden in New York. The name of his Boston emporium was later changed to the Boston Garden.

"that if they could find a view from the bathrooms, they'd put a seat there."

The ice plant, troublesome since the building's dedication, went out in a full burst of glory minutes after the Bruins-Black Hawks final game in 1967. "It was like a geyser," remembered Fitzgerald. "Dirty brown water shooting up fifteen feet. I could just imagine Bobby Hull skating by when it erupted. It would have sent him to the roof."

The Jacobs brothers sprung for the Garden's one major face-lift—a thorough cleanup, new entrances and ticket booths, and a widening of the downstairs lobby in 1976. But it remains the same Garden. The Horse downstairs is still serving before and after the games, the MTA Green Line still stops across the street, the commuter trains still empty out into North Station below. Virtually every major highway in New England passes within five minutes of the brown brick warehouse on the North End, and there are even a few places to park out back. But this is not your Cadillac-type of crowd.

"It's changed," said Naples. "There're a lot more kids now, people aren't as well dressed and no longer live and die with the Bruins. Every game there's someone wearing a Flyers shirt, or rooting for the Islanders, or someone else.

"But the crowd's still well behaved. I've seen how these people react to visitors. As soon as they find out they're from out of town, they're buying them hot dogs and beer and getting on them, but you know, in a nice way. They make those people feel good."

If the Bruins ever move, they'll have to move those people, too. Roger Naples saw the Montreal Forum modernized without losing any of its warmth 12 years ago, and he wonders why something similar couldn't be done with the Garden. It could, but estimates on a job of that magnitude run to $40 million. You can build a new arena for that, but you couldn't build another Garden. "Certainly there's no Byzantine splendor about the place," said Fitzgerald. "Opulence wasn't given much thought. It was built, like all the buildings of its time, as a place to watch sporting events. And in over thirty-five years, I haven't seen a better place to do it."

Maple Leaf Gardens

There are plans for a new arena in Harold Ballard's cabinet. "We drew them up a few years ago," said the president of the Toronto Maple Leafs. "Down on the waterfront, off Yonge Street. I figured twenty thousand, maybe as many as twenty-two thousand seats. Any more than that, it gets pretty hard to see. You're talking about following a three-inch disc.

"I don't know if we'll ever be able to do it. The money's hard to find. They almost have to be built by the government these days, the kind of money we're talking about.

"What I really want is more seats, not a new building. There's nothing wrong with the building we have now. It's the finest one on the circuit. And the most famous. The old [Montreal] Forum was a pretty famous place, but they left the damn old seats in the new one. They're so narrow you have to measure a customer's rear before you can sell him the seat.

"Naw, I'll take this place any time."

When Ballard's wife died in 1969, he locked up their house and built an apartment right off his Maple Leaf Gardens office. It is now not only his home, but his playground. In the predawn hours, Ballard will sometimes skate around the deserted ice surface shooting pucks.

Harold, the bombastic troll-under-the-bridge as he peers out at the game from his end-rink cubbyhole, his faithful companion King Clancy by his side, is the only Torontonian who maintains residence at the Gardens. Clancy goes home only at night. His current position mostly involves keeping Ballard company, but King played in the first game at the Gardens, and later coached and referreed there. He is as much a fixture as any of the girders.

The Gardens is Toronto's parlor room, as much a private 16,431-seat club as it is a hockey arena on nights the Leafs are playing. There has not been an unsold seat, the management claims, since 1946. Ballard says that some of the fans among the 8,500 on the season-ticket waiting list have been denied for 15 years.

Because the Leafs have gone as far as the semifinals only once since their last Stanley Cup in 1967, the "warm seats" as Ballard calls them, are better explained by habit than mania. The Canadiens' tradition may be richer in terms of championships, but the Forum is no more symbolic of hockey than the high brindle walls at Church and Carlton Streets in Toronto.

The original Maple Leafs, one of a variety of early professional teams in the Toronto area, folded. Today's team is a descendant of the Toronto Arenas, named after their home which, when built in 1912, was the first building in the city to have artificial ice. The Stanley Cup had become the exclusive property of the NHL when it was formed in 1917, and the Arenas in their premiere season were its first winners.

After three years, their name was changed to the St. Patricks. Another Stanley Cup followed in 1922, but by 1926, the St. Pats were out of money and dead last in the six-team league. They were rescued by Constantine Falkland Kerrys ("Conn") Smythe, the successful coach of the University of Toronto team. Backed by a syndicate, Smythe bought the St. Patricks for $165,000 and changed the name to the Maple Leafs.

The construction of their elegant new home—the Gardens—in 1931, took only five months, at a cost of $1.2 million. In Depression times, money was not easy to come by, but Frank Selke, Sr., a Smythe associate, used his connections with the financial people on Bay Street for the capital while Conn convinced the workers to take some of their payment in stock in the building. Maple Leaf Gardens opened on November 12, 1931, with a 2–1 Chicago Black Hawks victory over the Leafs.

Ballard, the son of a textile executive, was a Canadian speedskating champion in his youth, and later managed junior hockey teams. The coach of his Toronto Marlboros was Stafford Smythe, Conn's son. When the elder Smythe bought the team in 1948 and moved it under the Gardens' umbrella, Ballard moved into the building's management. He, the younger Smythe, and John Bassett, a local newspaper publisher, bought the Leafs and the building from Conn in 1961 for $2.5 million.

The Leafs immediately won three Stanley Cups in three years, and Ballard went to work increasing the Gardens' attractions and deepening its coffers. His first move was directed at the huge picture of Queen Elizabeth that Smythe had mounted on the end wall. Ballard wanted to use the area to put in more seats. "If people want to see a portrait of the Queen, let them go to an art gallery," said Harold. "What the hell, she doesn't pay me anything."

The Queen, who had lived long at the Gardens, was gone, but the building was so well constructed (there is not one obstructed-view seat) that aside from that one 4,000-seat expansion, Ballard has not had to tinker further with the original superstructure in his continual upgrading programs. "The building," he said, "was years ahead of its time."

The broad tiled hallways on both sides of the Gardens provided plenty of room to fill the walls with portraits and memorabilia from the Leafs' storied past, and enough floor space to have installed, in 1945, the first escalators in a sports arena. The Gardens was also the first to use the type of floodlighting now standard in stadiums, Herculite glass to replace the chicken wire around the rink, penalty clocks, and a computerized message board. Ballard even plans to replace the huge blue scoreboard with an animated one. A clientele which was the last to accept organ music during breaks in the game may turn up its nose at this, the last straw, in turning a hockey game into a carnival sideshow. But if Harold, described by the now 85-year-old Smythe as a carnival, wants it, he'll have it.

"If they don't like it," said Ballard, "we've got plenty of people waiting to get tickets."

For years, the Gardens on hockey nights was characterized more as a center for the Leaf performing arts than a place to go berserk over the local franchise. The crowd was exceedingly polite to visiting teams and rarely hard on the Leafs, but by the late 1970s, the noise level had grown.

Today, the rare obscenity is even heard, but the building continues to exude grace. It is immaculately maintained, the seats are upholstered, and the Hot Stove Club, a private eating and drinking place Ballard added in 1963, is richly appointed. In 1978, a row of elegant boxes was constructed near the ceiling.

The regular customers arrive by either subway or automobile, buying chestnuts from vendors outside the building, while others gather in front of their televisions on Saturday evenings. But even before the games were televised, Maple Leaf Gardens was home to people from Timmins to Saskatoon because, for more than 30 years, Foster Hewitt, the radio voice of "Hockey Night in Canada," invited them in. "From the gondola at Maple Leaf Gardens," Hewitt would begin every broadcast, and English-speaking Canada would be transfixed.

The original gondola, designed by Hewitt himself, required the announcer to crawl along a catwalk 121 feet above the ice, then straight down a marine ladder into the hanging booth. A steelworker eyeing the route while the Gardens was being built muttered, "I wouldn't go down that ladder for a million dollars." But Hewitt, who had selected the precipitous site as the best to watch the game, was undeterred.

Neither have the years of Leaf mediocrity kept fathers, sons, and now their sons, from their assigned places in the blues, grays, or greens. You know on which level you're sitting, not only because you've been going to it for 20 years, but by its color.

"The Gardens," says Clancy, "has class." That's the way Smythe wanted it, and the way it remains today.

Clarence Campbell, National Hockey League president from 1944–77, drops the puck for the ceremonial opening face-off between Buffalo's Danny Gare (left) and Toronto's Darryl Sittler, thus officially opening the Maple Leaf season. Toronto owner Harold Ballard looks on.

The Spectrum

Even as it rose in a miraculous 11 months, a town with an inferiority complex had a difficult time taking its new indoor sports facility seriously. One reason was its name, not Arena, Coliseum, or Stadium. But Spectrum.

"Very rarely, as it was going up, did anyone refer to it by its name," said Ed Snider, then a part of the group that had conceived the Flyers and their new home. "There was just a sort of cynicism about it, like there was about professional sports in Philadelphia."

The "big sardine can" in South Philadelphia, as one local sports columnist referred to it, opened on September 30, 1967, with the Quaker City Jazz Festival. Lou Scheinfeld, then Snider's right-hand man and now president of the NBA 76ers, remembers someone calling that day and asking if the new building was the same arena that used to be at 46th and Market streets. More prophetically, another caller wondered if The Spectrum was covered and should he bring a raincoat? Five months later, the answer to that question would have depended upon where the gentleman's seats were located. If it was under section one, he would have also needed a helmet. High winds whipped off a small area of the roof during a performance of the Ice Capades on February 17. The Spectrum, the indoor entertainment facility that was to be the city's bridge to top-name acts and a professional athletic renaissance, had turned into just another Philadelphia joke.

When hasty repairs failed, the mayor ordered the building shut down pending an investigation. The Flyers, who surprisingly were first in the expansion division, were forced to hit the road until The Spectrum was opened again for the playoffs. "It just kind of fit in," said Joe Watson, an original Flyer. "I remember how depressed I was when Philadelphia drafted me from Boston in the expansion draft. I didn't want to come. The city had a parade for us before the season opened and the people were standing out there making obscene gestures and yelling 'You'll be gone before December.'"

Three years later the Flyers were the Stanley Cup champions. Whether The Spectrum was the chicken or the Flyers the egg is an infinite argument, but today the building they play in ranks only behind Madison Square Garden in both bookings and profits.

The Spectrum's design is similar to at least five other arenas the NHL calls home, but what the Flyers have accomplished since their first Cup in 1974 has given the building at Broad and Pattison streets almost as much character and tradition as any of the pre-expansion haunts. "We had a lot to do with it," said Watson, "but don't underestimate the image created by Kate Smith."

The Flyers didn't win consecutive Stanley Cups on gimmicks, but The Spectrum management stumbled into one which ultimately made the site as recognizable as its hockey team. In 1972, Scheinfeld began instructing that Kate's rendition of "God Bless America" be played periodically to break up the pregame "Star-Spangled Banner" routine. Soon after, it was noted that on nights when Kate preceded the opening face-offs, the Flyers did not lose. After two years of this growing phenomenon, Scheinfeld got the idea to bring Miss Smith to center ice for the Flyers' opener.

"She was frightened," said Gene Hart, the Flyers' play-by-play broadcaster. "She had been out of the limelight for so long, she wondered how she would be accepted by almost an entirely new generation."

But she came, sang to a huge ovation, and the Flyers won again. Nine months later, the team was one game away from its first Stanley Cup, and rumors began circulating that Kate would be making another appearance. Scheinfeld played the suspense like Kate's organ, which was wheeled out onto the ice after the teams' warm-ups that afternoon. "Only time," said the Flyers' director of scouting operations, John Brogan, "I've ever seen an organ get a standing ovation. It was just sitting there and the people were going crazy."

The 1–0 victory prompted a two-day street celebration climaxed by more than two million persons gathering for a parade through center city. The next year, when the Flyers repeated their victory, the festivities were more orderly and much bigger. Philly

finally had a winner, and its depressed fandom leaped off the couch in pure cathartic joy.

When the team's faithfuls are properly wired up for the big event, there is no louder place in the NHL. The Spectrum's modern design does not sacrifice any coziness, and the ample parking and Broad Street subway station outside make the building not only a fun place inside but easily accessible.

"From my experience with the Eagles [as a vice-president], I thought there was no better place to watch a football game than Franklin Field," said Snider. "Of course there it's benches, and at The Spectrum we wanted theater seats, but we wanted them as close together as possible to contribute to the atmosphere. If not for building restrictions, we would have jammed more in."

When the Flyers outgrew the original 14,500 seat capacity by 1972, a third level was added to bring the total to 17,077. As the 1980–81 regular season ended, the string of sellouts was at 388 and stretched through every regular-season and playoff game from February 15, 1973. Snider's pay-cable television network brings most of the home games into 200,000 houses, but there are still nights when he could easily sell 30,000 seats, if he had them.

Since all but a few hundred are held by season-ticket holders, the atmosphere is clubby. And because they are expensive, the ambience leans toward high-toned and high-pitched. Not that it doesn't have its share of characters. Dave Leonardi, known better as "Signman," taunts the visitors from behind one goal, holding up cards such as "Insert Here," with an arrow pointed to the goal when the Flyers need one.

"The buildings in Montreal and Boston get you just as close to the action," said Leonardi. "But the fact that there are no walkways in front of any of the sections, just the outside concourse between the upper and lower levels, is a big plus. There aren't vendors or people walking in front of you going to and from their seats. Unlike a lot of the new buildings, just the game is in front of you, and that gives it intimacy."

But it's the people, not the bricks, that give this building character. "Some of the people here are a little too easily led by the scoreboard and organist," said Leonardi, "but there are enough crazies like me to give the place some atmosphere.

"A lot of the people who sit by me are school-teachers like me, or other professionals. If I didn't know that, I'd think they were vicious."

Although similar in design to at least five other NHL arenas, Philadelphia's Spectrum ranks only behind Madison Square Garden in New York in both bookings and profits. And no one argues the special role the Flyers and Kate Smith have played in making it so.

Chicago Stadium

Robert Gammie will swear there is no arena in the country built better than the Chicago Stadium. And he should know, because he was there, 51 years ago, supervising the laying of the bricks.

"It took a year," said Gammie. "We worked round the clock, two twelve-hour shifts a day. If you knew something about construction, you'd appreciate just how much care went into it.

"I damn near lost my life putting that thing up. A scaffold collapsed and it was a miracle we didn't go down with it. I took twelve stitches and was lucky I wasn't killed."

Though the Black Hawks awarded Gammie's heroism with only three Stanley Cups in those 51 years, his life has, otherwise, been a charmed one. Born in Scotland, Gammie says he was booked to immigrate to the United States upon the return of the original voyage of the *Titanic*. The boat went down like that scaffold did 17 years later, and Gammie settled instead for "a slow boat to China."

Settling in Chicago, he took a job laying bricks and had graduated to foreman when his company was contracted to build Paddy Harmon's sports palace on the West Side. "It was built five years after the ones in Boston and New York," said Gammie, "and it was far superior. The posts which support the roof are way back, where they don't block many views. The thing was an architectural wonder in its day and it's held up damn well. Except for the new seats, the thing hasn't changed at all."

And Gammie should know that too, because now 87, he has sat in the same location in the mezzanine since the building opened in 1929. "It's not the same seat," he said. "I wish it was. They put cushioned ones in a few years ago, but they jammed them together. Now there's twenty-six in my row. There used to be about fifteen.

"It's not the way it used to be, but a man's got to have his entertainment. I don't like football or baseball that much; I've just always liked hockey."

Gammie was a resident of the middle-class West Chicago neighborhood when the brick building with the stone facing went up. Now he drives from Downers Grove through blighted West Chicago to arrive at the fortress on 1800 West Madison. What became a bad neighborhood in the mid-fifties now appears to be no neighborhood at all. The Stadium is surrounded for two blocks by a moat of parking lots where houses burned down.

"There are some problems now, I don't mind telling you," said Gammie. "But it's safe. The security is excellent. We could probably use a new one somewhere with some escalators for the people who have to climb to the upper deck, but it's still a good place to watch a game."

Though Harmon ran short of cash and never finished the stands in the East End, the current ownership has not been reluctant to spend money on improvements. When the rest rooms were remodeled in the sixties, one Chicago publication said they were second only to those in the city's elegant Pump Room.

The place is almost immaculate, but when 18,000 persons regularly jammed the Stadium during the Bobby Hull era, they would have settled for seats in a pigsty just to watch the Hawks. There was talk of knocking the east wall out and adding more seats to make the building symmetrical and more profitable, but the work was never started.

"It was right after the riot [following the assassination of Dr. Martin Luther King, Jr.], and they used it as an excuse not to do the work," said Gammie. "I just think they didn't want to spend the money."

While those seats would have been useful 10 years before, any other spending to alter the nooks and crannies that make a grand old building home surely would have been wasted. The stairs leading up from the locker room are so steep that the goalie's head pops up like a jack-in-the-box when he leads the team onto the ice. The gate is so narrow, Tony Esposito in full dress has to squeeze through sideways. The old clock, with sweeping hands and unintelligible penalty times, finally was removed for the Hockey Hall of Fame in 1976, but the place still smells like beer and popcorn.

Harmon's mania for the grandiose also mani-

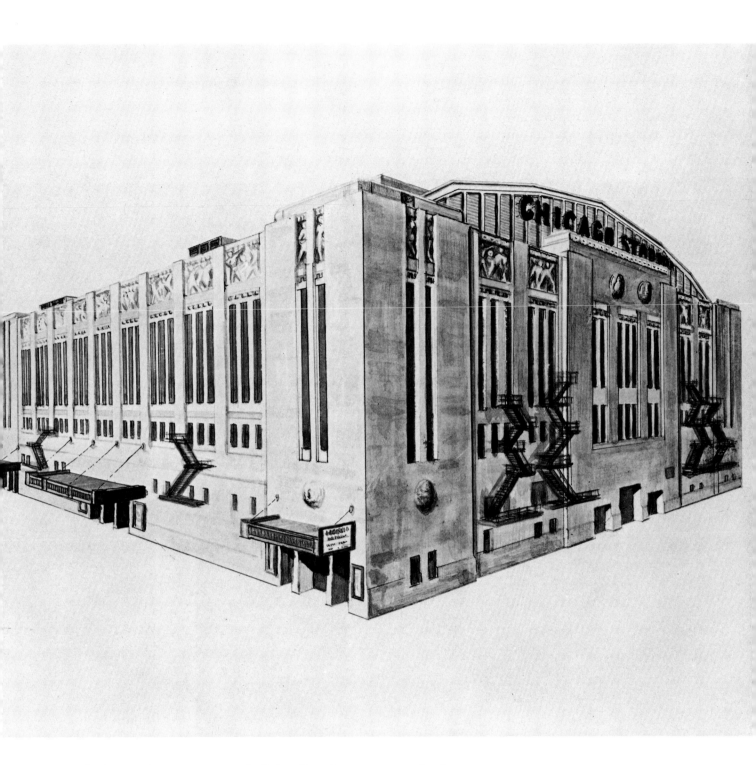

Chicago Stadium, built over 50 years ago by Robert Gammie, was constructed with support posts far in back so they wouldn't block the view of many spectators. It has undergone only one significant change since then, when more narrow but cushioned seats replaced the original ones.

fested itself in the music machine built into the Stadium. Today, the Black Hawks claim it remains the world's largest unified organ, with 25 keyboards, 883 stops and 40,000 pipes. From the day the building opened, it was entrusted to the gentle touch of Al Melgard, who played it until his death in 1972.

"Of course I knew him really well," said Gammie.

"Al could play that thing. Beautiful Scottish music, too, which I liked to think he played for me. The new guy bangs that thing so damn loud, a lot of people I know can't stand it anymore. That thing is powerful. One time some fans started a fight and it was getting way out of hand. Melgard pounded the organ so hard he smashed the windows in the place. He stopped the

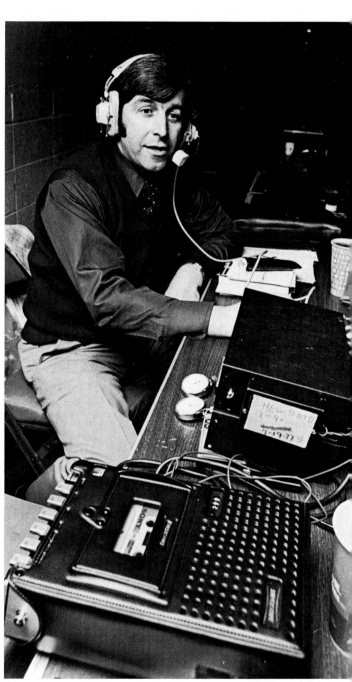

Above left: *The 1965 award-winning Black Hawks. Stan Mikita (left), with Ross Trophy; Bobby Hull with Hart and Lady Byng trophies; NHL president Clarence Campbell; and Pierre Pilote with Norris Trophy.* Above: *Black Hawks broadcaster Ron Oakes.* Left: *Stan Mikita (left) and Bobby Hull (center) in action.*

fight, but he was afraid he was going to lose his job."

If there was one thing Harmon liked as much as organ music, it was bike racing. The $7 million Stadium, an outlandish expenditure in those days, opened a year after its groundbreaking to a six-day cycling extravaganza. Later, political conventions, mayoral fund raisers, boxing and ice shows had their days, and even a super bowl was played there. It was called the NFL Championship game then, but in 1932, the Chicago Bears beat the Portsmouth, Ohio, Spartans, 9–0, on a 60-yard dirt field.

The wide cycling track was easily convertible to ice hockey, and Major Frederic McLaughlin, who had made his money in coffee, had his three-year-old Black Hawks to offer. McLaughlin had served in a World War I army unit that named itself after an Indian tribe, and when he brought the National Hockey League to Chicago in 1926, he borrowed its name—the Black Hawks. Constantly bickering over rental terms, the Hawks played three seasons divided between the bandbox Chicago Coliseum and the Chicago Arena before the opening of the Stadium.

Harmon's terms were steep, though, and McLaughlin, in the beginning, sometimes balked as the Hawks prepared for each season. "They were in and out of the place the first few years," said Howard Lavity, whose engineering firm today owns a block of 20 Stadium seats. "I can't be sure I saw the first game ever played there, but it was at least the second or third. I remember my father taking me as a kid. The place was a wonder. You can imagine how huge it looked to a ten-year-old."

Both Harmon and McLaughlin later hit hard times, and the Stadium was in receivership twice before James Norris, the owner of the Detroit Red Wings, got his partner, Arthur Wirtz, a Chicago real-estate entrepreneur, involved in hockey. Wirtz and Norris bought the Stadium in 1935, but by 1953, Wirtz was sole owner of both the building and the Black Hawks.

The team, which had won Stanley Cups with predominantly American players in 1936 and 1937, bottomed out to almost yearly last-place finishes. Legend explains why. When the impulsive McLaughlin reprimanded his coach, Pete Muldoon, for a playoff failure in the Hawks' first NHL season, an argument between the two resulted in Muldoon's firing. "I'll hoodoo you," said Muldoon in leaving. "This club will never finish in first place." The curse lasted for 35 years.

It was only after Wirtz took over and was given permission by Norris to hire away Tommy Ivan, who in six years as the Detroit Red Wings' coach had won six regular-season titles and three Stanley Cups, that the Hawks began to improve. Installed as the general manager, Ivan built a farm system that ultimately produced Stan Mikita and Bobby Hull. And though Muldoon's jinx held out until 1967, the Hawks did win a Stanley Cup after a third-place finish in 1961.

The franchise had hit gold. Hull became the most exciting player in the league for a decade, and there was not a seat to buy at the Stadium. Wirtz listed the attendance for every game as 16,666 to keep the Chicago fire marshal off his back, but many nights there were at least 2,000 more. The Stadium was the place to be whether you could see the game or not. The demand for tickets was so great that even the few seats located behind poles, offering no direct view of the ice at all, were sold.

The Hawks had made it to the 1971 finals, but let a 2–0 lead in the seventh game against Montreal slip away. Soon Hull's and other WHA defections began to take their toll. Today, as the team builds back to power, you can easily buy a seat, even read the scoreboard, but the vibrancy is gone.

"I remember *Esquire* magazine mentioning in a story during the fifties that there were no better-dressed women in the world than the ones at Chicago Black Hawks' games," said Lavity. "It was loud, but it had an elegance.

"I still go a lot. I travel in my business, and have seen games in both old and new buildings, and there still may not be a better place to watch one. A seat near the top in a place like the Forum would put you across Madison Street at the Stadium.

"It's a long climb up, but once you're there, you're above, and not back from the ice. The building itself is fine. Actually, it's in better shape today than it was thirty years ago. Maybe move it out to the suburbs, and you couldn't beat it."

Olympia—Joe Louis Arena

One delirious hockey fan in Chicago may be indistinguishable from his counterpart in Boston, but with the seats filled, each of the six castles the NHL called home for 30 years had its unique atmosphere. Detroit had Gordie and octopi. Howe threw elbows without regard for opponent or date, but ever respectful of tradition, Red Wing fans threw eight-legged fish on the ice only during the playoffs.

"It started in 1952," said Red Wings publicist Budd Lynch. "When the Wings won the Cup in the minimum eight games, a fishmonger brought the octopus, because he said it had one leg for each victory, and tossed it on the ice."

There are many recollections of the grand old red-brick building at Grand River and McGraw, each highly personalized, each indelible. "Thanks for the Memories" read the Olympia marquee after the Red Wings tied the Quebec Nordiques, 4–4, on December 15, 1979, the last NHL game in its 53-year history. But they could not let it go out in such a meaningless way, so the Red Wings opened it one more time on February 21 for what they called "The Last Hurrah." A team of Red Wing greats played a collection of NHL old-timers in a full 60-minute game so 13,000 persons could say good-bye.

The ultimate tribute to the Olympia's longevity was the fact that it fell only two months short of outlasting Howe's playing career. But its legacy is the people who skated and thrilled there.

"What do I remember most about the place?" asked Lefty Wilson, the Detroit trainer for the past 30 years. "Ovations. Like the last night. Ovations so loud, I swear the building shifted in the ground."

The Olympia was as sturdy as Gordie's shoulders, and as mean to visiting teams as his stick. And when it sat in the blighted neighborhood, alone and boarded up, two blocks off the expressway that Sid Abel traveled to get to work, he could not pass it without taking a nightly look. Abel played 11 Hall of Fame seasons there, coached there, managed there, did radio commentary there. Boards may now block the doors to the Olympia, but not to Abel's memory.

"I get sick everytime I drive by it," said Sid. "I loved that building. To me it was just a good hockey rink, excellent ice, knowledgeable fans, and all that excitement and tradition.

"The new place is beautiful, but a lot of people can't get used to it. I suppose, in time, it will warm up.

"When attendance at the Olympia fell off, they used the excuse of the neighborhood it was in. But it was mostly the team. There were a lot of years of rough sledding and a lot of the people who used to pack the place lost interest. There was nothing wrong with it the last few years. Most of the houses in the immediate area had been cleared out, and the [parking] lots were well lighted. It was safe. That building had a lot of good years left, but I guess you can't stand in the way of progress."

In Detroit, they use the term "Renaissance." The $28 million Joe Louis Arena, built on the riverfront next to a shopping center, offices, and a 73-story hotel, is surely a monument to the city's commitment to rebuild. The Arena, named after Detroit's native son, the former heavyweight champion of the world, boasts the largest seating capacity in the National Hockey League, 19,275, and when finished will offer many of the conveniences the Olympia never could.

"It's a new crowd," said Abel, now the Wings' broadcast color man. "A lot younger and a lot wilder. The old crowd could roar, but it was an intelligent one which appreciated good hockey on both sides."

Still, Tom Johnson, an all-star defenseman with Montreal and now a Bruins' executive, remembers Detroit as an intimidating place to play. "It wasn't that the Red Wings were mean," said Johnson, "they were just good, and it was never the most pleasant place to visit. You didn't win there very often.

"I remember [coach] Jack Adams's wife used to sit in the first row by the Red Wings bench and would let us have it. Tough old broad, maybe even tougher than Jack.

"The ice was always excellent, which didn't hurt a good skating team like ours. But the Wings knew how to play in that building. The corners were egg-

162

Top: *The first Detroit team ever to win the Stanley Cup, the 1935–36 Red Wings, included present Buffalo general manager Scotty Bowman (third from right, back) and manager-coach Jack Adams, whose name is given to the award for the NHL's coach of the year.* Above: *Detroit's Olympia opened in 1927; the last game played there was on December 15, 1979.*

shaped and when you threw the puck into them, it would come back out again instead of continuing around the back of the net. Gordie and those guys knew exactly where it was going and it was a helluvan advantage."

It took several years, though, before the Detroit team was good enough to exploit the nuances of its rink. The franchise was born on September 25, 1926, when a syndicate of Detroit businessmen purchased

Detroit's spectacular Renaissance Center includes the $28 million Joe Louis Arena (left), which opened on December 27, 1980. It has the largest seating capacity in the NHL, 19,275.

the players from the defunct Victoria Cougars of the Western Hockey League.

Construction of Olympia Stadium, at a cost of $2.15 million, was not completed until the following summer, sending the Cougars across the river to play their first season's home games at the Border Cities Arena in Windsor, Ontario.

Adams, a 10-year NHL all-star, began his 35-year career as coach when the Cougars opened up the Olympia on November 22, 1927, with a 2–1 loss to the defending Stanley Cup-champion Ottawa Senators. Detroit did not make the playoffs until 1932, when the team, in an effort to change its luck, was renamed the

Falcons by Detroit sportswriters.

"Things were so bad we didn't have enough money to buy a second pair of uniforms," Adams remembered years later. "I dug into my share of the playoff money one year to buy players. The Depression had hit. If Howie Morenz was on sale for a dollar-ninety, we couldn't have bought him. Then Mr. Norris came into the picture. It was a new ball game."

The Falcons were about to go into receivership when James Norris, a Chicago railroad, steamship, and cattle-ranch owner, purchased them and the Olympia in 1933. Norris had played amateur hockey in Montreal with a team known as the Winged Wheelers.

Their insignia, a red wheel attached to a wing, struck Norris as a natural for a hockey team representing the Motor City.

When Mud Brutuneau's goal, in minute 116 of sudden death, gave the Red Wings a 1–0 playoff victory over the Maroons in Montreal during Norris' first season of ownership, Detroit was on its way to its first Stanley Cup. The Red Wings repeated the next year, and in the next 21 missed the playoffs only once. But it wasn't until the arrival of an 18-year-old kid from Floral, Saskatchewan, that the powerhouse years began.

Gordie Howe, teamed with Abel and Ted Lindsay on The Production Line, led the Wings to four Stanley Cups in eight years. Though they yielded their early-fifties dynasty to Montreal's five straight championships, Detroit made it to three more finals before their decline began in 1966.

The Olympia's original 11,700-seat capacity had been inadequate for years, until 1965, when more than 2,000 seats were added by knocking out the building's rear wall. The rebuilding cost $2 million, but seats were usually considered a luxury. A wide concourse at the top of the upper deck provided space for at least 2,000 more to stand. That standing room was still used in the late seventies when big draws like Montreal and Philadelphia came to town. But on most nights, the capacity 14,200 was plenty for the Wings' needs.

The city, however, trying to pump life back into a comatose downtown, wanted the Red Wings as part of its new center. The deal Major Coleman Young offered Bruce Norris, who had taken over the club presidency upon his father's death in 1955, was too good to turn down. The Joe Louis Sports Arena opened on December 27, 1980, with the Red Wings losing to St. Louis, 3–2.

Gordie was finishing his 34-year career in Hartford, and there wasn't an octopus in sight. The new place was decidedly handsome and certainly full for the gala opening. But a warm house had been replaced by a cold complex. Still, Lefty believed it wasn't bricks that made the Olympia home. It was people.

"It all depends on how you go," he said. "Win a few games and twenty thousand could warm this place up nicely."

165

The Checkerdome

Almost 50 years after its dedication as the new home for the National Dairy Show, the big barn on Oakland Avenue prophetically came into the hands of the world's largest producer of animal feeds.

Through its checkered past, the St. Louis Arena proved capable of breaking just about anybody with the misfortune of owning it. It was left for the civic servants from Checkerboard Square, the Ralston-Purina Corporation, to ride gallantly to the last-minute rescue of the city's woebegone hockey team in 1978 and preserve the league's first post-1967 shrine.

"Somebody had to make a decision," said R. Hal Dean, chief executive officer of Purina. "Either we stepped in, or the Blues would leave town. That would have been a backward step for the city."

There never was anything wrong with the place that periodic soap, paint, and the air-conditioning system that was finally installed in 1979 wouldn't fix. With the Arena, renamed The Checkerdome, finally operational for events during St. Louis' muggy summers, it was no longer the drain on the hockey team that forced the Blues' original owners, the Salomons, into near bankruptcy.

Today, as St. Louis' beloved hockey franchise, the jewel of the league's first expansion, rebuilds toward its early glory days, the wooden dome is coming alive again. Which is heartening, because no expansion team, in any sport, was ever as immediately successful as the Blues. It seems like half the Hockey Hall of Fame passed through here in their final years before retirement, making the Blues not only the class of the six new teams but, for a time, even better than a couple of the old ones.

After their first season, the Blues were a virtual sellout, pumped to a frenzy by the league's most celebrated organist, Norm Kramer, and the standing, serenading fans. The Penguins and Kings were also born in 1967 with similar minor-league interest bases, but the Blues gave expansion an immediate legitimacy. All the way down to their name, and W. C. Handy's theme, the Blues were a natural.

"It was louder in that building then than it had ever been in Montreal," said Jacques Plante, who for two years shared the Blues' goal with Glenn Hall. "Just unbelievable. A standing ovation every time we took the ice.

"It just caught on like crazy. Every time, that first year, they got a big crowd, they'd have some spectacular game. Overtime or beating one of the six original teams. More and more people kept coming and soon it was full every night. Noise like I couldn't believe. They were two of the happiest years I had in hockey."

Only three years before, the property at 5700 Oakland Avenue had stood dark, damp, and, for the most part, empty. Hailed as an architectural marvel when it opened in 1929, its roof span was constructed with the principles that were still considered unique when the Houston Astrodome designers borrowed them 35 years later. The roof rested over space for 21,000 seats, by far the biggest indoor seating capacity in the United States.

It was built at a cost of $2 million by Benjamin G. Brinkman as the permanent home for the National Dairy Show. Brinkman went broke within two years, and the Dairy Show moved on after only one year. The building was still floundering in 1932 when the Flyers of the American Hockey Association moved in. Two days before the scheduled opener, the ice began to melt. An engineer, called in to check out the defective machinery, discovered that the only problem was the owner's nonpayment of the electrical bill.

Only because the temperature fell below freezing on the day of the game was it ever played. Every door and window in the Arena was thrown open, and the shivering crowd had the pleasure of seeing the only indoor hockey game ever played on natural ice.

The NHL moved its crippled Ottawa team to St. Louis two years later. Renamed the Eagles, it lasted only one year before failing financially and leaving the market. The lone AHA Flyers attracted a small but loyal following, and were at least paying their bills, which was more than many of the other AHA teams could handle.

166

The beautiful Checkerdome, so named because it is owned by the Ralston-Purina Corporation, is the official home of the St. Louis Blues, 1980–81's Cinderella team. When the house is full, 17,967 fans can view a game.

"One year," said Emory Jones, the Flyers' owner, "Wichita was supposed to open the season, but didn't have any players. The league president, William Grant, asked us to go to Wichita and play in their uniforms. A week later we did it again. By the third week, they still didn't have players so he called on us one more time. I had to remind him it was us who was supposed to play Wichita that week."

The Flyers lasted for nine years, disbanding when the AHA broke up in 1941. For six years, the Arena hosted no hockey until it was acquired by Arthur Wirtz, owner of the Chicago Black Hawks. Wirtz put a Central League farm club in St. Louis and, during some bad years in Chicago, moved some home games into the Arena. But he was losing money in both cities. The scheduled NHL expansion finally gave Wirtz the opportunity to unload the Arena.

One of the six new franchises was offered to St. Louis if the owner bought the Arena to go with it. Sidney Salomon, Jr., an insurance agent and former treasurer of the National Democratic Committee, stepped forward and then invested more than $2 million in the building, turning it into a showplace. Although the seating capacity was cut back to 14,500, the newly installed theater seats offered comfort. The lobby was tiled and a private dinner club added.

"The whole thing needed a bath," said Bob Burnes, executive sports editor of the St. Louis *Globe Democrat*. "Like you needed the sky to open up with rain to wash it down. I remember Sid taking me into the basement as the remodeling was beginning. There were boxes down there marked 1930 or 1931 that had never been opened.

"The Salomons had a fetish for cleanliness. The bathrooms were not only remodeled, they put an attendant in each one to keep them clean. It was one of the things they had to eliminate later when they ran into financial trouble."

The decline was excrutiating. In 1978, Salomon's final year, the new coach and general manager, Emile

Francis, was on his way to the dressing room before a game when he found an electrician trying to turn the power off. Francis ordered him out and saw that the bill was paid the next day, but by the end of the season, the Blues were dead broke.

Francis stalled the league while three or four local groups considered investing. When none could swing it, Ralston-Purina stepped in, spending another $1 million on the building's face-lift and saving hockey in St. Louis.

The Blues' instant success had forced seating capacity increases to 17,967, but even when the average attendance fell off to 10,000, the hardcore wore blinders to what the Blues had become. There were only those trophies in the lobby display cases to remind them.

"I want to see a hockey game," said Bill Meni, who has held tickets since the Blues' debut. "We never even considered not going. The crowds changed a little, there was some booing. One time we changed

our location because the people around us were more interested in causing a commotion than watching hockey.

"We had an original group of eight people going to every game to sit together, and now we're down to two. But it's picking up. We're going to have eighteen-thousand people back in there every night again, I just know it. The Arena—I still have to call it the Arena—has been a big part of my life. It made me sick to think we were going to lose it, but now I know we're coming back."

Opposite: *Center ice at the Checkerdome.* Below: *The St. Louis Arena, as it was called before 1978, was built at a cost of $2 million by Benjamin G. Brinkman to serve as the permanent home of the National Dairy Show.*

Memorial Auditorium

Buffalo's entrance into the National Hockey League in 1970 necessitated the raising of the 30-year-old Memorial Auditorium roof to add 4,813 seats. The cost was $11 million. Hell, if they had just waited a few years for the new Sabres to improve, the fans would have performed the service for free.

"The people here are just happy to have a team," said Scotty Bowman, who resigned as the Canadiens' coach in 1979 to become general manager of the Sabres. "Buffalo has been knocked so long, the Sabres are really a source of pride. These aren't the kind of demanding fans you have in Montreal. It's really a refreshing atmosphere."

The league, with an eye toward national television, went for mostly glamour cities in its first six-team expansion in 1967. So Buffalo, possibly the best minor-league hockey town of all during its 30 seasons in the American League, had to wait three more years.

When Vancouver and Buffalo were admitted for the 1970 season, a contest was held to name the team. Of 10,000 entries, the name Sabres came up five times, and the winners were awarded first-year season tickets. "There was some consideration given to keeping the name Bisons," said Paul Wieland, the Sabres' public relations director. "They went out their last year as champions and a lot of people wanted to continue the tradition. But Mr. [Seymour] Knox [the new team's owner] wanted something to indicate a major-league era was beginning. Sabres indicated blades and action. It seemed like the best suggestion."

The name fit almost as well as general manager Punch Imlach's fedora on his bald head. This marriage was made in heaven, which is almost as far up as the last rows of the Auditorium's seats.

The city-owned Aud seated only 10,000 when it was built at a cost of $2.5 million, in 1940, as a Works Progress Administration project. The hockey Bisons and college basketball were comfortable tenants for 30 years, but the move up to the big time necessitated a major-league building. The 24-foot roof raising, which the Sabres call the highest ever completed in the world, was delayed by a taxpayers' suit, but by

Buffalo's second NHL season, the additional seats at the top and some remodeling in the ends brought the capacity to an acceptable 16,433.

Though the fans, 12 percent of whom cross the Peace Bridge from Canada to attend home games, would have gladly suffered for a few years with their expansion team, the Sabres were competitive from day one and grew up fast. By 1973, they were in the playoffs, taking Montreal, the eventual champion, to six games. Two years later they upset the Canadiens and went to the Stanley Cup finals against the Philadelphia Flyers.

There had never been a hotter ticket in Buffalo than one for that series. And never a championship decided in a sauna. The temperature was in the high seventies and the lack of air circulation turned the Auditorium into a palace of sweat. Steam rose off the melting ice, necessitating several stoppages of play so helpers with bed sheets could skate around the surface dispensing the vapors.

The Aud was enshrouded like a Transylvanian castle, and when a bat flew in one of the open doors during the third game of the series, the setting was complete. It circled the ice for almost the entire first period until the Sabres' Jim Lorentz swatted it out of the air while manning his team's power play. Lorentz killed the bat, the Flyers killed the penalty.

The game, which dragged into overtime, was stopped 11 times from the third period on so the players could skate the fog away. But nearing dehydration, more and more team members chose to stay on the bench to rest and drink water.

The game ended almost 19 minutes into sudden-death and 5 minutes before midnight. Rene Robert picked up a rebound off Gil Perreault's shot from center ice that Flyer goalie Bernie Parent stopped, but later confessed he didn't see, and scored the winning goal from a wide angle. "The visibility was a little tough out there," said Robert. "It was the one time in hockey when the best shot was the one taken the farthest away."

The Flyers, winning all three games played in the

170

Opposite top: Buffalo's Memorial Auditorium was built as a Works Progress Administration project in 1940. Opposite left: Buffalo general manager Punch Imlach (right) hired Marcel Pronovost to coach the team in 1977, then was fired with him in 1978. Opposite right: Win or lose, Punch Imlach in his customary fedora, was a familiar face at Memorial Auditorium.

temperature-controlled Spectrum, wrapped up their second-straight Stanley Cup in a slightly cooler sixth game at the Auditorium.

Buffalo, however, is better known for its harsh winters than tropical Mays. In 1977, when high winds blew all the snow on Lake Erie over the city, virtually shutting down the town for a week, more than 100 Sabre employees, and refugees from the street, took shelter in the Aud Club for three days.

And as 25-foot drifts began hitting the airport, only 13 Sabres were able to get from their homes to the flight for a game in Montreal. The undermanned Buffalo team managed a 3–3 tie and was able to bus back to the socked-in city. But two home games the next week had to be postponed.

Even in good weather, hockey teams invading the Aud over the last 11 years have been left stranded by the Sabres. After four seasons of stagnation which eventually cost Imlach his job, Buffalo became a Cup contender again, and the Aud remained one of the league's premier pits for visitors.

Sharply banked seats and a playing surface that is 10 feet shorter than the regulation 200 feet by 85 feet provide a claustrophobic effect. "It helps 'cause we're used to it," said Bowman. "But they've never really had the team here to take full advantage of the smaller surface. Punch built a good skating club, but the Sabres have never been able to exploit the rink like the Bruins have in Boston."

Every hockey crowd has its share of rowdies, but the Sabres' lot is generally a gentle, appreciative, intelligent one. Its taunts are usually in good humor, its banners the most inventive in the league.

Imlach, as a joke, selected a fictitious Japanese player by the name of Taro Tsujimoto from the Tokyo Katanas in a late round of the 1974 draft, and the gag has been kept alive by four guys who call themselves "The Phantom Signmakers." Taro has a different saying for each game and opponent, such as, "Taro Says: The Old Gray Lemaire, He Ain't What He Used To Be." Or, "Taro Says: If Larry Had a Boatload of Knitters, Would Robinson's Crusoe?"

"We've gotten so much media attention," says Steve Hill, one of the signmakers, "that I'm afraid we can't be the phantoms anymore. Only my brother. He's never been photographed, yet."

"I'm a holdover from the Bison days," said Rich Ryan, who works at the Buffalo Ford plant. "I sold tickets for the Sabres in the early years. Now, it's a season sellout, so I'm just a fan.

"There's about ten of us who regularly go to the games. We sit behind the goal the Sabres shoot at for two periods so we can get on the visiting goalie. I think our greatest coup was the night of the [1978] All-Star game. There were these five guys a section over from us all wearing hats like Imlach's. On cue, we all yelled, 'Will the real Punch Imlach please stand up?' They all took off their hats at the same time, and were all bald. Broke the whole place up."

From the outside, a gray cement building created to keep people working during the Depression does not look out of place in Buffalo's bleak downtown decor. Inside, the multicolored seats and the Rich Ryans present a different picture.

"This city is people," Ryan said. "I wouldn't live anywhere else."

In recent years, the Buffalo Sabres have remained contenders through the skillful play of Bob Sauve (left), who shared the 1980 Vezina Trophy with teammate Don Edwards; Gil Perreault (right), who was the NHL's number-one choice in the 1970 amateur draft, and Rick Martin (bottom), scoring here against St. Louis. Perreault and Martin teamed up with Rene Robert to form one of hockey's most exciting lines, The French Connection.

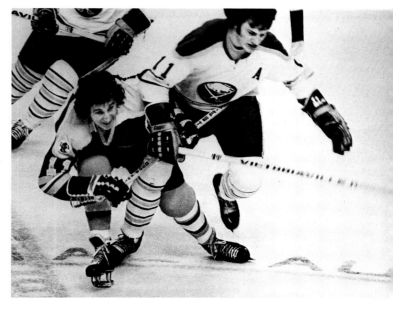

173

Madison Square Garden

When the fourth and present Madison Square Garden reaches obsolescence, the fifth will be built either in Westchester County or on the moon, depending upon which place the people of New York can reach most easily. And whether the attraction of the day is dancing elephants or laser hockey performed by robots in midair, the place will still symbolize entertainment and still go by the same name.

The Garden departed its second home on Madison Square in 1925, but Tex Rickard, the boxing impresario who picked up on the old site where P.T. Barnum's circus left off, was not interested in change, only more seats and dollars.

When Rickard's lease ran out, the owner, New York Life Insurance Company, announced plans that its new 40-story headquarters would be located on the lot where the Garden stood. Rickard decided to become his own landlord. His first idea had been a roof over the Polo Grounds in the Bronx, but his many friends on Wall Street thought it outlandish. Nonetheless, they did come up with $6 million for a building in Manhattan.

A trolley garage on Eighth Avenue between 4th and 5th streets, 25 blocks uptown from Madison Square, was demolished, and with Rickard's acquisition of the land going all the way to Ninth Avenue, construction of an 18,500-seat arena was begun. It was finished in 249 days and opened on December 15, 1925, hosting bicycle races. Actually, "Opening Night" lasted six days, and while boxing matches were always the most popular and profitable events, the finale of the extravaganza was an international spectacle—ice hockey. It featured the New York Americans, who had been created specifically for the occasion, and the Montreal Canadiens, members of the National Hockey League.

The attendance—17,442—startled Rickard, and although the profits from the first game were promised to charity, his promoting partner, Colonel John S. Hammond, did not have to hit Tex over the head with a stick to convince him of the game's permanent drawing power.

The National Hockey League had already come south of the border into Boston, where Rickard had financed the building of the Boston Garden, but he was anxious to move into New York. "Big Bill" Dwyer, who had paid $75,000 for the privilege, owned the Americans, so Rickard created his own house team. Tex's "Rangers" struck him as a natural.

Colonel Hammond had brought in Conn Smythe, the architect of the successful Toronto St. Pats, as his first general manager. Smythe quickly signed top-name players, but he could not get along with Hammond and walked out. The Colonel then summoned Lester Patrick, a hot-shot executive in the Pacific Coast Hockey Association.

With Smythe's players and Patrick's leadership, the Rangers were an immediate hit. On November 17, 1926, they played their first game at the Garden before more than 13,000, beating the Montreal Maroons, 1–0.

When, in Montreal for the following year's playoffs, Rangers' goalie Lorne Chabot was hit over the eye and carried off on a stretcher, the 44-year-old Patrick was forced to put on the pads. He allowed only one goal as the Rangers beat the Maroons in overtime and went on to win the Stanley Cup.

Meanwhile, the tenant Americans brawled more but won less, clearly becoming New York's second team. Dwyer was convicted of rum-running in 1935, and the franchise was sold to Red Dutton, a former defenseman and later president of the National Hockey League. Attendance continued to decline and after one last fling as the Brooklyn Americans in 1942, the team expired.

The Rangers had helped Rickard through the loss of fight revenue during the Depression. Even when hard times came on the ice after the 1939–40 team won the franchise's last Stanley Cup, the people kept coming. Though the Rangers made the playoffs in only 8 of the next 26 years, the Garden remained a vibrant place.

In the early fifties, a psychologist named Dr. Tracy was convinced he could bring the Rangers out of

The New York Rangers and the Madison Square Garden crowd share the glory after Peter Stemkowski scored at 1:29 of the triple overtime, giving the Rangers a 3–2 victory over the Chicago Black Hawks in their Stanley Cup semifinal game on April 18, 1971.

their doldrums through hypnotism. The Rangers, more amused than mesmerized, took the Bruins 3–3 into the third period that night, but lost on a long shot that hopped past goalie Chuck Rayner. "You've got to let me at the 'goolie,'" Dr. Tracy insisted as the Rangers showed him to the door. "He's not relaxed."

Neither was Phil Watson, the fiery French coach who inherited the team in the mid-fifties. Watson was so upset with one Ranger performance that after a Garden game he ordered his team back onto the ice for a full practice. The departing crowd was so stunned by the Rangers' appearance thay stayed to jeer, which may have been what Watson had in mind.

But even on nights when they didn't go back to the ice, the Rangers took abuse from angry fans gathering outside their locker-room window on the 49th Street side of the building. Standing on the sidewalk, they'd let their heroes know what they thought of the evening's performance. And Watson would usually yell back.

A night out with the Rangers began with a subway ride and an orange soda at Nedick's in the Garden lobby, and ended with a stop at Al Mueller's for a nip or two on the way home. It included at least a glance at "Sinbin" Sally Lark, an interior decorator from Brooklyn who faithfully sat in the seat next to the penalty box; Gladys Gooding, whose heart left her beloved Brooklyn Dodgers only during hockey season; and an unidentified lady who once made Toronto's Wild Bill Ezinicki's nickname come to life. When the Leaf leaned over near the boards to get ready for a face-off, the lady couldn't resist temptation, and stuck him with her hatpin.

For more than 34 years progress was limited to the installation of Herculite Glass. But in 1960, the Garden corporation announced plans for a new building at a yet-undetermined location. The Pennsylvania Railroad suggested air rights on the site of its station at 33rd Street between Seventh and Eighth avenues, and eight months later, the deal was finalized.

The new Garden would be not a blockhouse with seats rising from a floor, but a $116 million arena, auditorium, and office complex. Demolition of the old Penn Station was begun in October 1963, and the circular new Garden, with its 9 multicolored levels, 11 escalators, endless corridors, theater, exhibition hall, and bowling alley, rose 13 stories above the street.

When the Rangers beat the infant Philadelphia Flyers in the first hockey game at the new Garden on February 18, 1967, a week after closing the old place with a 3–3 tie against Detroit, the view looking up from the ice level was considerably more impressive than the one from the seats to the arena floor.

The new Garden was decidedly beautiful, but the seating's gentle taper left the diehards a lot farther back from the action than above it. "I've been coming to Ranger games since 1943 when I was fifteen years old," said Paul Gardella, who works for the New York Supreme Court. "I'd like to someday see a Stanley Cup, sure, but first, I'd just like to be able to see the game better.

"I'm not against progress, but I liked the old place better. Even the crowds have changed. You used to see women in evening gowns and men in tuxedos. You never heard a four-letter word."

The Rangers were a much-improved team, rebuilt to give the new Garden a winner. And the people came. But while making the playoffs for 12 straight years, the Rangers remained ultimately frustrating. A memorable triple-overtime Garden victory over Chicago in 1972 sent them to the finals for the first time since 1950, but Bobby Orr, in one of the most breathtaking individual performances in Stanley Cup history, led the Bruins to the championship in six games.

But a Ranger fan's breath is generally not taken for long. The Garden, said the New York *Herald Tribune* back in Rickard's time, is "not a building but a state of mind." Obviously, the hockey fans of New York lost theirs over the building's team a long time ago.

"I'm a screamer. My wife is a wild woman. Our kids are all grown now and this is our entertainment. Tuesday and Saturday nights at the Coliseum. I wouldn't miss a game, even during the tax season."

Though the Islanders wear a New York emblem, they play out of a place called Uniondale. And that, to a Manhattanite, might as well be Wichita. The Islander fan replies that he might as well be watching the game from Wichita if he has to buy a seat in the top level of the Garden. "I'd take the best seat at the Garden over the best at the Coliseum," said O'Shea. "But I'd take the worst one at the Coliseum over the worst at the Garden."

The Garden slopes, the Coliseum rises. The

The fourth and current version of New York's famous Madison Square Garden, located above Pennsylvania Station between Seventh and Eighth avenues, is a $116 million arena, auditorium, and office complex.

Garden is splendorous, with four different shades of seats, the Coliseum stark, with only two. The Garden's trappings are show biz, its fans sometimes crude. The Coliseum is modern but unpretentious.

Things have gone down at the Coliseum that would be considered too far off Broadway to play the Garden. In 1979, a fast-food chain was offering free chili to all fans able to present a ticket stub for a game in which the Islanders scored more than five goals. When the Islanders scored number five one night against the Rangers, the scoreboard took up the cause, flashing "Chili" every time the Islanders ran up another goal. The game ended 10–4 with an angry Torrey, apologizing to the Rangers for the gauche behavior. "They can have their chili," said the Rangers' Don Murdoch. "I hope they choke on it."

And though the Islanders were accused of doing exactly that when the Rangers upset them in the 1979 semifinals, the extra year's wait only made the championship's arrival that much more joyous. Nystrom's overtime goal gave the Isles a 5–4 victory over Philadelphia in the sixth and deciding game.

"May 24, 1980," Simon Rubin pronounced with a reverence usually reserved for VJ Day. The parade four days later drew about 40,000 persons, a modest crowd by Stanley Cup standards, and the one-mile route to the Coliseum would never be confused with a Broadway run. It was almost as if invitations had been sent out only to the Islanders' closest friends.

They were children of the suburbs, not the city. And when they grew up strong, Long Island was proud.

Nassau Veterans Memorial Coliseum

Madison Square Garden is the greatest show on earth, the Nassau Coliseum a county fair. The big blue ribbon the New York Islanders won in May 1980 is worn over their fans' hearts, not paraded through ticker tape down Broadway.

"We nurtured them," said Simon Rubin, an East Meadow CPA. "We lived with them. We suffered through them. We screamed and we held our breath for them. When they were hurt, we hurt, and when they won, we won.

"We hugged and cried. It was the culmination of the spectator's dream."

Stanley Cups can do that to you. They can make Wantaghs and East Meadows and Westburys into one big Long Island and make an eight-year-old, $31 million undistinguished mass of steel and cement into a home. A home of champs.

Both the Rangers and the Islanders go by the name of New York, but while Islander fans celebrated, Ranger fans marked the fortieth season without a Cup on their calendars and waited for next year. The creation of the Islanders in the 1972 National Hockey League expansion had torn at a few old hockey hearts out on the Island, but within two years, the lines were being drawn. Some Ranger fans stayed, others defected. On nights the Rangers visit the Islanders, about a quarter of the fans still root for the old team, but Charles O'Shea, who owns two funeral parlors on Long Island, has buried the Ranger in him forever.

"To me the last straw was losing the finals that year [1970] to Boston," said O'Shea. "I have no more allegiance to the Rangers whatsoever. I started over again with the Islanders. It was like watching a little baby grow up."

O'Shea, who had been first in line at the basketball Nets' ticket office the day it opened in 1969, was assigned Islanders' season ticket number 1 when they went on sale in 1971.

Both teams were owned by Roy Boe, a garment company owner who began his sports empire by buying a Westchester semipro football team and moving it to Long Island. In 1969, Boe bought the American Basketball Association Nets, who played in the ramshackle Island Garden until the Coliseum opened in the spring of 1972. In 1971, at a cost of $12 million, half of which went to the Rangers as a territorial indemnification, Boe was awarded the hockey franchise at the Coliseum.

Boe was no longer around when the championship arrived, having sold the Nets to New Jersey ownership to pay Islander bills, and then later lost his hockey team in a tide of red ink. The 1979 reorganization of the Islanders was led by John Pickett, a minority owner under Boe. There was never a question of the Islanders going out of business, but general manager Bill Torrey, who had built the team from scratch, walked a fiscal tightrope in the final days of the Boe regime to keep it all together. The Coliseum faithfuls, who had suffered gladly in the early years, would be rewarded yet.

"I grew up in the Bronx and saw some hockey games at the Garden as a kid," said Rubin. "But I was mostly a Knicks basketball fan. The idea of the Islanders though was intriguing. They were a fledgling little thing, but they had immediate status. They were in the NHL. Not a team like the Nets trying to get into the NBA. This was major league for Long Island, and I wanted to be part of it.

"I didn't buy season tickets right away, but my wife and I went to almost all the games the first year. The Islanders were so bad, it was wonderful. Just wonderful. We used to live to see how bad they could be each night. But even in the second year, when a Denis Potvin and a Bob Nystrom arrived, you could see what the addition of just a few players was doing. The team was respectable. Then came this series of magnificent draft picks. [Bryan] Trottier, [Clark] Gillies, [Mike] Bossy. There were a few years when we wondered whether they would ever get over the hump and win it all, but when they did, it was indescribable.

179

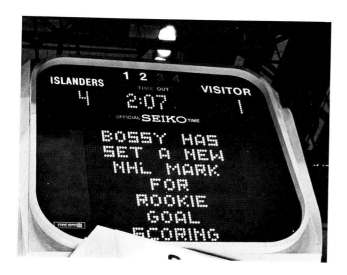

Above: *Nassau Veterans Memorial Coliseum, home of the New York Islanders.* Opposite: *Islander fans, mostly suburban dwellers, celebrate their team's first Cup.* Left and bottom: *The scoreboard at the Coliseum both illustrates and educates. Here it gives fans a look at Bobby Nystrom, playoff hero, and Mike Bossy's feats.*

Top: *Islander fans prefer the Coliseum to the Garden because the seating rises at an angle that keeps them closer to the ice.* Right: *A Bryan Trottier booster.* Opposite: *Duane Sutter (left), Denis Potvin, and Steve Tambellini ride with their team in a Long Island victory parade hosted by 40,000 of their "closest" friends.*

182

6
Dream
Team
Profiles
by Jay
Greenberg

This chapter is only a display case. It is the exhibits themselves that make tickets to see them play or books about what they do priceless. These are the role models, 10 perfect examples of hockey players, selected not by position but by function. It is an all-star team selected not just by form but accomplishment. It ranges from a wrist named Mike Bossy, to an artist named Guy Lafleur, to a fist named Tiger Williams. They are the best at what they do, not in all cases because of skill level but in the determination they bring to their jobs.

Nobody skates with more grace than the Canadien's Lafleur, but no one drives himself as unrelentingly or effectively as Boston's Terry O'Reilly. There are many forwards who carry out defensive assignments, but no checker controls games like Montreal's Bob Gainey. His teammate, Larry Robinson, is as complete a defenseman as has ever played the game.

Mike Bossy is accruing goals at a faster pace than anyone in National Hockey League history, and no defenseman since Bobby Orr has controlled a game offensively from the blue line better than Bossy's Islander teammate Denis Potvin. While Bobby Clarke has had a few peers on the ice, the leadership he has exerted upon the Flyers over a decade has been unparalleled.

Bigger mouths and bigger fists than Vancouver's Dave Williams have opened up faces, attracted their share of outrage and disappeared, but even in his sixth NHL season, Tiger produced another 200 penalty minutes. If not undefeated, Williams remains undeterred. The purists will cringe at Williams' inclusion with the deities of this chapter, but his is a role performed as effectively as the other nine. Recent legislation has curbed some of the impact of the league's strong-arms, but as long as the body check remains legal and the use of fists penalized only by five minutes, the intimidators are a significant part of the game.

The 10 members of this Dream Team have accounted for a total of 20 Stanley Cup rings, but fate has not been as kind in placing others with championship casts. In the case of Chicago's goaltender, Tony Esposito, three times a first-team all-star in 11 NHL seasons, this seems particularly cruel. Though some have, in brief stretches, played more spectacularly than Tony, no one has been as consistent.

Which, paradoxically, brings us to the baby of the group, Edmonton's 20-year-old Wayne Gretzky. To delete him on the basis of date of birth would ultimately date this book. Because in Gretzky's first season in the NHL, he was its Most Valuable Player.

So while the Hart Trophy portends Gretzky's greatness, the others, in their unique ways, have already reached theirs. Even so, they remain at the top, both of their own games and of *the* game.

Let us celebrate their presence.

The Shooter

His wrists don't look so special. **Mike Bossy** does not have the clubhouse boy shake hands with visitors for him. He does not sleep in padded mittens, or put a notch in a nail at the end of one of those long, bony fingers every time he scores another goal. That would not be natural. While red lights twirl, flashbulbs flash, scoreboards short-circuit, and Bossy holds up the puck with which he scored his latest one, there is no aura, no pretension about him. Mike Bossy is, among all the things he does so well and without thought, naturally friendly.

Still, there is something about him, a sense of who he is and where he has to go, that has as much to do with the nets he fills as his physical gift. "I know I've been given a talent," said the Islander's right winger. "I know there other people who have been given talents—like lawyers, professional people—who weren't able to come through and make the most of them. I did. I like to think if I wasn't a professional hockey player I could make it as a golfer or tennis player. I think maybe if I had started very young the way I did with hockey, I could have been good at them."

If there were choices, then growing up in Montreal obscured them. We have 10 different stories of 10 unique talents in this chapter, but they all start the same way. Borden Bossy gave Mike a toy hockey stick a few days after he was born, flooded the backyard, and bought him skates when he was three. "We put him in a church league when he was four," recalls his dad.

Preceding pages: Despite an upside-down landing, Mike Bossy smiles as he scores an overtime goal in the 1978 quarterfinal series with Toronto. Opposite: *The Consummate Defenseman. Montreal defenseman Larry Robinson uses his six-foot three-inch, 210-pound frame to the ultimate advantage. He moves the puck well and hits hard. He says, "Nothing is more important than winning."*

"Playing against boys who were six or seven. He scored twenty-one goals in the first fifteen minutes."

Bossy's pace, in three NHL seasons since joining the league in 1977, is only a little slower. He has recorded 53-, 69-, and 51-goal years. His first 100 NHL goals came faster than anyone—Gordie Howe, Maurice Richard, Phil Esposito, Guy Lafleur, and Bobby Hull included—in history. At the present rate—averaging 57 a year—Bossy will break Gordie Howe's record of 801 by the time he's 34.

Expansion and dilution make comparisons nebulous, but the truth is that no one has ever packaged numbers of goals the way Bossy has.

"I don't think an analogy can be drawn between Mike and anyone elso who has ever played this game," said defenseman Gerry Hart, Bossy's former teammate. "He just has an uncanny ability. You've got to be born with something like that and I don't think it can be explained. I think we're all a little bit in awe of him."

Bossy's shot is hard, but it wouldn't hurt nearly as much as, say, Detroit's Reed Larson's. He skates quickly, but wouldn't come close in a race with Guy Lafleur. Bossy is accurate, but line up 20 pucks, 30 feet out from a goal and have him shoot for targets, and Philadelphia's Reggie Leach would bury him. But start a game and Bossy is more like a machine. Blink and you miss the show. The mechanical baseball arm comes over at regularly scheduled intervals, and Bossy, receiving a pass from Bryan Trottier, gets his shot away. Iron Mike's wrists never get sore; he never stops moving.

What Bossy has, simply, is the quickest release in the game and as great a sense around the goal as anyone who ever played. "If you know what I mean by a natural," said ex-Islander goalie Chico Resch, "he's got as clear an impression of the goal and what's happening around it when he has the puck as anyone ever could.

"Lafleur relies on his stickhandling and skating, and of course he's got a good shot in close. But Bossy relies on that sixth sense of knowing completely what's happening between him and the goal, and then reacts accordingly. A lot of other guys may have that ability, but they can't execute it like Bossy can."

And few who do can explain it. "Very rarely do I think about what I'm doing when we have the puck,"

said Bossy. "I try to go out there and play instinctively, do what comes natural instead of thinking about set plays.

"If the situation comes when I have time to think, I do. But that doesn't happen very often, there isn't much time to think. It has to be instinct. I used to shoot pucks a lot when I was young, but not now. I think it's a waste of time. The more I practice the more I'll try to pick spots, and if I start doing that, I'll start aiming. I don't want to do that."

There is no sense in looking for what will eventually come. Bossy has never gone more than six games without getting a goal and perhaps only once, when he, Trottier, and Clark Gillies were shut down in the Rangers stunning semifinal upset victory in 1979, was he subjected to any period of failure.

A year later, he scored 10 playoff goals and the Islanders won the Stanley Cup. If he has set a high standard, he considers himself worthy of it. "But there are nights," said Bossy, "when things aren't going so well that I'll go home and sit in a room all by myself and look at all my scrapbooks and look at all the things I've done and at least it makes me smile. I've always been kind of a ham that way.

"People have come to expect a lot of me. I expect a lot of myself. I don't know, after the three years I've had, maybe people will expect me to score ninety."

He was intrigued by his own choice of numbers.

"Ninety goals," Mike Bossy said. "Now *that* would be impossible."

The Plugger

The bluest Bruin collar merges into the kind of face you see on seamen, leprechauns, bodies perched on barstools and seated in the Boston Garden balcony. It's a South Boston face, which means more people than **Terry O'Reilly**'s mom like it. Truth is, it's too nice for Terry to treat it the way he does.

By the time the Bruins abbreviated involvement in the 1980 Stanley Cup playoffs was over, O'Reilly looked like Fred Munster. Both eyes were black, his front teeth caps were gone, a cut ran down from the corner of his mouth, and he talked like he had a potato in each cheek.

O'Reilly had started four different fights with the New York Islanders' Clark Gillies and had taken a puck in the face. Terry did not so much surrender at the end of five games, he simply ran out of gas. "I might have to see a plastic surgeon after my career is over," he laughed later in the summer. "I guess I looked pretty rugged.

"It's not a question of deciding whether it's worth it. It's just that sometimes I get into a situation where I can't see any alternative. When the Islander series was all over, I stopped and thought about it, and asked myself what would I have done differently? And I couldn't think of anything.

"The situations were there where Clark and I had the scraps. You'll see that in any playoff series. The physical aspect usually comes out at the beginning and it has to be settled. You can't go through a seven-game series with two teams and not have some challenges. You either have to confront it or walk away from it. And if our team had walked away we wouldn't have been able to beat the Islanders, because they've got the players who can play the skating, playmaking game. Our only alternative was to beat them physically and we didn't do it."

Since the time Terry was 12 there has been no other way. He had been a goalie from age 8, until he decided chasing the puck, not stopping it, looked like more fun. "Those were pretty formative years," he said. "I'm sure losing them set me back. I don't know whether I ever would have been a more natural skater. I've caught up, to a degree, but whether I'd be beyond where I am now, it's hard to say.

"To play professionally, I had to get past the point where I was thinking about where my feet were. Maybe thinking isn't the right word. Worrying probably is. I had no control over them."

There was no other way but plodding straight ahead. He considered his junior career in Oshawa more as a means to a college scholarship than to the pros, so he was surprised to be a first-round selection by the Bruins in 1971. "I have not seen that much of him," said then-general manager Milt Schmidt on draft day. "But I get the word from the scouts that he will go through the end of the building for you."

Getting there in time to have some effect on the game was something that would have to be worked on. And O'Reilly now had to do it the hard way, while playing professionally.

"In junior hockey I found myself in the corners scrapping for the puck," he said. "I wasn't capable of anything else. Here I was playing professional hockey and having trouble staying on my feet. It scared me, all the talent I was up against, so I just had to work."

He took power-skating lessons, following a series of exercises 10 times in each direction—stopping, starting, going forward and backward. "I wasn't playing much in the games," he said. "It had to be done through practice."

Don Cherry came, Phil Esposito and Bobby Orr left, and a new Bruin era had begun. The Lunchpail A.C., Cherry called it, and O'Reilly, improving steadily, emerged to stardom at just the right time to become its leader and symbol. Within three years his point totals had jumped from 35 to 90. His relentless drive made him not only an example of what hard work could accomplish, but the prototype of the guy who would do whatever was necessary to win.

And as is so often the case, his style belied his off-ice personality. O'Reilly collects and restores antiques and furniture, treating his treasures with considerably more care than his body. "I don't think you start seriously considering your body as something sacred until you get older," he said. "Maybe I'll improve my habits of personal care as time goes on. I look at some of the things I've done the way I play the game and I'm quite sure it's taken years off my life. But when you're on the ice competing, you don't give that a second thought.

"Some guys can play the game casually, skate up and down the wing and capitalize on mistakes, never break a sweat and never have to be aggressive. I've watched Bobby Clarke. That head down on every stride, just putting so much effort into everything he does. If all the guys who have natural talent played like him, I don't think Clarkie and I would have jobs."

The singers, they say in the locker room, should sing, and the dancers dance, and O'Reilly would never confuse the category into which he fits. "Through my career I've played with and against guys who I always thought were so much better than me and [I've] seen a lot of them come and go. They just didn't work at it.

"You go on a long two-week trip and catch a little

bit of the flu and play two nights in a row and then sit on the bench wearing damp equipment and catch chills, you really don't want to go out on the next shift," he said. "Sure that happens. But for every low there's a high. You go out sometimes and feel like Superman.

"When I do feel down, I try to tell myself the guy sitting across from me might be feeling the same way. And if he isn't, I'll catch him some other night."

The Leader

Time has still not separated the legend from the boy. The halo remains perched above his head, his stick still slashing someone's shins. Whatever changes 11 years have brought upon the man-child whose indomitable drive lifted the Philadelphia Flyers to consecutive Stanley Cups, are subtle.

Bobby Clarke was 31 when only 21, and now that he is 31, he's still only 21. He always was wise beyond his years and yet he hasn't aged one bit. As Fred Shero, his former coach, used to point out, hockey players are men playing a little boy's game. And there remains no bigger man and no smaller boy than "Clarkie."

The thought has occurred to him, though, that sooner or later he'll have to go to work for a living. Which is why in the summer of 1979 he wore out the rugs in his huge Cherry Hill, New Jersey, home deciding whether it was time to begin moving into management by becoming a playing assistant coach.

To Flyers coach Pat Quinn, who had inherited a team in transition the year before, there was no other logical candidate. "Players have been looking to him for advice and leadership for ten years," said Quinn. "So why not?"

Still, Bobby, who had been stung by whispers about his supposed role in management decisions when he had no such official function, hesitated.

"He paced for three days," said his wife Sandy. "He talked to everybody he knew, both in and out of hockey. He talked to every teammate he could find. He was so worried they would take it the wrong way."

They didn't, for two reasons. One, the Flyers

The Consummate Talent. Guy Lafleur, handsome, graceful, and humble, is revered by fans and awed by his teammates and opponents. He has speed and agility that dazzle and never let up.

accepted that no matter what his input had been into player moves of the past, it was now officially part of his job. And second, it worked because he is Bobby Clarke and remains, six years removed from the Flyers' last Stanley Cup, and five from his third Most Valuable Player award, one of the dominant players and personalities in the game.

Even without the championships, without the approaching 1,000-plus career points, without all the tributes piled upon his reluctant head, he would be no less fascinating. His skills have often been underrated, but never his impact. If his Hall of Fame plaque says nothing more than "he played the game," the way he played would still set him apart from everyone else.

"He's the symbol," said Darryl Sittler, "of what the perfect player should be. I don't know where he gets all his energy. It's amazing."

"He may have made the biggest impact on the game ever," Shero once said. "I don't think there has ever been another player to have such an influence on a team. Other superstars whose teams have won were inspirational, no doubt. But they never had the same conditions as Bobby. There were only so many teams and the players around them weren't exactly nothing. But here's a guy who lifted an expansion team to a championship for the first time."

Six years later, a newer, sleeker model of the Flyers returned to the Stanley Cup final series. And Clarke inhaled deeply with a new Flyers team reaching out for its own glory rather than an old one reaching back. He was intoxicated by the rebirth. It always was his bottom line. Fame, fortune, or fatigue had not affected him in the interim. It was the Flyers all the time.

"If I ever lose enthusiasm, I don't think I can be a decent player," said Bobby. "I don't think I can get by on individual skills. I don't think I would have played too many years the way things were going. Now I feel like I could play forever.

"I think, though, that I've changed, too. I don't think I'm as tense about things as I used to be. It used to drive me crazy if someone didn't work hard in practice or someone had a bad game because they weren't working hard. After you've played so many years you realize that everybody's not the same. You have to accept it or you'll drive yourself crazy."

So, it's not the new job but the 11 years that have affected what few changes are noticeable in Bobby. He's mellowed. That's obvious because fewer Flyers are seen walking into the dressing room wearing tailored slacks and leaving with them cut off at the knees. Clarke's chewing tobacco stains are now safely in his spitoon and no longer on teammate's shoes.

"On game days," said Quinn, "he's a player. I don't talk to him at all between periods. But at other times, I need his advice. Overall, his suggestions are always good, his rapport with the players is excellent."

Clarke takes every fourth shift, instead of two out of three as he did earlier in his career, and even has been talked by Quinn into skipping some optional practices. Sometimes he'll even admit he's tired. And the diabetes, the public mention of which once angered him, is now open for discussion.

"When I first started in the league, I didn't want to be singled out or have people using it as an excuse when I had a poor game. I've grown up a little bit about it. I can't hide it. I don't want to hide it.

"If I can help somebody else, particularly a child, by talking about it, then I want to. The problem is that because I'm Bobby Clarke people think I have some kind of a secret to be able to perform with it. There is no secret. I just have to take care of myself.

"But I am aware that people who have it are more susceptible to blindness and heart conditions and kidney problems. That's something, like everything else in my life, that goes with the territory. Again, it's not something that's sure to happen to me. I know people who have diabetes who live to be eighty or eight-five. Others die young.

"But it's never been a consideration in the way I live or play. I just do things the way I'm comfortable. I have to live with myself."

And the Flyers with him. It is their incessant challenge. "He doesn't have to say anything," said Paul Holmgren, Clarke's closest friend on the team. "You just watch him. You see a guy like Bobby Clarke, who has won everything already, refusing to let up for a second, trying to win more. How could a guy like me not do the same thing? I'd be embarrassed not to."

"All I want," said center Ken Linseman, "is that man's respect. To me, to have that would be the ultimate compliment."

Because of his great speed and balance, it isn't often that Guy Lafleur is knocked on his head. It takes a player of the caliber of New York Islander Denis Potvin to topple him.

New York Islander Mike Bossy, despite an occasional trip up, scored his first 100 goals in the NHL faster than anyone ever before. No one has been able to package goals the way Bossy has.

The Shooter. Mike Bossy has never gone more than six games without scoring a goal, simply because he has the quickest release in the game and as great a sense around the goal as anyone who has ever played the game.

195

The Goalie

Within a year, three of the masters—Ken Dryden, Gerry Cheevers, and Bernie Parent—were gone. In searching for the heir apparent we need not scan the future, but look backward instead. He is found where he always was. In goal at the Chicago Stadium.

Tony Esposito notes the irony but understands the circumstances. "A great deal has to do with who you play for," he said. "I've done a lot of the things I've wanted to in hockey. I have three Vezinas, but the Stanley Cup is the one thing I don't have. I haven't given up, I think we're on the move now.

"Dryden was very capable, but I'll tell you this. He was blessed to be on the right team, in a position where he didn't have all those rebounds. He was a good first-shot goalie, but not a good rebound goalie. I'm not saying he wasn't good, but he came with the right team at the right time.

"I used to come into some of those rinks when we had our bad years and the shots would be forty-two to eighteen and fifteen of ours would be from the blue line. Hell, that would be a cakewalk. You could blow one goal and it would mean nothing, 'cause your team is going to get you three and four.

"I've had good teams and I've had bad teams. When you have a good one, you say, 'Thank God.' But I can remember feeling sorry for the other goalie, too."

Then the World Hockey Association took Bobby Hull from the Black Hawks, and by the next year Whitey Stapleton was gone, too. Age and complacency set in and soon Tony-O became that guy to be pitied. And once the decline was underway, Esposito never had the chance to disprove all the "buts" that had come up when the Hawks were powerful and his name was bandied among the best.

There was his style, stoop shouldered, pads forming a "V," which made the stand-up stuffed-shirts shake their heads. There was, in the early days, as solid a defense as has ever been put together, which some argued masked Tony's weaknesses. There were two trips to the finals and that haunting goal Jacques Lemaire scored from outside the blue line to turn around the 1971 seventh game.

"It aggravated me; there was no way he should have beaten me from there," said Tony. "We had them, two-zero. Bobby Hull hit the crossbar and the puck came right back out, and soon after Lemaire scored that goal.

"Yeah, it would have meant that one Cup I don't have, but I don't think history has been bad to me. I know I'm still playing. And I think I've been more consistent than many other goalies in the game today.

"There have been others who have been great for a few years, but they lost their nerve or lost the edge at a lot younger age than it's happened to me. I think that's how you judge performance. By the guy who can endure. I'm not saying I was better than anybody, but I know I've been around twelve years in the league. And will continue to be. When I'm done playing, and I have no projection—I think it could be as many as eight to ten more years without any problems—then people will judge."

But maybe it would still be those years when the Black Hawks declined that should count the most. "It was getting depressing, we were going nowhere," he said. "I never quit but it was embarrassing to me to associate with a team not even in contention.

"The key is the mental concentration. You lose some of that excitement from the first few years, and then you have to start working at it. I had to give more. You see so many guys who can't do it after a few years."

Twelve years have changed only the people around him. It's still the same Tony, staring through his best friends and teammates on the afternoon of a game. He needs a mask only for protection, his face at game time is almost as inanimate as plastic. He'll bark and grumble at the same reporters immediately after a game that he'll greet warmly the next day.

"After steak time comes, from then on it's all business," he said. "I worry only about myself because I know what I have to do to get myself ready. I do have a problem afterward. I don't try to be rude, I just need that time, especially after a loss, to be by myself. If you lost this kind of an edge, you're satisfied. And that's when you level off.

"I feel great. I think I move as well as I did when I came up with Montreal in 1967. You don't lose your agility, or your strength or reflexes, maybe a little speed, but then I don't have to do sprints."

Now he's 36, and it would be as glorious as it would be ironic for him to move into his prime time with the Hawks recharged.

But the truth is there's been nothing wrong with him all along. The record book shows 72 career shutouts (eighth on the all-time list) and a 2.65 goals against average. In no year since 1971–72 has Esposito played in any less than 63 games. And in too few of those did he see less than 30 shots. It has been hard to keep standing for all those rebounds.

"I don't think I'm really unorthodox," Esposito said. "You can play more stand up playing for Montreal. Ken Dryden never worried about rebounds. If I didn't, I could stand there like a board, too. They see twenty a game and two rebounds, it's fine. You get two-on-ones and rebounds like I have, you have to hang back.

"I may play a different style, but I play by the rules, if you know what I mean. I know when its time to go down. I don't make the move until the puck is played. I don't go out there and play guessing games. Billy Reay [his former Chicago coach] told me I could read the plays and be in position better than anyone he's ever seen.

"I told him I never really thought about it. I just did it."

The Consummate Defenseman

Defensemen come in all sizes, shapes, talents, and temperaments, performing according to varied roles selected for them by their teams. **Larry Robinson** argues that it's all subjective anyway, that his two Norris Trophies as the league's best defensemen were nice, but not necessary. And hardly definitive.

"I don't think about how I consider myself," said Robinson. "I don't like to blow my own horn. I've just always considered the team ahead of personal goals. So therefore it's important for a defenseman or a forward to be able to do both—contribute both offensively and defensively."

Which is, Robinson's reluctance nothwithstanding, exactly our point. "You look at all the things a defenseman has to do," said Scotty Bowman, his former coach, "and Larry Robinson does more of them better than anybody. That's why he's the best defenseman in the league."

The consummate defenseman in today's game must lead an attack as well. While Robinson has never produced the point totals of a Denis Potvin, he has been responsible for a good share. And ultimately, he is the best all-around defenseman in the game today because he is the most consistent.

A search for another classification—the purely defensive defenseman—failed to find anyone who performs those particular duties near Robinson's class. There are some promising defensemen of this type on the horizon, and a few heading into the sunset, but at this time all the best defensive defensemen are good both ways.

"If you're just defensive and your team is down," said Larry, "you're not going to be that much help getting them back into the game. Some teams may prefer to have defensive defensemen because their game is geared that way.

"I pride myself in being able to play any kind of game the situation requires. You want to play a hitting game, I can play a hitting game. You want to play a wide-open game, I can do that."

Doing it all, in Robinson's case, has meant an average of 14 goals and 50 assists a year, and 5 Stanley Cups in 8 seasons with the Canadiens. For a gangling farm boy passed over by 13 teams in the 1971 amateur draft, this isn't too bad, even if Larry is not willing to admit it.

He was a little awkward as a junior, and further confused some scouts by spending time on wing. The Canadiens, though, knew he was a defenseman. They did not so much polish this diamond in the rough as they mounted it on the drill press and let it do some industrial-strength drilling. Inconsistency is standard at that age, but the Canadiens' real concern was whether Larry would be willing to use his 6-foot-3, 210-pound frame to his best advantage.

Complaints that he didn't hit enough had been all but silenced by 1976, when the Canadiens, two years removed from hockey's Holy Grail—the Stanley Cup—finally had their shot at the aborigines who had

197

Opposite: *The Plugger. Boston's Terry O'Reilly is the perfect example of excellence accomplished through hard work.* Below: *The Leader. Bobby Clarke, Flyers' player-assistant coach, has had few peers on the ice, but over the past decade his dedication and leadership have been unmatched.*

stolen it the previous two years, the Philadelphia Flyers.

In one memorable sequence, Robinson lined up Philadelphia's Gary Dornhoefer as he attempted to cross the blue line. A crack, thought to be Dornhoefer's back, was heard throughout the Forum. It turned out to be the boards, which required a 10-minute delay for repairs. The Canadiens won that series the Flyers' way, grinding out three one-goal victories in a four-game sweep. Robinson, reaching out like an octopus for Flyers and pucks for more than 30 minutes a game, was the major reason why.

Three years later, Montreal had won three more Cups. Robinson and veterans Serge Savard and Guy Lapointe stood along the blue line like redwoods, making up probably the best defensive nucleus ever to play on one team. But, on most nights, Robinson has been the most complete player.

Because he performs in Montreal, comparisons to Doug Harvey, the former Canadien great who was the pre-Orr consensus pick as the game's all-time defenseman, were inevitable. "The only thing that's important to me," Robinson insists, "is not whether I can ever be as good as Harvey was. He was the best in his time, and I'd like to be the best today. All I really want, though, is to win as many games as Harvey did. The rest of it doesn't matter, it's not important. Nothing is as important as winning.

"The writers picked me for two Norris Trophies and I'm very proud of them, but I don't think they are able to pick out the finer points. You look at most of the defensemen who have been picked for the Norris Trophy, they've been guys who score a lot of points. Sometimes, that can be unfair."

So is life in the NHL, if your job is fore-checking Robinson. Hardly anyone directly challenges him anymore. It is considered far more prudent, if not more successful, to sneak behind him. Larry hits harder than anyone, moves the puck as well as most, and uses his size to the ultimate advantage. Those arms are long enough to stretch five times around the Stanley Cup. And only grudgingly, when the law of averages and injuries finally ended the Canadiens' reign in 1980, were they able to pry Robinson's fingers from it.

Though certain he could have done more to reverse the result, being told he was as good as ever would be a compliment Larry could finally handle as well as a puck. "Being consistent is the ultimate test of any hockey player. I don't think it's possible to prepare yourself mentally for every game during the regular season, but once one starts, everything falls into place. You have a job to do, and thinking about something else will either get you hurt or force you out of a job.

"The safety catch against complacency is how demanding a game this is. I always look at it as if I have to earn my job every year. By doing that you're a lot more conscious of what you have to do.

"You start out every year with one goal in mind, winning the Stanley Cup. Nothing else matters more. They hand you that Cup and it makes all the bruises, the cuts, the bangs, the travel, and the sleepless nights all worthwhile."

With five Cups by age 29, one would think Robinson would rest well. His goalies always have, knowing Larry was there.

The Offensive Defenseman

The latest in a long line of "next Bobby Orr's" came into the National Hockey League in 1973 with a puck on his stick and a yoke on his back. The Islanders, one year removed from birth, the winners of only 12 games the season before, were dead weight, but no heavier than the burdens **Denis Potvin** placed upon himself.

The truth was, no defenseman since Orr had come out of junior hockey with this much talent, and few 19-year-old heads are equipped to put the association in its proper perspective. While the league standings and Denis' personal record indicated Potvin and the Islanders' standing were following a healthy progression, Denis' head could not keep pace with his body or point totals.

His aloof manner did not help warm up his teammates, and his published criticism of Orr's being named the Most Valuable Player in Bobby's last hurrah, the 1972 Canada Cup, turned into a nightmare. Potvin had seen himself as something special since age 14, when Orr's name first appeared in the

Opposite top: *The Fighter. Vancouver's Dave ("Tiger") Williams claims there aren't many guys in the NHL who are in better condition than he is.* Opposite left: *Bobby Clarke scored his one-thousandth point during the 1980–81 season.* Opposite right: *The Checker. No checker controls the game like Montreal's Bob Gainey.*

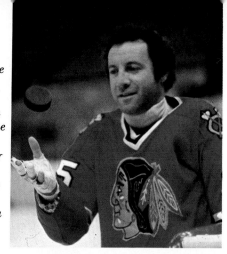

Right: *The Goalie. Tony Esposito of the Chicago Black Hawks has won three Vezina trophies and has over 70 career shutouts.*
Below: *Esposito, making a glove save, demonstrates the concentration that has made him so consistent over the past 13 years.*
Opposite: *The unorthodox Esposito style, stoop-shouldered, pads forming a "V," makes some purists scowl.*

same paragraph with his, and that international series was viewed by Denis as his coming-out party.

"Anytime I did something in junior," said Denis, "I heard, 'Orr did it . . . Orr did it.' After a while, you say, 'I did it . . . Denis Potvin did it.' I let it get to me."

A locker-room apology smoothed things over with his teammates, and three Norris Trophies as the league's best defenseman left no reasonable doubt Denis had lived up to expectations. But inner peace would not be possible until his team, growing stronger by the year, won its Stanley Cup.

Just when the Islanders, coming off two devastating playoff upset losses, were about to be written off as forever cooked by playoff pressure, the title came in 1980. Ironically, it was a season in which Potvin had missed 49 games with a thumb injury, but it was hardly a coincidence that upon his return he played arguably the best, but surely the most team-oriented, hockey of his career. The fact that he also had grown into the Islanders' captaincy three years after his severe alienation from his teammates made the triumph that much more satisfying.

"I felt it [the Cup] was something that had to happen to make me personally happy with my career," said Potvin. "I know that sometime in my career I did it. I don't have to face playing fifteen years, and winning individual awards and never playing on a team that went all the way. . . .

"The individual awards are great, but they don't mean as much as team supremacy. If that's changed over the years, it's probably been mostly in perspective with the changes in the club. In the early years, looking to win a Stanley Cup was really out of focus, so you try and motivate yourself in different ways. I won the Rookie of the Year award, for instance, and that was a goal I had set for myself. But as years went on team developed."

In other words, as the Islanders grew up, there was a Bryan Trottier to move the puck to rather than a Germain Gagnon. And no longer the reason for Denis to always carry it himself. The result was a little less flash and a little more efficiency. The truth is few NHL defensemen play a better defensive game than Potvin, and to term him the league's best offensive defenseman is probably damning him with faint praise. The better way to put it is that no defenseman today has better offensive skills.

"Moving the puck and keeping our forwards moving is essential in my game," said Denis. "If I didn't do that, I'd be taking away a large portion of it. The offensive part of my game, really, I don't worry too much about. I go through periods where I feel my shots should be going in more, but that's typical of anybody who gets five or six a game.

"To say I'm the best offensive defenseman implies that one part of my game is better than the other. I'd like to be known as the best defenseman, period, in the league, if there's a choice. I've worked hard to combine both aspects of the game. In past years I've given up some of my offense. Our team doesn't need blind rushes and I'm a better positional player if I don't carry it as much. It's also a lot harder on the body."

The quintessential Potvin is best displayed on the Islanders' league-leading power play. An orchestra needs a conductor, a five-piece combo only a count-off man, and Denis not only directs, but plays. Oh, can he play. It's a two-minute concert. The pivot, the passes feathered into the open Mike Bossy inside the opponents' box, the clearing shots knocked down and sent down the boards so Trottier can start the play again. Potvin feeds more teammates than a short-order cook, then sneaks up the slot to take a bite himself.

"I think if you had your choice of any five players from all the teams in the league to put on one power play," said Flyers' coach Pat Quinn, "you'd pick the five the Islanders already have together. And it has to start at the point, with a guy who moves the puck efficiently like Denis."

"Borje Salming is good," said Bill Torrey, the Islanders' general manager. "There's no question young [Ray] Bourque of Boston is a helluva talent. But yeah, there's no question, if you look within the most recent framework, Denis is the best. Just look at the record.

"When he's going, he has the moves and an excellent shot. The wrist shot, when he uses it, is devastating. But where he stands out above anyone, maybe as good as anyone ever, is that passing ability. It's not just touch, it's that tremendous strength. He gets it there."

When the Islanders finally got to their nirvana with a six-game Stanley Cup victory over the Flyers, Denis had stared the last of his ghosts down. He had 6

Wearing the captain's "C," which he relinquished when he took over the role of assistant coach, Bobby Clarke inspires his teammates through his own example rather than by the titles he holds. Toronto's Darryl Sittler calls him the "symbol of what the perfect player should be."

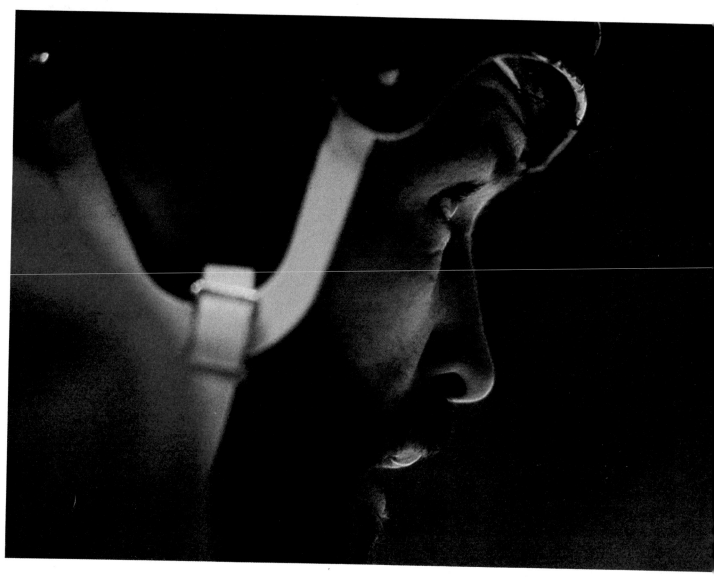

Opposite: *Montreal's Larry Robinson demonstrates his
stickhandling ability against the New York Rangers.
Considered the best all-around defenseman in the game,
Robinson has been a significant factor in the Canadiens' five
Stanley Cup victories in Robinson's nine years with the team.*
Above: *The Offensive Defenseman. Denis Potvin, New York
Islanders' captain, has already won three Norris trophies as
the NHL's best defenseman. No defenseman today has better
offensive skills; he passes well, rushes with the puck, and has a
devastating wrist shot.*

goals and 13 assists in the playoffs, including an overtime goal to win game one and another in the 5–4 clinching victory. Orr had been out of the game for two years and Denis had not only grown up but out of Bobby's needlessly oppressive shadow.

"Sure, Orr changed the game," Denis said four years ago, "but I'm for more positional play. He may be flashier and a better skater, but I'm a harder hitter and there are things I can do that he can't."

Verbal jousts with legends would get him nowhere. The insecurity was silly. And ultimately, conquerable.

"I'm over it now," he said. "When rookies come into the league they are now calling them the next Denis Potvins. All of a sudden I see life on the other side and realize it isn't really that important.

"I felt in those early years I had so much pressure on me. I didn't need that; it was scary. When they said, 'Here comes the next Bobby Orr,' I said, 'My God, if I don't do what Orr has done, I'm going to get down on myself and get bad press and people are going to say he didn't live up to expectations.'

"I just thought, 'Where can I go with my own talent?'

"I'm not rebellious anymore. I'm not bitter about anything. I think I'm a very emotional person, but it's controlled in a way that it comes out when it's important. It's me, playing my game. And I see the Orr comparisons now as not a very important thing."

The Magician

A limited number of times a century, a brain outraces a hormone and the world marvels. In the rarest of cases, the child prodigy is given the equal gift of an early maturity to handle his genius. And **Wayne Gretzky** handles it. He handles it so well that he's almost too good to be true.

He was skating before he was 3, joined a team of 11-year-olds at 6, was interviewed for the first time when he was 8; he shared a head table with Gordie Howe at 10, scored 378 goals in 85 games when he was 11, was called the next Bobby Orr at 12, and left home

to play junior hockey when he was 13. He had an agent at 14, graduated to Junior A and was profiled in *Sports Illustrated* at 16, signed his first professional contract when he was 17, and became a millionaire on his eighteenth birthday.

"I feel very lucky," said Gretzky. "I have lived two lives where most people only get one. As a hockey player, I spend most of my time with adults and I learn a lot from them. But in the summers, when I go back to Brantford [Ontario], I'm with kids my own age that I've known since before I left. I am a normal kid."

What Wayne Gretzky has accomplished on a hockey rink is not, in any sense of the word, normal. Not at 19. Not at any age.

In his first National Hockey League season, Gretzky was voted its Most Valuable Player. What's left for middle-age, his twenties, is not an encore, but the main event. Let your imagination run wild and Wayne may take you there.

"You get one like him every ten years," says Gretzky's coach with the Edmonton Oilers, Glen Sather. "There is a Howe and a Hull and an Orr, and there is Gretzky. He adjusts to all situations well because he is very mature. Don't let the age fool you."

Two months into the 1979–80 season, when the last doubts about his ability to play well in the NHL had disappeared, Gretzky set a goal. Wayne had finished third in the WHA scoring race the season before and, tired of hearing about how life in the better league would be more difficult, wanted to finish at least third in the NHL, too.

"I was reading an article about myself two hours before a game at Maple Leaf Gardens," Wayne said. "It was complimentary—all about what a good year I had last year in the WHA. The story predicted I'd probably do okay in the NHL, but the last line said while I'd finished third in scoring in the WHA, there was no way I'd do it in the NHL in my first year.

"I don't think there's any way to beat Jesus [Marcel Dionne] and God [Guy Lafleur]. They're better than I am. But the rest, well, I think I'm as good as they are."

So Gretzky went out and played the second half of the season as if he were the second coming, finishing with an astounding 137 points. Dionne had the same, but he won the title by scoring 53 goals to Gretzky's 51, while Lafleur, who missed six games with an

Tony Esposito, three times a first team all-star during his long career, gladly finds help from his defenseman in covering up a loose puck in front of the net.

The Magician. Wayne Gretzky, a skating prodigy who learned to skate before he was three years old, plays with the elegance of Jean Beliveau and has a touch likened to that of Stan Mikita. The Edmonton Oilers' Gretzky is at his best behind the net. Defensemen freeze, Gretzky's wings move into the slot, and he puts the puck onto their stick.

injury, came in with 125. And a lot of hockey people still wondered how Wayne did it.

The Gretzky calculator, even when it was only the hand-held size, never really featured ringing bells and flashing lights. It just simply, quietly, continued to add up. At level after level, despite cautions about his adjustments, the infant among children, the child among adolescents, the teenager among men, Gretzky produced.

"The only time I ever felt overmatched," said Wayne, "was that first year, when I was six. I scored only one goal the entire year. Otherwise, I've never had any problems adjusting."

Even scouts, fixtures at Brantford pee wee games from the time Wayne was eight, couldn't figure it out. "When you grade the talents we normally look for in young players, the shot, the size, and the speed, it's almost spooky how he does it," said one. "The puck just comes to him."

Or, more precisely, Gretzky knows exactly where the puck is going and simply waits for it to arrive. And if it eventually finds its way behind the net, Wayne is at his best. Defensemen freeze, Gretzky's wingers move into the slot, and the puck is on their stick. When a game is over, the scoresheet shows Wayne with a goal and two assists. And everybody swears they never saw him do it.

"He only looks eighteen," said Sather at the start of the season. "Actually he's thirty-two and came back in somebody else's body."

But if that were true, Gretzky's is not the body one would select. Listed at six feet, 165 pounds, he actually looks at least 10 pounds lighter. "Mental maturity he has," said Sather. "Physical maturity, it'll take a few more years. Sure I had my doubts when I heard about a seventeen-year-old kid playing pro hockey. Look at all the underage drafts that have flopped.

"Their development is uneven at that age, both physically and mentally. But this kid is special. He can be as good as he wants to be. And I know just how much he wants it. What he has is a gift very few players who have ever played this game ever had. What makes him special? What made Einstein special?"

There's a little bit of Jean Beliveau's elegance about Gretzky, as he moves upright, eyes darting,

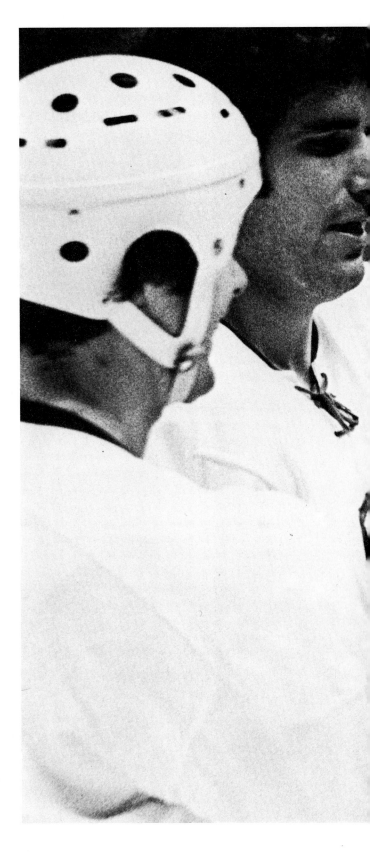

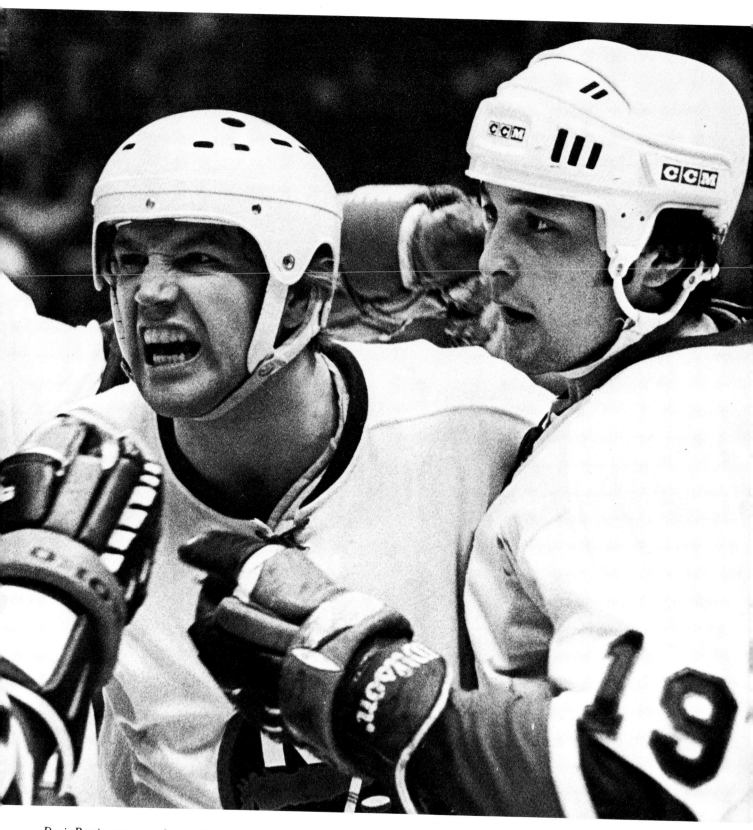

Denis Potvin appears to be psyching himself up as he growls at his brother Jean, also a defenseman for the New York Islanders. Holding Denis back are teammates Clark Gillies (left) and Bryan Trottier.

213

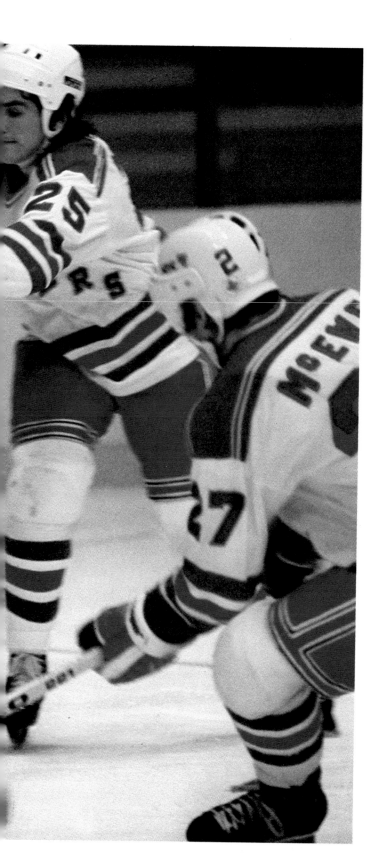

Montreal Canadien Bob Gainey, whose play has inspired the establishment of the Frank J. Selke Trophy for the NHL's best defensive forward, has been called "the most mechanically perfect hockey player in the world," by Soviet coach Victor Tikhonov. Above: Gainey and his Canadien teammates share the thrill of their 1979 Stanley Cup victory over the New York Rangers.

215

across a blue line. Stan Mikita, in his heyday, didn't play with a puck; it was his yo-yo on a string. And Wayne's touch is similar. But a Guy Lafleur, swathed in Clearasil, he is not. There are 30 to 40 players in the NHL who skate faster, and almost as many who can excite an audience more than Gretzky, but they accomplish far less. There are times when you don't see Gretzky at all. And then he'll slip, no slither is the better word, away from his check, and the puck is on somebody's stick and in the net.

"His biggest asset is the ability to control the puck and himself," said goalie Dave Dryden, his former teammate. "He'll wait for that mistake and make it count. You can't compare him to anyone else. He's unique."

"How good is he?" said Dennis Sobchuk, another former teammate. "Ever try to catch a feather?"

On his eighteenth birthday, Gretzky signed a 21-year contract with the Oilers. It runs out in 1999, which is why he wears the 99 on his back.

"I don't think he'll ever become complacent," said Sather. "He's got too much pride. Early last year in a game with the Islanders he made a bad mistake. The guy scored and it was his fault. He looked down and then looked at the bench, and I shot him a look that said 'Don't even think about coming back to the bench until you get it back.'

"Twenty-one seconds later, he scored."

The Checker

It is not an effortless stride but it is, nonetheless, graceful. While Guy Lafleur's feet push off behind him, leaving a trail of vapors, **Bob Gainey**'s push sideways, his head down, his knees pumping.

There is nothing deceptive about it, no shifts at three-quarter speed, just a sprinter in magnificent full glide heading straight for the tape. Three steps into gear, there are not many players in the National Hockey League who could catch the Canadiens' left wing, but that is not the point. It is Gainey who is usually doing the catching.

His is not a role, but a dimension. There are players on each NHL team who effectively carry out checking assignments, but none of this type who control games like Gainey. He has brought the checker out of the closet, taken a dump truck kind of job and turned it into a sports car, prompted composition of ballads for formerly unsung heroes. And, by his brilliance, even inspired an official league trophy.

They could not, after all, name it after him. But in three years since the establishment of the Frank J. Selke Trophy for the league's best defensive forward, they have not been able to find anyone else to win it, either.

"Maybe at one time a player of my type was overlooked," said Gainey. "The trophy brought some attention to it, and now if anything, it's the opposite. I've been called underrated so much, I'm afraid I'm overrated."

But not by any winger who has had Gainey's straitjacket fitted upon him over a seven-game series. Not by anyone who has ever tried to knock him off his skates. Not by a defenseman who has forgotten that Gainey, when the situation calls for it, can score goals. And certainly not by the best minds in the game. One of them, Viktor Tikhonov, the coach of the Soviet national team, calls Gainey "the most mechanically perfect hockey player in the world."

Mechanically, in the Russian sense, means complete, but when, after decades of research, the Soviet sports laboratory announces the production of the perfect hockey player, the rising curtain will unveil on Gainey's clone. He has never been named to an NHL postseason all-star team, but repeatedly on Soviet-North American tours, Gainey has been the best North America could answer with.

"You look, not just at the Russians' speed, but their strength on skates," said Scotty Bowman after the Soviet triumph in the February 1979 Challenge Cup, "and the only player we have to match up against that is Gainey."

It is not completely a coincidence that Gainey learned to play his game under the closest thing North America has to offer to the scientific Soviet sporting mind. Roger Neilson, who coached Gainey in junior hockey at Peterborough, did not endorse the Soviets' free-wheeling style, but he was years ahead of his time in teaching and training methods. Neilson, now coach of the Buffalo Sabres, did not take Gainey's raw 17-

year-old speed and harness it toward scoring. A few looks at Bob firing wide on breakaway after breakaway gave him better ideas.

"We had a strict system," said Gainey. "Maybe two or three of our talented guys were allowed to freelance, but just a little.

"A scoreless tie, to us, was a point. If we got a break and scored a goal or two, we'd win. We did have offensive plays, but it was all very controlled. When Roger laid it all out to us, a lot of things didn't seem right, but it wasn't long before we could see what it was doing for us.

"I could skate, but I wasn't a very good offensive player. I didn't have the hands, the touch. So I looked at this as an opportunity for me to excel at something else."

Of course when the Canadiens passed over myriads of all-Canadian kids with 100-point totals to make Gainey the eighth player taken in the 1973 draft, there were raised eyebrows. But after only six games in the minors, Bob proved a lot more ready to play in the NHL than some of the prodigies picked ahead of him.

"The emphasis, as soon as I reported to my first Montreal camp, was on learning," said Gainey. "They never expected me to do anything I couldn't. I was insecure, sure, but it was implied that if they didn't want me, I wouldn't be here so soon."

By the next season, he was drawing the opposition's top right-wing gun and, even without hands, was scoring his standard 15 goals a season. While other checkers shadow or agitate their men, pick up loose pucks and get them out to center, Gainey does considerably more. He follows his man as far back as advisable, but knows when to release to fill a passing lane. And when he picks off the puck, or digs it from a corner, he keeps it, not zigzagging or ragging, but hitting a breaking teammate or carrying it himself and refusing to be knocked off his feet. The odd rush culminates with a burst down the left wing and wide-angle drive for the far corner. A few times a year it even catches the net, but if it doesn't, Bob has already picked up his man at center.

"One guy checking just doesn't work," he said. "It has to be a five-man thing. And I always felt if you were no offensive threat at all, you couldn't be effective, either. If they have no fear of you, you can't hurt them. They'll just keep taking it in your end and

sooner or later they'll score."

If his recurring rescues of the North American honor were not evidence enough of his effectiveness, four Stanley Cups are. When the fourth one, in 1979, was proving the most difficult, Gainey was at his best. When Montreal, which had barely gotten by Boston on an overtime goal in the seventh game of the semifinals, lost the first game of the finals to the Rangers, then fell behind in the second, Bob simply took over.

He was everything you'd ever want a hockey player to be, skating and hitting, and even scoring six playoff goals himself. It was firsthand evidence that should the Canadiens ever find the insanity to change his role, he would surely be a consistent 30-goal scorer.

"They do expect some offense from me," said Gainey. "Scoring the eighth goal in an eight-to-one game doesn't strike me as very meaningful, but if I got five a year and they were all significant in us winning games, I'd think I'd had a good offensive season.

"You can't be one hundred percent either way. A good offensive player is at thirty to thirty-five percent defense. Me, I'd probably be twenty-five percent offense.

"I've never felt underpaid or lacking in recognition. I'm secure about what I do. The game is entertainment and the goal scorers sell tickets. It's the other players, though, who win championships."

Just as he did in 1979 against the Rangers. That series was hardly one isolated dash out of Lafleur's or Larry Robinson's shadow. It was, heart and soul, the utmost Gainey.

The Fighter

Any year's draft will produce 10 to 15 guys like **Dave ("Tiger") Williams.** They are big, willing, unpolished, and uncompromising. Belligerence will usually get them to the National Hockey League, but only competence will keep them there.

So they come, leave their mark on someone's face, and go. Either they get tired of bruising their

Dave Williams of Vancouver has averaged just under 300 penalty minutes per season during his career. However, he has also earned respect by scoring at least 30 goals in each of the past two seasons. Opposite: Williams struggles with Buffalo defenseman Bill Hajt (left) for position in front of the Buffalo goal.

hands, or their wives tell them how ridiculous they look, or someone a little stronger and a little more willing comes along to take their place. The smarter ones use the limited time available to create a buffer zone around themselves and learn how to operate in it. They either go legit, or they go to the minors, and only a few dodge the gunfighter's bullets and remain the way nature presented them as 19-year-olds.

"I don't think I've mellowed," said Williams. "But the league has. The rules are more rigid, the officiating more consistent. The system has mellowed more than the players.

"Most of the new rules are pretty good. A lot of them are about fifteen years too late. But the one [passed in the summer of 1980] where they're making all the players not involved go into a neutral area, I can't agree with. The one thing they forget is that this is a team sport. If your teammate is involved in an altercation, you should be there if he ever needs you. I want to be beside my teammate when he needs me. A good hockey team is a good marriage."

Dave Williams has lasted six years not by averaging 291 penalty minutes a season, anybody could do that. He's still there because he's always been where he's needed. The rest of the occasional histrionics are a charade, as is his self-proclaimed undefeated record. "The game has changed and you have to change with it," he said.

"Anybody can throw knockouts. You don't have to be all that clever to do that. But you have to work on the other parts of your game. A lot of guys just got too involved in the one aspect of it. You have to do more than one thing to play in the league.

"I'm mainly average in all departments as a hockey player. But there aren't many guys in the NHL who are in better condition than I am. I feel mentally strong, too. I don't have many highs and lows over eighty games. I can maintain the same attitude."

During the 1979–80 season, Williams scored a personal-high 30 goals, his best in six seasons, but in his previous four years he never finished with less than 18. When his tramping style and pugilistic notoriety did not fit the image wanted by a new Leaf management, he was traded in midyear to Vancouver. Toronto wanted speed, the Canucks wanted self-respect. "He knows," said Vancouver Coach Harry Neale, "how to win. His dedication is unparalleled by anyone in this league. He's a pretty good hockey player and he gives a damn. And he goes out every night and proves it.

"He's a leader. Guys are attracted to him as a person. If you lived with us for a year you'd know why we made that trade. There aren't many guys like that. And when you get one, you're lucky."

While refreshed with the scenery change, Tiger says that with the Canucks he's learned the burdens of being a main man rather than an accessory. "I can appreciate what guys like [Bobby] Clarke and [Darryl] Sittler go through. They not only have to play well, but make sure things go smooth. Before, in Toronto, all I had to do was show up; here there's that added pressure. They need people who can do things the right way and help the young players out."

His nose, flattened "like a beer can that someone stepped on," in the words of Leaf-owner Harold Ballard, suggests that there are more than 27 chronological years on Tiger. If there had been a silver spoon in his sandbox, he probably would have used it over his playmate's head. Summers during his junior years in Swift Current, Alberta, were spent working as an oil rigger.

"Fifteen hours a day," said Williams, "and it was a tough buck. If a few players in this league who don't give it all they have could work at a job like that for a couple of months, it might change their attitude a little.

"I just got back from a hunting trip [it pitted Tiger and a bow and arrow against bears] and I was at a logging camp. I'm talking logs as big as this desk I'm sitting at. Guys work hard, but they get paid pretty well. Every job has it's good and bad, but one thing I envy about them is there's no pressure. They do their work and go home. They don't have to answer to twenty million people. I feel that pressure more than when I first came up. The team is investing a lot of money in you to improve and try to better each year's performance. The older you get the more they want out of you. Until you get old, and then they don't want you at all.

"Anyway, I appreciate the opportunity I've been given. If it wasn't for hockey, I'd just be a guy in the work force now. Probably in oil. Maybe I'd be the head of Chevron by now."

A sense of humor like Williams' and the showmanship that goes with it run shorter in the NHL than petroleum on the continent. "The Penguins," said Tiger one year when the Leafs faced elimination in a best-of-three series "is done like dinner." The Leafs won and a year later were found going into Long Island for the seventh game of the series against even greater odds. "The Islanders," said Tiger, "is worse than done like dinner. They're burnt like toast. They're so far out in left field they're out of hand-grenade range."

The Leafs won that one, too.

Hockey, to the Tiger Williamses of the NHL, is a blue-collar job, but $125,000 supports his wife and two children more than adequately. There are few dekes about him. Tiger skates straight ahead, and off the ice he performs the same way. He is the consummate family man, doesn't smoke, drinks little, and jokes that Swift Current is such a good place because it has 28 churches for its 6,000 residents.

But he does take the fighting seriously. When in Toronto, he worked out regularly in a boxing club, and, in fact, has a younger brother who is one of Canada's top amateur boxers. And mounted with the bear heads on his wall is a cherished autographed picture of Muhammed Ali.

The scoreboard on many nights comes up against the Canucks, but Williams has never admitted to a personal defeat in a fight. "The only fights I lose are with the parking-ticket man," he said. "I always lose my five bucks no matter what I tell him.

"Draws? Well, everything is in the eyes of the beholder. My eyes only tell my brain what I want them to tell it. I don't know if I'll ever get tired of fighting. Maybe if there gets to be no reason for it, I'll probably stop. I guess that's the bottom line."

Thirty goals answer a lot of finger waggings, giving a legitimacy to the roles of players like Williams. One once broke into tears seeing the word "goon" used against him in a magazine article, but Dave Williams is still Tiger because he never worries about his reputation, never questions his purpse.

"I'm not crazy," he said. "If I was, would I wear a helmet? There are twenty guys in the league who are loonier than me." But not as effective or willing over his period of time.

"What people say has never bothered me in my life," he said. "You never take anything seriously unless it comes from somebody who really knows you well. I was told that a long time ago, but I live by it. I don't worry about what anybody says. The only thing a hockey player needs is respect from his teammates. If you don't have that you're in trouble. If you do, everything is apple pie.

"We all have a job to do. I dislike guys for a lot of reasons but I've got a lot more feeling for the guys who play like me. I know the way they're thinking. But anybody who plays in the NHL, no matter what team or what position, I have respect for him because I know how he got there. There's four hundred guys in the league and four thousand guys trying to get in.

"We're all out there trying to do a job, a job which is very competitive. Business is just as competitive, maybe more. You have to learn to be a cut-throat in business, too. Only here we can do it physically and get away with it. There's always going to be the Mean Joe Greene. Every sport has got them. Even basketball. If everybody played the same way, it would be pretty damn boring. Aggressive hockey, or however you want to refer to it, will never die. Especially in the States. People like it too much."

The Consummate Talent

God created hockey. And then he created **Guy Lafleur.** Or was it the other way around? Either he was born to play this most graceful of team sports or the sport was put there to be played by this most graceful of athletes.

The game is not always pretty; it can be played on many levels, but one could argue that in its purest sense, it only marks time between eras until a Lafleur comes along. Fortunately, there seems to be a master scheme. When age takes a Jean Beliveau, a Bobby Orr is in his prime. When Orr's knees rob both him and us of a full career, there is a Flower in bloom in Montreal.

What Lafleur does transcends statistics or standings, raising hockey to an art form that belongs on stage or in a museum. Even the name, which connotes something beautiful, is perfect. The circumstances which delivered him to Le Canadiens were guided by hands more divine than former-general manager Sam

Unquestionably hockey's most exciting player is Montreal Canadien Guy Lafleur. Whether Lafleur is passing or skating into position to receive one, he exhibits a grace and style that are uniquely his own.

Pollock's. No one man is bigger than the hockey business, but it's only a "good" game without a Lafleur. There may be as many as 10 dominant players in the NHL at any time, but we're lucky if there's one consummate talent.

And when he is also handsome, graceful, and humble, revered by a people, held in awe by teammates and opponents, his presence surpasses just sport. This is a perfect accident—people are supposed to have failings. But bowing at the shrine of the best hockey player of our day, we cannot bring ourselves to look for any.

"You notice," said teammate Rod Langway, "that Guy doesn't sweat. Unreal. He walks on the red carpet all the time; walking on water is somewhere down the line. Number ten. The Flower, that's it. He's in the garden all by himself."

And except for his first three years in the NHL, which was the last time anyone caught Lafleur looking human, he always has been. Guy Damien Lafleur was cloned in Jean Beliveau's image in 1951 in Thurso, Quebec. He wore Beliveau's number four through his youth and followed the footsteps of the Canadien great 20 years later to Quebec City for his junior career. And he came to Montreal in 1971, heralded as Beliveau's successor. Pollock had traded one of his better players, Ralph Backstrom, to Los Angeles to insure that Oakland (whose draft choice the Canadiens owned) would finish behind the Kings, and last in the NHL. Everything went without a hitch, even when Lafleur scored a creditable 28 goals his first year.

But then Lafleur slipped to 28 and 21. "I admit I had doubts," said Scotty Bowman, then the Canadiens' coach. "Claude Ruel [his assistant coach] always said that when Guy was twenty-five he was going to be an accomplished, complete hockey player. Claude would tell me that when I kept asking, 'Is he going to come through?'

"I'll tell you what slowed him down, he was a shy kid, so he never popped off, never said anything, and he had to deal with all the pressure himself."

"I think it was a case of him not knowing how good he was," said former-Canadiens' goalie Ken Dryden. "In practice, he would make moves that left you speechless, but he didn't have the confidence to do it in a game. In a game he would make the orthodox play instead of what he was capable of. I suppose he

thought he couldn't get away with things he did in juniors. In most guys' cases, it's true. But obviously Guy Lafleur isn't most guys."

The turning point came when Beliveau, a vice-president in the Canadiens' organization, criticized Lafleur softly but publicly. The advice, to work hard, was taken by Guy in the right way.

"He didn't say anything that he hadn't already said to me privately," said Lafleur. "It was good. It gives you a wake-up—like I'm going to show that guy, you know. I was missing too many chances and saying, 'Oh, forget it.' I wasn't going after the puck, saying, 'Oh, what's the use?' because I didn't have the confidence. I wasn't doing everything I could."

He finished the following year with 53 goals and 66 assists, despite missing 10 games with a hand injury. In the six seasons since then he has continued to average 54 goals, but that's putting art into columnar tables. What Lafleur does should not be recited in numbers, but in music.

"Beliveau was something special, like Guy, but when I think of the two of them alongside each other, Lafleur is ahead of Jean with all the things he does," said Jimmy Roberts, a teammate who witnessed the blossoming and is currently an assistant coach with the Buffalo Sabres. "What I really can't believe about him is the way he's going at top speed all the time. I mean, he'll get caught out here at the end of a shift and he's just as fast and as quick as he was when he first went onto the ice.

"I haven't seen anyone else who can do that. You think of other big names . . . Hull for instance. He had that blazing shot and he could hold you off with that big arm of his. Or Howe— he was around when I was breaking in and he was something. But Lafleur— he's the most exciting player I've ever seen.

"He's different. Beliveau did certain things. Hull, Howe. But Lafleur, he does it all. The few times he comes out flat he surprises everybody because it happens so rarely."

Lafleur's new assertiveness on the ice also portended a subtle change of personality. Twice in the last two years, he shocked his worshippers with outbursts of verbiage. Once he demanded a renegotiation of his contract. The following year he criticized Ruel, who had stayed on after Bowman's departure as an assistant coach to Bernie Geoffrion, of interfering with

Geoffrion's job. Only because it was Lafleur who had spoken up were there no lingering resentments.

"I don't think there was one player who resented what he did [about the contract]," said Scotty Bowman. "Because it was Lafleur, they figured he should get everything he wanted."

So the image, which requires little caretaking, remains intact, even with the emergence of a public personality. "Maybe I'm thinking I wasn't talking enough before," he said, a few months after the Ruel criticism. "I haven't changed my thinking, I'm now third on the team in seniority and maybe I feel the

leadership more. Like with the thing with Ruel and Geoff. Maybe I'm the only guy who is in a position to say anything. I don't want to put anybody down. I just wanted us to be proud. When things are going bad, the easiest thing in the world is to let the season go by and not say anything."

But the outbursts are still rare. The real Lafleur is working very hard at practice, is visiting sick kids in Montreal hospitals, refusing to be used in the French separatist movement, selling yogurt, cologne, and ice skates, and being a daddy to five-year-old Martin. And while no longer embarrassed at questions about his gift, he is still at a loss to explain it.

"You play the game when you go out on the ice," he said. "I don't think about it, you can't plan it. Oh, you have to pay attention to who you are going to check, but on offense you just go. One-on-one on a defenseman, I have no idea which way I'm going to go—until the last moment when it just happens.

"Yes, it's a gift. But you have to work hard at it. As far as my place in history, there's lots of time to think about that. I'd like to play ten more years and what comes will come. But it's hard to see myself doing what Gordie Howe or Maurice Richard did. I'd be very proud of these things, if they come in time, but right now the team comes first."

As does his public. The obligations were unnecessarily tough on him for many years, until he realized he had the grace to handle them. Being perfect and being Guy Lafleur is not so hard after all.

"It does get tough sometimes because I've got a family," he said. "But for myself, personally, I love it. I appreciate everything I've got. I love my job. I love skating. I love running the game."

Because Denis Potvin's offensive skills are so outstanding, his defensive ability is often overlooked. Here, he helps out former Islander goaltender Chico Resch in front of the net, blocking a high shot with his shoulder.

225

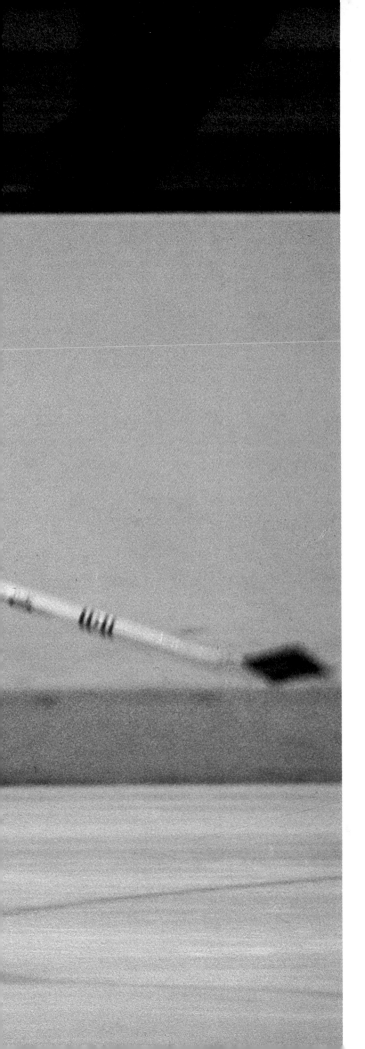

7
Dream Team
Players' Poll

There are approximately 420 men in the National Hockey League, who play a total of 840 regular-season games, plus nearly 100 preseason and 65 playoff games. Hockey is their game, but it is also their life—and livelihood—at least for the time being. Theirs is a profession whose job description includes slap shots, fore-checks, face-offs, stickhandling, fast skating, bumps, pains, agonies, ecstasies.

The men who fill this job description are already accomplished in their chosen field. They've learned the ropes and paid their dues in collegiate, junior, minor-league, or European play. Some, of course, are better than others. But how does one measure the truly great ones who at times seem to be performing the impossible on the ice? How do these players rate against each other and against the other superstars in the NHL? You've no doubt seen and heard the opinions of fans, sportswriters, and radio and TV broadcasters, but what about the players themselves? Who do *they* think are the best among their peers?

The answers to these questions are provided in this chapter in a poll conducted among NHL players before the 1980–81 season. The poll, which was conducted especially for this book and covers a wide range of categories, represents, by position or performance, hockey's finest, according to those who should know.

The results of the players poll aren't necessarily surprising, but they are certainly intriguing. Wayne Gretzky, the "boy wonder" of the Edmonton Oilers, won in more categories than any other player, as might be expected. He did *not*, however, finish atop the category of Best Center. That honor went instead to the New York Islanders' Bryan Trottier. Indicative of just how stiff the competition was is the fact that Marcel Dionne of the Los Angeles Kings, one of hockey's premier players for the past decade, failed to win a single category. Nor did Mike Bossy of the Islanders who, since entering the NHL in 1977–78, has scored goals at a faster rate than anyone in hockey history, having never scored fewer than 50 goals in a single season! And while the NHL's outstanding youth were well recognized in the results of the poll, Bobby Clarke, the indomitable leader of the Philadelphia Flyers for more than a decade, won more categories than anyone but Gretzky.

And so, with apologies to Richard Dawson and "Family Feud," our survey said...

BEST LEFT WING

1 Charlie Simmer

2 Steve Shutt

3 Clark Gillies

BEST CENTER

1 Bryan Trottier

2 Marcel Dionne

3 Wayne Gretzky

BEST RIGHT WING

1 Guy Lafleur

2 Mike Bossy

3 Lanny McDonald

Preceding pages: *In a special poll of NHL players, Bobby Clarke was voted the Most Enthusiastic, the Hardest Worker, the Best Fore-checker, and the Best on Face-offs, but no one asked about slap shots.* Opposite: *Charlie Simmer.* Top: *Guy Lafleur.* Above: *Bryan Trottier.*

BEST DEFENSIVE FORWARD

1 Bob Gainey

2 Bobby Clarke

3 Walt Tkaczuk

BEST OFFENSIVE DEFENSEMAN

1 Denis Potvin

2 Borje Salming

3 Larry Robinson

BEST DEFENSIVE DEFENSEMAN

1 Larry Robinson

2 Serge Savard

3 Dave Burrows

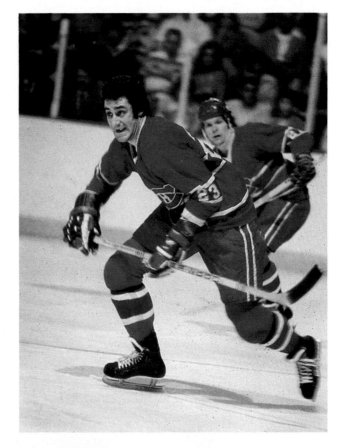

Top: *Bob Gainey*. Left: *Denis Potvin*. Above: *Larry Robinson*. Opposite top: *Terry O'Reilly*. Opposite bottom: *Tony Esposito*. Opposite right: *Wayne Gretzky*.

BEST CORNERMAN

1 Terry O'Reilly

2 Wayne Cashman

3 Paul Holmgren

BEST GOALTENDER

1 Tony Esposito

2 Don Edwards

3 Mike Palmateer

PLAYER WITH THE BEST HOCKEY SENSE

1 Wayne Gretzky

2 Marcel Dionne

3 Ulf Nilsson

231

BEST FORE-CHECKER

1 Bobby Clarke

2 Doug Risebrough

3 Bob Gainey

BEST BACK-CHECKER

1 Bob Gainey

2 Al MacAdam

3 Bobby Clarke

BEST ON FACE-OFFS

1 Bobby Clarke

2 Doug Jarvis

3 Phil Esposito

BEST WRIST SHOT

1 Lanny McDonald

2 Denis Potvin

3 Danny Gare

BEST STICKHANDLER

1 Gil Perreault

2 Marcel Dionne

3 Guy Lafleur

HARDEST HITTER

1 Barry Beck

2 Denis Potvin

3 Clark Gillies

BEST SLAP SHOT

1 Reed Larson

2 Larry Robinson

3 Guy Lafleur

Opposite top: *Bobby Clarke*. Opposite left: *Bob Gainey*.
Opposite right: *Lanny McDonald*. Top: *Gil Perreault*.
Right: *Reed Larson*. Above: *Barry Beck*.

233

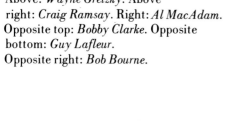

Above: *Wayne Gretzky*. Above
right: *Craig Ramsay*. Right: *Al MacAdam*.
Opposite top: *Bobby Clarke*. Opposite
bottom: *Guy Lafleur*.
Opposite right: *Bob Bourne*.

234

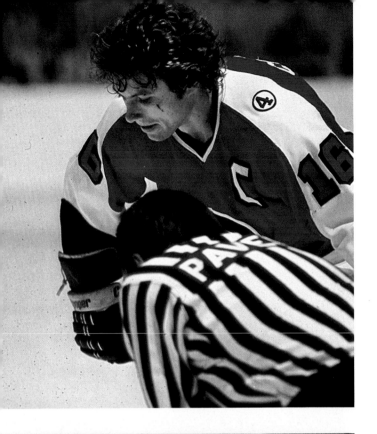

BEST PLAY MAKER

1 Wayne Gretzky

2 Bryan Trottier

3 Marcel Dionne

BEST PENALTY KILLER

1 Craig Ramsay

2 Don Luce

3 Bob Gainey

MOST UNDERRATED PLAYER

1 Al MacAdam

HARDEST WORKING PLAYER

1 Bobby Clarke

2 Eddie Johnstone

3 Terry Ruskowski

MOST ENTHUSIASTIC PLAYER

1 Bobby Clarke

2 Terry O'Reilly

3 Bob Kelly

FASTEST SKATER (Tie)

Guy Lafleur

Bob Bourne

BEST LINESMEN

John D'Amico

Leon Stickle

BEST REFEREE

1 Wally Harris

2 Bruce Hood

3 Andy van Hellemond

BEST COACH

1 Scotty Bowman

2 Al Arbour

3 Fred Shero

BEST GENERAL MANAGER

1 Bill Torrey

2 Lou Nanne

3 Scotty Bowman

FAVORITE ARENA

1 Montreal Forum

2 Maple Leaf Gardens

3 Madison Square Garden

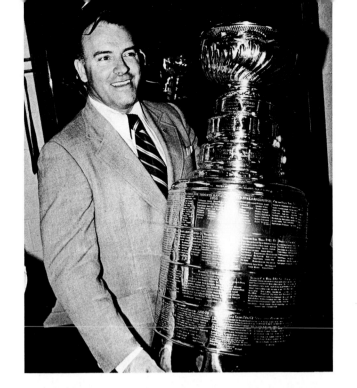

Opposite top: *Wally Harris (left)*. Opposite bottom: *John D'Amico*. Opposite left: *Leon Stickle*. Top right: *Scotty Bowman*. Top left: *Bill Torrey*. Above: *Montreal Forum*.

237

Wayne Gretzky's abilities were singled out by NHL players in more categories than any other player.

MOST NATURAL TALENT

1 Wayne Gretzky

2 Gil Perreault

3 Guy Lafleur

PLAYER MOST VALUABLE TO HIS TEAM

1 Wayne Gretzky

2 Guy Lafleur

3 Marcel Dionne

BEST YOUNG PLAYER (under 23)

1 Wayne Gretzky

2 Ray Bourque

3 Bobby Smith

IF YOU WERE STARTING AN NHL TEAM FROM SCRATCH, WHICH CURRENT NHL PLAYER WOULD YOU FIRST SELECT?

1 Wayne Gretzky

2 Guy Lafleur

3 Bryan Trottier

8
Ice Flakes
Hockey's
Characters
by Frank Orr

He's there every night that the Toronto Maple Leafs play a home game, on the street close to Maple Leaf Gardens, as much a fixture of the hockey scene in Toronto as blue-and-white sweaters, or "Hockey Night in Canada" telecasts, or sellout crowds.

"Psst, wanna buy a ticket?" That's his pitch. The man, middle-aged and reasonably well dressed, is a ticket scalper. He purchases tickets from a variety of sources at their face value and sells them at a high profit, often a 400 percent mark up, to hungry fans anxious to see a game in an arena where no seat for a regular-season or playoff game in the National Hockey League has not been sold since the end of World War II.

Hockey writers often check the street market with him on their way into the Gardens, then mention in their game reports the demand for tickets.

"A tough ticket tonight because there's a convention on with guys from the small towns who wanna see the Leafs play," he'll say.

"I just got sixty bucks each for a pair of golds [face value is $15.50]."

Or he could say: "Slow night tonight and I'm goin' to be lucky, very lucky, to get face value for a whole handful of these suckers."

The ticket scalper is just one of the many characters one encounters on the hockey scene around the NHL. From the directors' lounges to the dressing rooms to the streets outside the rinks, there are a variety of people who are, well, different.

Flakes, nuts, kooks, oddballs, comedians, hedonists, blithe spirits, carousers. Describe them any way you want, but the guys who are slightly off the sidewalks of the norm supply the game with a large amount of its appeal.

Concentrate on the majority of hockey people and you will yawn a great deal! They will answer your questions with the standard cliches, never departing from the answers that have been used since the game was played on natural ice.

An example is the postgame press conference with the coaches: "We didn't move the puck, we didn't fore-check, back-check, or work hard enough," the losing coach will say.

"We moved the puck, we fore-checked, back-checked, and worked hard," will be the winning coach's comment.

That's why Harry Neale is regarded as a treasure by the majority of sportswriters who cover the NHL. Neale is the head coach of the Vancouver Canucks and his postgame conferences are a splendid stand-up comedy routine. "We're losing at home; we can't win on the road," Neale announced one night. "My failure as a coach is that I can't figure out any place else to play our games."

The majority of the owners of big-league hockey teams these days resemble bankers in their pinstripe suits. Many look like guys who carried briefcases to kindergarten. Ask an NHL owner a simple question and he's likely to counter with a crisp "no comment," or supply an answer that contains little you didn't already know.

Harold Ballard doesn't think that way. Ballard, 77, owns the Toronto Maple Leafs. Ballard has been called "The Mouth That Roared." He's also been called a few less flattering names by his fellow owners and the players on his team.

Ballard is a throwback to another era, when the men who owned sports teams (he also owns the Hamilton TigerCats of the Canadian Football League) were big-league promoters. Ballard is a master of the craft. He earns large amounts of publicity for himself, Maple Leaf Gardens, and his teams, with his outrageous statements. It's a slow news day? Phone Ballard and ask him what he feels about frontal lobotomies, women's liberation, or hockey. He'll give you an instant column.

Ballard held his hockey team in the spotlight through much of the summer of 1980. He had a long-running feud with the team's best player, center Darryl Sittler. Ballard called Sittler "a cancer on the team" and said that Sittler "would never play for the Leafs again."

Just before training camp opened, Ballard earned an enormous amount of publicity by calling a press conference to announce that Sittler, who had a no-trade contract, would be with the team in the 1980–81 season.

"Half this game is mental; the other half is being mental," said Jim McKenny, the Maple Leafs' resident wit and philosopher through the 1970s before he took his high-class comedy act to Switzerland in 1979.

One NHL veteran player backed up McKenny's assessment that there's a little "basket-case" in most

Thus, this is not an attempt to embrace the entire field of flakes. Instead, it's one man's favorites among the dozens who have crossed his path in travels down the old hockey trail.

Does any normal human become a goalie?

Perhaps a writer's biases and prejudices should be stated up front. This one has a soft spot in his heart— and perhaps in his head—for goaltenders, probably because he was one himself. In fact, I might be the only goalie in the history of hockey ever to have a fan urinate on him during a game. At the time, I figured that if it were criticism of my goaltending, it wasn't very subtle.

The incident happened in something called the Ontario Rural Hockey Association Intermediate D series, a league for teams representing small farming communities. The rinks were small, natural-ice bullrings and, in one tiny Ontario village, the spectators stood on a small platform that extended out over the ice surface above the net at one end of the building.

Now, a goalie needs unshatterable concentration and I was able to sustain mine when the spectators dribbled coffee, soft drinks, and cheap booze on me. I lost it totally in the third period when a spectator decided to relieve himself in my direction.

NHL goalies never have had to endure that indignity, except, figuratively speaking, from their teams' management and the defensemen in front of them. However, playing goal in hockey must be the single, most difficult task in sport.

"The only job in sport that's worse," said Lorne ("Gump") Worsley, a splendid NHL goalie for two decades, "would be as the javelin catcher on a track team."

The profession of goaltending is a trifle of absurd. A man with his body covered in mattresses stands in front of a fishnet while other men shoot pieces of frozen rubber at him.

A theory once was presented that goaltending was not a profession that attracted chaps who didn't really fit into the parameters of the so-called normal.

"How about Ken Dryden?" someone replied. Dryden was the NHL's dominant goalie of the 1970s, the anchor of six Stanley Cup championships won by the Montreal Canadiens.

"Oh, sure, Dryden was normal!" I offered. "Just

hockey players. "Being a hockey player really extends one's boyhood," the man said. "Many times when I get up in the morning, I look in the mirror and say to myself, 'What are you going to be when you grow up?'

"If you take it all seriously, all the fuss and furor, nonsense and garbage, you'll go crazy, anyway. So it helps if you're a bit nuts to start with. You save a great deal of wear and tear on yourself getting that way."

The list of hockey players who have qualified for the "character" designation is a long one. Hockey always has had a strong "flake" element, men who marched to their own drummer, some of them long after the band had stopped playing the tune.

Players, owners, coaches, ticket scalpers, trainers, general managers, scouts, ice makers and Zamboni drivers all have qualified for the flake/character list. To try and mention them all, of course, is impossible unless the book is as long as *War and Peace*.

Preceding pages: *A familiar face to those who have attended a New York Islander home game is their number-one fan, "Lord Stanley." Above: Lorne ("Gump") Worsley, whose consistent good nature made him one of the best-liked men ever to play hockey, played for the Canadiens for six years, four of which they won the Stanley Cup.*

243

about every goalie plays as the number one for an NHL team while taking fulltime law school studies at the same time."

Johnny Bower was normal, except the he played in the NHL until he was 45 years of age, maybe even 48 because Johnny never was 100 percent certain of his age. Glen Hall was normal except that he threw up before most games and often between periods. Jacques Plante was normal, too, except for 2,314 idiosyncracies. Andy Brown was normal except that he never wore a face mask and he raced stock cars in the off-season.

"Is goaltending a normal job?" Plante asked. "Sure it is! How would you like it in your job if every time you made a mistake, a red light went on and fifteen thousand people stood up and yelled 'you ass—.' "

The tendency is to think that the so-called modern goalies are much more straight-laced than their predecessors. Sure they are!

John Garrett of the Hartford Whalers is a good goalie of the 1980s. He studied Latin in school and once said: "It's a good language to have. If I ever meet an ancient Roman, just think of the great conversation I'll be able to have with him."

Denis Herron was Dryden's replacement in the Canadiens' net when The Lawyer retired to the legal profession in 1979. Skinny at 5 feet 11 inches and 160 pounds, Herron once tried to add weight to his frame by drinking several thick milkshakes every day. He gave himself a gallstone, not a chubby body.

Even in a distinguished field of goalie-flakes, Gilles Gratton stands out. Gratton, in fact, would have stood out as a flake in any field.

Gratton never made it big in hockey. He played with the Toronto Toros of the old World Hockey Association, the New York Rangers and the St. Louis Blues in the NHL. His list of flake achievements is much longer than his list of hockey accomplishments.

Gratton was into reincarnation, meditation, playing the piano, streaking, and once said he planned to become a porno movie star. He once meditated nonstop for 48 hours and made headlines with his statements that hockey players were paid far too much.

What had happened to him during his several previous lives influenced him his current one, Gratton claimed. When he was with the Rangers, Gratton informed John Ferguson, the team's general manager and coach at the time, that he was unable to play in a game because of a leg injury.

"When did you hurt your leg?" Ferguson asked.

"I was a soldier in the Franco-Prussian war and was wounded in the leg," Gratton replied. "It still bothers me from time to time."

Gratton had a tiger's features painted on his face mask. Why not? Gratton had been a tiger in one of his earlier visits to earth.

"Things all got a little out of hand with Gratton one night," Ferguson said. "During the warm-up, one of the Ranger players came to me and suggested that I not play Gratton in the game. 'He's growling like a bloody tiger behind the mask,' the guy said.

"I figured Gilles was just goofing around, but early in the game a fight broke out near our net. If I hadn't seen what happened, I wouldn't have believed it.

"Gratton took off his mask, dropped his gloves, and skated around hunched up like an angry cat, snarling and holding his hands in the claw position. He jumped on someone like a cat pouncing on a mouse."

Gump Worsley was inducted into the Hockey Hall of Fame in 1980, a popular selection because Worsley was one of the best-liked men ever to play the game. The Gumper had a consistent good nature, plenty of fast lines, and ability to stop the puck.

Worsley's NHL career had three distinct segments—ten seasons with New York Rangers when, for much of the time, that team was at the bottom of the standings; six glorious years with the Canadiens that included four Stanley Cup triumphs; and four good seasons with the Minnesota North Stars, the team for which he now works as a scout and goalie coach.

Chubby at five-foot-seven, 185 pounds, Worsley never ducked an issue, never hesitated to answer a question. His Ranger days were a succession of feuds with coach "Fiery" Phil Watson, a large part of the war inspired by Watson's dislike for the size of the Gump's girth.

"Worsley is nothing but a beer-belly," Watson once roared.

"As always, Watson doesn't have the faintest idea what he's talking about," Worsley shot back. "I never drink beer, only good Canadian whiskey."

The Rangers of the 1950s were a small, effete-

Hartford goalie John Garrett, who studied Latin in school, once said, "It's a good language to have. If I ever meet an ancient Roman, just think of the great conversation I'll be able to have with him."

245

checking team, and when Worsley was asked which NHL team gave him the most trouble, he replied, "The Rangers." One summer, Worsley operated a small restaurant in his hometown of Montreal. The menu listed The Ranger Special—a chicken sandwich.

Worsley was one of the last NHL goalies not to wear a face mask.

"Would it have been fair not to give the fans the chance to see my beautiful face?" Worsley said.

"Seriously, I had troubles adjusting to the mask because I had played so long without one. When I wore a mask, I kept losing sight of the puck when it was at my feet. Eventually, I got accustomed to it enough to wear a mask. It sure saved a lot of stitches."

Worsley once was smacked in the face by a slap shot off the stick of the Chicago Black Hawks' Bobby Hull, the NHL's most feared weapon. "I was lucky because the puck hit me flat," Worsley said. "If the edge of the puck had hit me? Well, if that had happened they would have called the undertaker and had him measure me for a box."

Jacques Plante is the choice of many as the finest goalie ever to play the game, and his mathematics in a 17-year career with the Canadiens, Rangers, Blues, Maple Leafs, and Bruins back up that view. In 837 regular-season games, he sported 2.37 goals against average and, in 112 playoff games, he lowered that figure to 2.16.

A serious, intelligent man, Plante's flake status was achieved unintentionally. He pioneered several innovations to the goalie's craft, notably the wearing of face masks and skating away from the goal crease to field loose pucks.

"I got sick and tired of being hit in the face with pucks, so I wore a mask," Plante said. "Management opposed it, but it wasn't their faces that were being stitched all the time.

"In semi-pro hockey, I played behind a defense that had two guys who couldn't skate backward and two who couldn't pivot. I could skate better than any of them so I started to skate out to clear loose pucks. When I did it with the Canadiens, management figured I was just showboating a little."

When the Canadiens visited Toronto, Plante objected to staying in the team's hotel, claiming that something in the atmosphere affected his asthma. On one trip, the Canadiens allowed him to stay at a different hotel the night before a game, but Plante showed up at the arena with his asthma in full bloom.

"I had a dream that I was sleeping in the team's hotel and when I woke up in the morning, my asthma had flared up," Plante said.

The royal family of mayhem

Gus Plager was a fine amateur hockey referee in the hockey hotbed of Kirkland Lake, a gold-mining town in Northern Ontario. A rough and ready man, Gus sired three sons—Barclay, Robert, and William—who were chips off the old granite. Barc, Bob, and Billy Plager, hockey's royal family of mayhem and fun, were immensely likable, easygoing chaps who tackled all challengers for a decade in the NHL.

I was working for the newspaper in Guelph, Ontario, in 1959 when Bob Plager, 16 years of age at the time, arrived for the training camp of the Guelph Biltmores, the junior farm club of the New York Rangers. Barclay already was established as a junior star and flake with Peterborough Petes in the Ontario junior league and very little time was required to determine that brother Bob had the same tendencies.

I met young Bob, escorted by Poppa Gus, outside the Guelph Arena.

"Ask him!" said Gus after the introductions.

"Who's the toughest guy on this team?" Bob said.

I told him and Bob replied; "Well, pop, that's the guy I gotta beat up a few times in camp to make this team."

During a Peterborough-Guelph game, Bobby and Barclay staged a fight that ranks among the longest, toughest, nastiest, and most damaging in hockey history. They fought with sticks, fists, and even tried a few kicks. They fought on the ice, in an arena corridor, and in the dressing room. They both were cut and bleeding at the finish.

When another player tried to intervene, the referee warned him: "Stay out of it! If you touch one of them, they'll both turn on you!"

After the game, Barclay approached Bob in a restaurant and everyone expected the furniture to fly.

"Barclay just wanted to borrow five bucks and to tell me that our mother was browned off because I wasn't writing letters home often enough," Bobby said.

"Heck, we had worse fights than that at home in the back yard," Barclay said. "I'd beat up Bob, Bob would beat up Billy, and Billy would go down the street and beat up our cousin."

"I wish I'd been there when those jerks had that fight," said younger brother Billy when he heard about the battle. "I would have whipped both their asses."

Eventually, Barclay and Bob wound up with the St. Louis Blues, mainstays of that club's defense when the Blues were in the class of the NHL's six 1967 expansion teams. Billy joined them for parts of three seasons and later spent NHL time with the Atlanta Flames and Minnesota North Stars.

The Plager boys were equal parts of malevolence and put-on. Barclay had the most hockey talent and intensity. He was a good big-league defenseman for a dozen seasons. Bob was a slow skater but an extremely smart player who parlayed a minimum of pure talent, toughness, and desire into a good career. Billy was plagued by injuries and his career ended in the mid-70s.

Bob became one of hockey's best comedians, famous for his practical jokes and the wild tales he told reporters.

"In our hometown of Kirkland Lake, they called our father 'Squirrel' because he raised three nuts," Bob said. "If we had a disagreement, Gus would send us to the backyard to settle it."

Bob claimed that he and Barclay, in the best brotherly fashion, took Billy under their wings.

"We taught him that it's much better to give than to receive, a good lesson for any young man to know," Bob said. "Once Billy complained about all the cuts he was getting from high sticks. We told him his timing was bad in throwing body-checks, and with our guidance, he only had fifty stitches one season."

In a game at Vancouver, Billy acquired a lengthy cut on his head. "When I saw something pouring out of the cut, I knew he was okay," Bob said. "It wasn't blood; it was sawdust. No Plager is hurt when he gets hit on the head. What have we got up there to hurt?"

Bob Plager once missed a Blues' plane on a road trip and when he caught up with the team in the next town, general manager Lynn Patrick asked for an explanation before fining him.

"Geez, Lynn, my wake-up call never came," Plager said. "When I did wake up and realized I'd missed the plane, I looked up toward the heavens and said, 'Why me, Lord, why me?'

"All of a sudden, the ceiling cracked open and a big hand came through the plaster with a finger pointing right at me. A big, loud voice said, 'Because you brown me off, Plager!' "

Barclay Plager was the man who said what has become the hockey fighter's credo. "It's not how many fights you win that's important," Barc said. "It's how many you show up for."

The last public appearance by the battling Plager brothers happened during the 1972–73 season when Barclay and Bob's involvement in a scrap in a St. Louis restaurant earned headlines.

"Barc and me had made a public-relations appearance for the Blues at, of all things, a ladies' club," Bob said. "The ladies were quite impressed. They couldn't understand how such well-mannered, handsome, presentable young men could be involved in such a rowdy game as hockey.

"On the way home, we stopped to have something to eat. We ordered alphabet soup and the waiter spilled it on my good suit. I didn't like the words the noodles spelled, we got into a little beef, a couple of punches were tossed, and somebody called the cops. However, it was all sorted out very quickly.

"I couldn't help thinking what those ladies at that club, who figured we were such nice boys, thought when they read about it in the papers."

Barclay Plager coached the Blues for two seasons until health problems caused by an old head injury forced him to give up the job early in the 1979–80 season. Both he and Bob now are scouts for the team.

"Maybe none of the Plagers will be in the Hall of Fame," Bob said. "But we did prove that with clean hearts and minds, good living, and devotion to duty, it's possible to succeed."

A sense of humor doesn't hurt, either.

The Sunshine Boys

Harold Ballard is 77; Francis ("King") Clancy is 78. But they seem to be everywhere in the NHL and many other places to boot. Ballard is the owner of the Toronto Maple Leafs; Clancy has a "lifetime" contract as a team vice-president. Mainly, though, he's Ballard's sidekick and traveling companion.

Bickering with each other and calling each other unflattering names, Ballard and Clancy operate at an energy level that would shame many men a third their age. They're on the go nonstop, traveling to all Leaf road games, NHL governors' meetings, side trips to Las Vegas or Atlantic City for a turn at the tables, attending horse races whenever possible, and viewing games and workouts of the Hamilton TigerCats, the Canadian Football League team Ballard owns.

"Mainly, we have fun, King and me," Ballard said. "We've got nothing else to do, anyway."

Ballard is one of the world's great sports fans with a fan's outlook toward his team and players. He alternates between killing them with kindnesses when they win and booting them in the backside when they lose.

"Ballard should tape his ankles so he won't turn them, jumping on and off his team's bandwagon," a Toronto writer once said.

Among his fellow NHL governors, Ballard is viewed with mixed reactions. A few find him amusing with his outrageous statements and bombast. A few others, notably Ed Snider, owner of the very progressive Philadelphia Flyers' organization, barely tolerate him because they see him as an impediment to any progress the NHL might attempt to make.

"Harold Ballard is not one of my favorite people," Snider said.

Ballard's act is to oppose just about everything the board attempts to do. He'll make public statements about "the Johnny-come-lately guys who don't know a hockey puck from a door knob" or "the dumb owners of teams who don't know how to promote their clubs well enough to make money but want to feed off those of us who do."

On an assortment of important matters to the league, notably the 1979 merger with the four surviving teams from the World Hockey Association, Ballard is the last holdout just about every time.

"I just can't understand how these people think," Ballard said. "The bloody WHA caused us nothing but trouble, stealing our players, pushing salaries and costs sky-high, and forcing us close to belly-up with huge legal costs to fight them. Now they want to take these other guys into our league. I just don't understand it."

At the finish, on the merger issue as he has done

on so many other issues he has opposed, Ballard threw in the towel and said he would make it unanimous.

At the press conference to announce the peace settlement between the two leagues, Ballard sat at a table, holding a sign that said, "Now, let's kill all the lawyers." Ballard's method is to turn everything into a confrontation, a hassle he can milk in the publicity mills.

Ballard's blustery vendetta with NHL president John Ziegler, who took over the job in 1977 after the 31-year reign of Clarence Campbell, has not been without its "lighter" moments.

When Ziegler ordered all NHL teams to place the names of the players on the back of their sweaters, Ballard at first refused to do it. Ziegler fined the Leafs for not obeying the league rule. Ballard then had the players' names placed on the sweaters, but in dark blue, the same color as the team's road uniforms.

At least once each season during a Leaf losing streak, Ballard can be counted on to blast the team in the strongest possible terms and to pull a couple of outrageous stunts. In the 1975–76 season, Ballard's "eggs" speech became as famous in hockey as Richard Nixon's "Checkers" speech did in politics. At the time, Swedish-import Inge Hammarstrom was a Leaf, a swift, slick winger who had problems handling the heavy traffic in the corners of NHL rinks.

"Inge Hammarstrom could skate into a corner with eight eggs in his pocket and not break one of them," Ballard said.

Late in the 1978–79 season, Roger Neilson, now head coach of the Buffalo Sabres, was the Leaf coach, and the club was in a prolonged slump. Ballard fired Neilson in a television interview after a Thursday-night game in Montreal, even though he had no idea at the time who would be hired to replace Neilson. All day Friday, Neilson went through an assortment of interviews and analyses on why he had failed to transform the Leafs into a contender. Meanwhile, Ballard was attempting to hire a replacement.

His first choice was Eddie Johnston, at the time coach of the New Brunswick Hawks, the American League farm team the Leafs shared with the Chicago Black Hawks. The Chicago club, which had Johnston under contract, refused to allow him to take the Leaf job.

When the Leafs appeared for a Saturday game at Maple Leaf Gardens, no announcement had been forthcoming from the Leaf front office on who would coach the team. Just before the start of the game, who should appear behind the bench but Roger Neilson?

"I just did it to shake up the team," Ballard said.

The reality of the situation was that the Leaf players, with team captain Darryl Sittler as the spokesman, had convinced Ballard that, at a point late in the season, the club had a better chance for success with Neilson at the controls than a new coach.

Later, Ballard revealed that he wanted to have Neilson appear behind the bench as the "mystery coach" wearing a balaclava mask which he would remove to the cheers of the crowd. Neilson, of course, refused to be part of such nonsense.

Not even a conviction on fraud and theft charges involving Maple Leaf Gardens funds in 1972 lowered Ballard's profile. He served one year of a three-year jail term and, when on a one-day pass from prison, attended a press conference to announce the signing of Sittler to a new contract.

Asked about life in the jail, Ballard couldn't resist the urge for a little put-on. He said it was like living in a country club, that he played golf every day, lounged by the swimming pool, and had filet mignon for dinner at least four nights a week.

When his statements were reported, a great many people took Ballard seriously and the newspapers were flooded with letters to the editor about the pampering of convicts by the Canadian penal system.

Ballard's peppy little sidekick, King Clancy, is hockey's senior citizen, a fixture in the NHL for 60 years. Clancy was 18 years of age in 1921 when he began his NHL playing career. A 135-pound defenseman, the irrepressible Irishman was purchased by the Leafs in 1930 and since then has been a fixture around Maple Leaf Gardens, except for the 11 seasons in which he was an NHL referee.

The common denominator in all of Clancy's hockey activities—player, referee, coach, and executive—was fun. As a player, he was a feisty little terrier who tackled all comers.

"Clancy only weighed a hundred thirty-five pounds, but a hundred twenty-five of it was heart," said Conn Smythe, the man who built the Maple Leafs and Maple Leaf Gardens.

As a referee, Clancy ruled more by good humor and quick banter than by a thorough application of the rules. In 11 seasons, he handed out only five misconduct penalties. If a player swore at him, Clancy swore right back.

Clancy's exchanges with the fans are legendary:

A fan in Boston once yelled at him, "We named a town near here for you, Clancy. It's called Marblehead."

A doctor who sat in a rinkside seat at Maple Leaf Gardens gave Clancy a verbal ride repeatedly. Finally, Clancy gave it back: "Maybe I'm not perfect, Doc, but I don't bury my mistakes like you do."

Clancy coached in the American League for several seasons, then coached the Leafs for three years in the 1950s before moving into the executive suite with the team in 1960.

"The King and me are going to be around until we get the chance to drink some booze out of the Stanley Cup won by the Maple Leafs," Ballard said.

"When you're on your way in, you're on your way out"

Often, the reasons why a man takes a job as coach of an NHL team are a trifle difficult to figure out. Longevity isn't one of them. In the 1980–81 season, the league's senior coach from the point of continuous service with one team was Al Arbour, who had been at the

The mask of Gary Bromley is in a class of its own.

controls of the New York Islanders since the 1973–74 season.

"As a coach, you must always remember one small fact: when you're on your way in, you're on your way out," said Punch Imlach, who was general manager and coach of the Toronto Maple Leafs (twice) and Buffalo Sabres.

"It all depends on how fast the old wheel is turning. Any coach, or general manager for that matter, must realize that his only end is to be booted out into the street."

The job of coaching has undergone large changes in the past decade. When the NHL had six teams, most coaches were former players who moved behind the bench when their playing careers ended. The expansion of the NHL from 6 teams to 18 teams between 1967 and 1974 and the birth of the World Hockey Association changed the picture considerably. Teams looked outside the ranks of ex-players for coaches and, in the 1970s, teams began to hire coaching staffs, instead of leaving the job to one man.

In the 1980–81 season, the 21 NHL teams had a total of 48 coaches, but one fact of coaching life remained the same: it's a tough way to make a living.

Perhaps Toe Blake, the most successful coach in NHL history, who guided the Montreal Canadiens to 8 Stanley Cup triumphs in 12 years, said it best. During one of his few losing seasons, Blake snapped: "Once I was a very happy man. Now I am a bitter man, a very bitter man."

When Blake gave up the job in 1968, he said, "It was a treat to be able to sleep at night for the first time in a dozen years."

Bryan Watson, who took the job of coaching the Edmonton Oilers in the 1980–81 season after a 17-year playing career, discovered the facts of coaching life very quickly. "When I was a player, I'd be down after a loss, of course," Watson said. "Mainly, though, I had to worry only about my own performance and if I'd played well myself, it eased the sting of losing.

"But as a coach, there are no such escapes. When my team loses, I can't say, 'We lost but I coached well.' Instead of one player, myself, to worry about, I have twenty to worry about now."

"Maybe a man who becomes an NHL coach is the same as one who becomes a racing driver," an NHL coach once said. "They both figure they can beat the odds and have a long career."

Coaching an NHL team takes its toll on many men. Easygoing, relaxed chaps become tight and tense. Men with pleasant, laid-back personalities become surly and uncommunicative. Gray hair appears in increasing amounts.

Few are the coaches who retain their sense of humor for long. Don Cherry and Harry Neale are two exceptions.

Cherry had an 18-year playing career, all in the minor pro leagues except for one game in the 1955 Stanley Cup playoffs with the Boston Bruins.

"When I was a kid, I prayed for enough talent to be a pro hockey player," Cherry said "I forgot to say NHL, though, because they only gave me enough to make minor pro hockey.

"I never made much money playing in the minors. I worked at construction jobs, even running an air-hammer one summer, to pay the bills. I once sold used cars for one day. When I found out how many lies you had to tell in that business, I quit."

Although Cherry had three successful seasons as coach of the Rochester Americans in the American League, "Don who?" was the question heard most when he was named coach of the Bruins in 1974.

That didn't last long. Through five stormy, windy years, Cherry guided the Bruins to four divisional titles, two Stanley Cup finals, and within an overtime goal in the seventh game of upsetting the Montreal Canadiens in a memorable 1979 semifinal. In that time, Cherry became just about the number-one personality in the NHL, the most quoted, outrageous coach, because he never forgot that hockey is part of the entertainment business.

Cherry's Bruins were not slick and flashy. They were a grinder team succeeded on immense ambition, not finesse.

"We're a lunch-pail team," Cherry said. "Guys who wear hard hats and carry lunch buckets to work can identify with us because we have to work hard at our jobs just the way they do."

Cherry became an immense favorite with the media, the most-quoted man in hockey. He loved the postgame bantering with the press and never failed to provide an assortment of lively quotes. He made a celebrity out of his dog Blue, a bull terrier. Cherry claimed that he consulted Blue on hockey matters and

Opposite top: Flake or not, Ken Dryden drank from four consecutive Stanley Cups (1976–79) with the Canadiens, then retired to become a lawyer. Opposite left: Maple Leafs' Harold Ballard (seated, right) and King Clancy kept an eye on their former coach, Roger Neilson (standing), who had an on-again, off-again relationship with them. Opposite right: Gilles Gratton believes he was a tiger in a former life.

when he returned home after a loss, his dog shunned him.

"Blue is a fighter, the way I want my players to be," Cherry said.

One of Cherry's favorite players was Stan Jonathan, a chunky little winger who was perhaps the best fistfighter in the NHL. Cherry paid Jonathan the ultimate tribute by hanging a picture of Blue over his locker in the Bruin dressing room.

Cherry was the NHL's best-dressed coach, possesser of a large wardrobe of suits, some velvet. He often needled his coaching peers, especially Scotty Bowman of Montreal, about their wardrobes. "Can you imagine?" Cherry snorted during one Stanley Cup final. "Scotty Bowman is the coach of the best hockey team in the world and he wears Hush Puppies!"

Cherry's approach was to isolate himself and his players on a dressing-room island, apart from the front office and management. During his five-year stay with the Bruins, his relationship with general manager Harry Sinden slowly deteriorated to the point where they didn't speak for one and a half years.

"We appreciated the job Don did in marketing himself and the team," Sinden said. "But did the front office have to be the target for all his jokes?"

At the end of the 1978–79 season when Cherry's contract with the Bruins ran out and the team didn't offer him a new one with large enough figures on it, Cherry hired on with the Colorado Rockies, one of the NHL's sad-sack teams.

Cherry's hype increased attendance in Denver by 150,000 in the 1979–80 season, but the team finished in a tie for last place in the 21-team league. Once again, Cherry encountered problems with the front office. At the conclusion of the season, the Rockies fired Cherry from the coaching job, although he was paid $135,000 for not coaching in the 1980–81 season.

"They presented a six-page indictment of my shortcomings," Cherry said. "It was enough to make me doubt myself. I'd worked my ass off promoting hockey in Denver and the attendance increase indicated some success."

When the Rockies sacked Cherry, he said he wasn't worried because he knew he would have another coaching job "within ten minutes." Those 10 minutes were long ones. Cherry's hockey activity in the 1980–81 season consisted of appearances as an

analyst and color commentator on telecasts of NHL games.

"I'll be back," he said. "Back in 1978, the other coaches in the NHL named me as the best coach in the league. Sooner or later, someone will remember that and I'll be back in the business."

Would he change his approach, notably his wars with management?

"Wouldn't change a thing because I only know one way to do the job," Cherry replied.

Harry Neale was a fine junior defenseman with the Toronto Marlboros in the 1950s, but he opted for a college education and never did make it as a pro player. He coached U.S. college hockey at Ohio State University and junior hockey in Canada, before moving to the WHA with the Minnesota Fighting Saints and, after that team folded, the Hartford Whalers. In 1978, he was named head coach of the Vancouver Canucks of the NHL.

Neale is a serious, intelligent coach who just happens to be a very funny man, a master of the one-liner. His sense of humor, combined with his vast hockey knowledge, has made him a much-in-demand lecturer at hockey seminars and coaching clinics.

"Where's it say that you can't have a little fun doing this job?" Neale said. "This job can drive you nutty if you don't have a few chuckles along the way."

One of Neale's coaching wrinkles is to have his players plan and run practice sessions. "I've picked up some good ideas from the drills the players used," Neale said. "It's a funny thing, but a couple of players I've had on my teams who almost drove me crazy because they were so lazy in my workouts were real whip-crackers when they ran the workouts."

Neale's throwaway lines in interviews are gems. Here are a few examples:

"Our best system of fore-checking last season was to shoot the puck into the attacking zone and leave it there."

"We have too many guys who are small but slow."

"We had a couple of defensemen whom we would like to rush once a game—then we'd have to replace the pucks."

After Curt Ridley, the Canucks' goalie at the time, injured both knees on one play, Neale was asked if he'd ever seen such a happening before. "No, I never have," Neale said, "It's pretty good, too, because the NHL record is three."

After watching Ken Linseman, the talented little trouble-causer of the Philadelphia Flyers, try to aggravate every opponent with his chippy tactics, Neale said: "He's either the bravest or the stupidest player I've ever seen. It's difficult to tell because the line between bravery and stupidity is a very thin one."

In the 1980–81 season, Neale had Dave Dunn and Tom Watt as his assistant coaches. Dunn was a journeyman defenseman in the NHL and WHA who had a business and economics degree and was a professional-caliber guitar player. And he wasn't too shabby in the one-liner department, either.

"When I played hockey, I had a unique skating style: my feet never left my ankles," Dunn said.

Watt had a distinguished coaching career with the University of Toronto Blues, winning 9 Canadian championships in 13 years.

"It's great to have two assistants to share the blame when things go badly," Neale quipped. "When things are going good, I don't want them around when the glory is being handed out."

Hockey's Jekyll and Hyde

Encounter Carl Brewer far away from hockey and he'd come across as a serious, intelligent, well-read man, a devoted father and a smart businessman. But place Brewer within a half mile of the hockey milieu and Carl comes, well, a trifle unstuck.

During the 1979–80 NHL season, the initial shock wore off quickly when it was announced that Brewer planned a comeback with the Toronto Maple Leafs, the team on which he had walked out back in 1965. Brewer was 41 years of age at the time, his head completely void of any hair, and he had been out of big-league hockey for seven years.

"I just wanted to prove to myself that I could do it and the Leafs gave me the chance," Brewer explained. "Besides, I wanted to die as a Maple Leaf and if they were the last team I played for in the NHL, then I'd have realized that ambition."

Brewer did play in 20 games for the Leafs and conducted himself rather well. Not that it was difficult to accomplish that with the Leafs in 1979–80, a team that was in consistent upheaval under general manager Punch Imlach.

Brewer's on-ice action with the Leafs ended in March of that season when he spoke out publicly in support of Leaf center Darryl Sittler, who had a season-long feud with Imlach.

"I admire Darryl Sittler because he was able to bear up under the pressure and play his game," Brewer said. "I caved in under the same sort of pressure fifteen years ago."

In the early 1960s when Imlach's Leafs won three consecutive Stanley Cups, Brewer was an all-star defenseman on the team, a superbly skilled player with great speed and puck handling skill. But his career never ran smoothly, because he and Imlach butted heads frequently. In 1963, Brewer had a contract dispute with Imlach. Brewer left the team and attended the training camp of a Canadian college football team.

During the Leafs' training camp for the 1965–66 season, Brewer departed for good in the middle of a scrimmage session. He claimed the pressures of hockey were causing his hair to fall out.

Brewer, appropriately, was one of the first players to challenge the NHL system. He wanted to be reinstated as an amateur to join the Canadian National team and won that right in a lengthy confrontation with professional hockey. Later, Brewer was playing-coach of the Muskegon Mohawks in the International League, saw NHL action with the Detroit Red Wings and the St. Louis Blues, played and coached in Europe, and in the 1973–74 season resurfaced in Toronto with the old Toros of the World Hockey Association. "The owners always played chess with the players," Brewer said. "I had a bit of fun playing chess with the owners."

A deep fear of flying and airplanes was added pressure for Brewer. He often needed a little time in the airport bar to work up his courage for the flight ahead. When Brewer attempted to negotiate a comeback contract with the Leafs in 1971, one of his contract demands called for the club to supply him with a few belts of good Scotch on all flights. He had the unusual view that if he sat as close as possible to the flight deck on planes, the better were his chances of surviving a crash. During his season with the Toronto Toros, to face a flight on a 747 from Vancouver to Toronto, Brewer paid the difference between an economy and first-class ticket out of his own pocket to sit close to the crew.

After his usual tune-up in the airport bar, Brewer settled into his first-class seat where he had a couple more courage-bracers. When the plane leveled off at cruising altitude, Brewer went into the washroom, removed his clothes, donned his bathing suit and splashed water all over his body. He walked back to the economy cabin, a towel draped around his neck, and said, "If any of you folks back here want to come up to first class and use the swimming pool, be my guest."

The Toros' players were on a charter flight after a game at Ottawa, but Brewer was late. One of the players noticed a wheelchair rolling across the tarmac toward the plane and, sure enough, its occupant was Brewer, covered in a blanket. He rolled the wheelchair under the plane, stabbed at the tires with an umbrella and, content that the craft was structurally sound, boarded for the flight to Toronto.

Brewer's 1980–81 farewell whirl with the Leafs wasn't an especially happy experience. He was regarded as a spy for Imlach by the other players, who gave him the nickname "CIA."

Leaf defenseman Dave Hutchison, later traded to the Chicago Black Hawks, was benched for a game in which Brewer played. "It's really a joke, having Brewer on this team," Hutchison said. "Hell, there are many players in this league who would prefer to play an entire season against Brewer than one game against me."

"It was a laugh that they thought I was a spy for Imlach," Brewer said. "I guess they don't know anything about the relationship between the great Punch and me. There really isn't one."

Although Brewer's NHL time had reached an end, he wasn't finished in hockey. He spent the summer of 1980 playing in an off-season league in West Germany.

The elongated boyhood

If the player who said that a hockey career extended one's boyhood was correct, then the fact that some hockey players occasionally behaved with boyish zest was understandable. The list of player-flakes is a long one, men playing a boys' game.

Of course, the money isn't juvenile. In the 1980–81 season, the average annual salary in the NHL, including pensions and other fringe benefits,

was $108,000.

"Being a pro hockey player is a strange way to earn a living," Bob Plager once mused. "It's a very fragile career that can be ended very suddenly by an injury or the fact that the team's owner doesn't like the color of ties you wear.

"You have to be a combination of boy and man, I think, to make it. They tell you when to go to bed, when to get up, and what to eat as if you're twelve years old. Because you're a pro player, the hangers-on are incredible, people who just want to be around guys who are in the limelight.

"So it should be no big surprise when, occasionally, some player acts a little goofy. If you take it

After a 17-year playing career with six teams, Bryan Watson discovered the coaching facts of life very quickly when he became Edmonton Oilers' coach in 1980–81.

seriously all the time, you'll go a little daffy, anyway, so you might just as well do it on your own."

Mike ("Shakey") Walton was unique among flakes: he had the papers to prove it. During his stormy days with the Toronto Maple Leafs in the late 1960s, a psychiatrist said that playing for the Leafs was pushing Walton toward the twilight zone and that, for the sake of his mental health, he should be traded.

When the Leafs traded Walton to the Boston Bruins, the Bruin players had a couch placed in front of his locker when he joined the team. The Bruins (twice), the Minnesota Fighting Saints of the WHA, the Vancouver Canucks, St. Louis Blues, and Chicago Black Hawks also decided that they didn't want to push Walton over the brink, so they traded him.

Walton's problem was that management never figured he was serious enough about the game, especially the defensive side of hockey. "I had a few chuckles now and then and management always viewed that as an indication that I wasn't serious enough," Walton said.

"Maybe I liked to laugh and clown around too much, but I always felt I worked hard. It seemed that if you always looked serious and didn't have any fun, they always figured you were working, even when you weren't."

Wayne Cashman combined the two factors—hard work and fun. Although the Boston Bruin winger has mellowed a little in his 30s, Cash was a mite wild, on and off the ice, in his early years in the NHL.

Cashman was a superb corner man, at his best in combat in the pits. He played left wing on a line with Phil Esposito. Espo worked the slot in front of the net; Cash patrolled the corners and produced many passes for scores by big Phil.

In fact, Cashman claimed that corners were a large influence in his life. "I have to live in a house on a corner lot and anytime I drink too much—and that's not very often—I just go to a street corner and I know everything will be fine," he said.

"When I die, I hope they bury me in the corner plot of the cemetery because if I'm in the corner, I'll be able to rest in peace forever."

The Boston police once stopped Cashman's car and discovered that he had overindulged. When they took him to the police station, Cash asked if it were true that he was allowed to make one telephone call.

The police said that it was, Cash made his call, and the cops thought he had called his lawyer.

Twenty minutes later, the delivery man for a Chinese restaurant arrived at the police station with an order of food for Mr. Cashman.

Bryan ("Buggsy") Watson was one of the great pests in NHL history, a chippy, aggressive player who drove opponents crazy with his tactics. He was the NHL's career penalty-minute leader for a time until Dave Schultz passed him.

Watson parlayed a great sense of humor, a slender portion of talent, and a fat slab of desire into a 17-season NHL career and, in 1980–81, the head coaching job with the Edmonton Oilers.

Watson gained his first notoriety with the Detroit Red Wings when he was assigned to "shadow" Bobby Hull, the scoring star of the Chicago Black Hawks, in several playoff series.

"It was funny, but every time we played Chicago, the Black Hawks had Bobby Hull checking me," Watson quipped.

Watson also was one of hockey's best citizens, a willing worker for charities, especially those involving mentally retarded children. He won the Charlie Conacher Memorial Trophy for his humanitarian efforts and worked on special projects for the Kennedy Foundation in Washington. Watson was also one of the leaders in the NHL's involvement in the Special Olympics, coaching several floor hockey teams.

"One summer, I stayed in Pittsburgh when I was with the Penguins and did some promotion work for the club," Watson said.

"They asked me to help coach a floor hockey team of retarded kids. I was reluctant at first, but it didn't take those great kids very long to hook me. Being involved with those kids is the most rewarding thing I've ever done in my life. I got far more from them then I ever was able to give them."

Watson supplied perhaps the most novel explanation for missing the net on a breakaway of any NHL skater. When he was a Washington Capital, Watson had an in-alone chance from center and missed the net by approximately 40 feet. When he returned to the bench, Tom McVie, the Cap coach at the time, asked, "What the hell happened, Buggsy?"

"Coach," Watson replied, "I couldn't get my stick out of cross-check."

Photo Credits